Anasazi Ruins
of the Southwest
in Color

ANASAZI RUINS
of the SOUTHWEST
in COLOR

William M. Ferguson and Arthur H. Rohn

Foreword by Richard B. Woodbury

The University of New Mexico Press
Albuquerque

Library of Congress Cataloging in Publication Data
Ferguson, William M.
    Anasazi ruins of the Southwest in color.

    Bibliography: p.
    Includes index.
    1. Pueblo Indians—Antiquities. 2. Pueblos. 3. Indians of
North America—Southwest, New—Antiquities. 4. Southwest,
New—Antiquities.
I. Rohn, Arthur H., 1929–
E99.P9F47   1986   979.01   85-29035
ISBN 0-8263-0873-2
ISBN 0-8263-0874-0 (pbk.)

Printed in Japan

Contents

Illustrations

Foreword

Everyone's first visit to the southwestern United States is an occasion for enthusiasm, often for love at first sight and lifelong infatuation. This is true not only today and for recent visitors but also for some of the earliest easterners to visit the Southwest. Although their comments were expressed in sober, scientific terms, the members of the various U.S. government exploration parties in the 1840s and 1850s reacted enthusiastically, as, for example, in Lt. James H. Simpson's report in 1850, which included a lengthy account of Chaco Canyon. Although on a campaign against the Navajo, he spent most of four days examining the main ruins and making measurements of them, and he describes ceilings, walls, windows, and other features in great detail. The expedition's artist, Richard H. Kern, had time to make careful plans and drawings, which appeared in the final report (some of them in color), the first accurate views of the great ruins of the Chaco Canyon available. When Capt. Lorenzo Sitgreaves was sent in 1851 to find a wagon route to the Pacific, he had Richard Kern with him, and one of Kern's illustrations for the government report is the first published view of Wupatki ruin, near Flagstaff. The Chaco ruins and Wupatki have not changed much since these early views, some walls tumbling a bit more and some rooms damaged by the digging of looters. But one thing has changed: as this volume makes clear, we need not today invoke wandering Aztecs to explain the Southwest's ruined pueblos.

When the large-scale government geological and topographical surveys of the West began, after the Civil War, archaeological sites were not neglected. Photographs by W. H. Jackson, the pioneer who worked with wet-glass plates as large as twenty by twenty-four inches, and drawings by William H. Holmes who soon shifted careers from art to archaeology, were included in the government reports of 1876 and 1878, and brought the first general attention to the ruins of the San Juan area.

Unfortunately, another expression of enthusiasm for the Southwest's past beginning at least a century ago, was digging in the ruins, collecting "relics" for pleasure or profit. A San Francisco newspaper story in 1884 describes a visit to Walnut Canyon, near Flagstaff, by tourists returning from Grand Canyon: "In one of the first dwellings that we visited we struck a bonanza . . . a storeroom . . . for the whole row of dwellings. We dug for an hour or more, and found . . . beans, gourds, reeds, arrows, bowstrings, coarse cloth, a child's sandal . . . a measuring stick with notches at regular intervals, bone needles. . . . In visiting other ruins we added to these relics, and came away heavily laden."

It was in December 1888 that Richard Wetherill and Charles Mason, searching for straying cattle, discovered the Mesa Verde ruins that they named Cliff Palace and Spruce Tree House. Reports of their digging, with its spectacular finds, traveled rapidly, and by 1891 Gustav Nordenskiold arrived from Sweden to excavate systematically at Mesa Verde. His handsomely illustrated and popularly written report, *Cliff Dwellers of the Mesa Verde,* was published in 1893 and helped further to arouse public interest. But even his careful observations and shrewd insights could not repeople the ruins with the activities of the past, as archaeologists can today, and as Ferguson and Rohn describe here. Archaeologists were, at that time, digging up specimens for museums, and ideas about them were rudimentary.

Even before this, scientific and scholarly organizations in the eastern United States were starting the serious investigation of pueblo ruins—such as Adolph Bandelier's visit to Pecos in 1880 under the auspices of the Archaeological Institute of America. His report, published the next year (more promptly than many archaeological reports today) is still a valuable source of information on this famous ruin. At the time of Bandelier's visit, it was only forty-two years since the last seventeen inhabitants of the once populous town had given up and moved away to join another village.

By 1882 efforts to provide protection for southwestern ruins had begun, stimulated in part by Bandelier's account of extensive vandalism and looting at Pecos and elsewhere. The first legislation proposed was unsuccessful, but by 1906, the Antiquities Act was passed by Congress. Even though at first enforcement was ineffective in most instances, the 1906 act eventually led to stronger laws, and in recent years there have been successful convictions of archaeological looters. Most private land is still unprotected, but today, as this volume makes clear, there are at least a few ruins in every part of the Southwest that are legally protected and accessible to the visiting public.

As important as protecting ruins on government land was the creation of a system of federal (and later state) archaeological parks and monuments, beginning in 1889 with Casa Grande, the great four-story adobe structure in the Gila River valley of southern Arizona. In 1891 the Colorado legislature petitioned Congress to protect the ruins of Mesa Verde as a national archaeological park and finally, in 1905, legislation was signed by Theodore Roosevelt creating the park.

Thanks to this combination of early public interest in pueblo ruins and successful protection of at least a few from vandalism and commercial looting, today's visitor to the Southwest can experience some of the same excitement and admiration that stirred travelers a century ago. And whether for those who travel by armchair or in more mobile ways, the authors of this volume have provided the ideal guide.

The stay-at-home traveler has both pictorial and descriptive material with which to enjoy a trip to many of the Southwest's Anasazi ruins. And the active traveler has the detailed explanations of an expert guide to ancient pueblo life in all its aspects, with photographs to add the orientation and frequently the aerial perspective that make even the best preserved and familiar ruins more comprehensible. The general background and the local details are amply provided. Visitors need both to fully understand and enjoy archaeological sites; merely "looking at" them is not enough.

My own "favorite" ruins are all here, although I might have written on them at much greater length, probably too great length, crowding out some that are equally deserving. I should confess that, like others, on my first visit to the Southwest I became hopelessly fascinated and delighted with it. As an inexperienced undergraduate I had the good fortune to join the staff of Harvard's Peabody Museum in 1938, which was excavating the prehistoric and historic Hopi site of Awatovi, and have felt since then that every summer that did not include a visit to the Southwest was somehow incomplete.

But here is a chance to visit ruin after ruin, summer or winter, and to plan a tour to include favorite places to revisit and new ones to explore for the first time.

This is, of course, not the first book on southwestern ruins for the general reader, nor will it be the last, but it certainly does everything in one volume that the beginner or the old-timer can want. Indeed, the only thing left to ask for, I think, is another volume to cover the rest of the Southwest—Mogollon, Hohokam, and all.

Richard B. Woodbury

Preface

The Anasazi Indians of the Southwest represent 2,500 years of cultural continuity from the early Basket Makers of 700 B.C. to their modern descendants, the Pueblo Indians. The pueblos and cliff dwellings built by these ancient people during their halcyon days between A.D. 1000 and 1500 are the most spectacular ruins north of Mexico. In this volume, all of the significant and accessible Anasazi ruins are photographed and described in detail. Many of the photographs are aerial views, which show the interrelationship of the structures within the site and the intrinsic beauty of the setting. A pueblo ruin photographed from the ground appears to be little more than a pile of rocks, but from the air the plan of the structure, its rooms, kivas, and great kivas can be easily seen. The aerial photographs reveal the full extent of the original village or town, not just the excavated portion. The ancient fields sometimes can be seen near the habitations.

The magnificent ruins of Anasaziland are located in a variety of settings: Chaco Canyon in the middle of the desert of northwest New Mexico, Mesa Verde on the forested high mesa in southwest Colorado, Canyon de Chelly and the Navajo monument's ruins (Kayenta) in cliffs deep in canyons of eastern and north Arizona, Wupatki on the north slope of the San Francisco peaks near Flagstaff, and Bandelier with its living shrines in the rugged canyons next to Los Alamos. Also included in the book are many other accessible Anasazi sites, each of which is important to the Anasazi culture and exciting to visit. Examples include Aztec Ruin with its restored great kiva and Chimney Rock Pueblo built on a narrow ridge 1,000 feet above the valley floor in southern Colorado in a setting that rivals that of the temples of ancient Greece.

This volume looks at the extant ruins of the Anasazi culture from Basket Maker II (before A.D. 500) to the end of Pueblo IV, when the Spaniards arrived—the beginning of historic times. Many of the major ruins are preserved in the national parks and monuments and cover the phases from Basket Maker III to the end of Pueblo IV (600 to 1540). Because of the number of excavated ruins, the emphasis in the book lies with Pueblo III times at Mesa Verde, Chaco Canyon, Kayenta, and Canyon de Chelly. Pueblo IV coverage is less extensive. These ruins are found at Bandelier, Pecos, Salinas, and the Hopi Mesas. The contact and amalgamation of the Anasazi with their southern neighbors, the Mogollon, Sinagua, and Hohokam, during the 1200s is displayed at Wupatki.

The book is composed of a series of descriptions and essays, any one of which is substantially complete within itself, with illustrations, photographs, and text forming a unit. One can read it from start to finish, or use it as a reference. The Introduction is a series of sections relating to the Anasazi culture, their architecture, clothing, tools, food, and diseases. We then look at the Anasazi culture of Pueblo III (1100 to 1300) in Chaco Canyon, the Northern San Juan which includes Mesa Verde, and Kayenta, including the ruins of Tsegi Canyon and Canyon de Chelly, and discuss the Great Migration of the 1200s from these three regions to the Rio Grande valley and the Little Colorado River valley of the Hopi and Zuni where the Pueblo IV Anasazi culture flowered until the arrival of the Spaniards. The effect of the early Spanish contact appears in the coverage of Gran Quivira and Pecos.

The most reliable tool for reconstructing the life of the ancient Anasazi is to consider the culture of the Pueblo Indians of historic times. They are the descendants of the ancient ones. We look at the way these Pueblo Indians live, their social organization, rituals, mores, myths, and legends. From these sources we can extrapolate about how their forebears lived in prehistoric times.

The Anasazi were a people almost unique in the world: their culture was egalitarian. There were no kings, chiefs, nobles, warrior class, or elite. They were farmers who constructed masonry pueblos and cliff dwellings, hunted small game, and planted and harvested corn, beans, and squash. They were a neolithic people without a beast of burden, the wheel, metal, or a written language, yet they constructed magnificent masonry housing and ceremonial structures, irrigation works, and water impoundments.

We include illustrations of rock art, painted, pecked, and carved on cliff faces and building walls and examples of their delicate jewelry and beautiful ceramics.

There is strong disagreement among Anasazi scholars concerning interpretations of the Anasazi culture. Without written records, there can be no definitive answer to many of the enigmas of the past. We have endeavored to present contradictory theories and have not endeavored to defend any particular point of view. The principal thrust of this book is to display and explain the magnificent Anasazi ruins of the Southwest and the culture of these ancient peoples.

William M. Ferguson
Durango, Colorado

Arthur H. Rohn
Wichita, Kansas

Introduction

The Anasazi

Anasazi is the name given to the prehistoric Indians who inhabited the Four Corners area of southeastern Utah, northeastern Arizona, southwestern Colorado, and northwestern New Mexico for a 2,000-year period from about 700 B.C. to the arrival of the Spaniards in the Southwest. The Anasazi descended from older Paleo-Indians and may have been a fusion of Shoshoneans from the Great Basin, Tanoans from the western plains, and Keres from the mountains. These Indians were not indigenous to North America; their ancestors—and the ancestors of all of the Precolumbian peoples of the Western Hemisphere—came from Asia across what is now the Bering Strait between Siberia and Alaska on the land bridge. Dry land was created because the water trapped in the great glaciers of the Ice Age had lowered the level of the world's oceans. These migrants followed the ice-free corridors south across what is now Canada into mid-North America and Central and South America.

For most of their known history, the Anasazi occupation centered around the Four Corners in the drainage of the San Juan and Little Colorado rivers.

Anasaziland covered most of the high Colorado Plateau: the geographic area bounded by the Rocky Mountains on the north and east, the Great Basin on the west, and the Sonoran Desert on the south, or in terms of modern landmarks, the territory inside a line beginning at Pagosa Springs, Colorado, extending northwesterly to Monticello, Utah, southwesterly to the Grand Canyon, southeasterly to Springerville, Arizona, easterly to Grants, New Mexico, and northeasterly along the Continental Divide back to Pagosa Springs.

Two additional small regions occupied by the Anasazi lie east of the Continental Divide in northern New Mexico—the territory around Taos, and the Chama River valley from Chama to Española. Following the Great Migration of the late 1200s, Anasaziland had receded to the Rio Grande valley from Taos to Socorro, the Zuni River valley of west-central New Mexico, and the four Hopi mesas near Keams Canyon, Arizona.

Prior to the Great Migration, the Anasazi occupied four main regions:

(1) Northern San Juan. This region includes the portions of southwestern Colorado and southeastern Utah lying north of the San Juan River. The San Juan has its headwaters in the high, rugged San Juan Mountains near Pagosa Springs, Colorado, from whence it flows southwesterly past Farmington, New Mexico, and then loops northwesterly into southeastern Utah where it joins the Colorado River at Lake Powell. In this region are Chimney Rock, Aztec Ruins, Mesa Verde, the Ute Mountain Tribal Park ruins, Hovenweep, and other Montezuma Valley sites.

(2) Chaco Basin. The Chaco Canyon ruins lie in the center of the Chaco Basin of northwestern New Mexico. This Anasazi region includes the area drained by Chaco Wash and is bounded on the east by the Continental Divide and on the west by the Chuska Mountains; it lies between Farmington and Crown Point. In this region are Chaco Canyon, Salmon, Pueblo Pintado, and other Chacoan outliers.

(3) Kayenta. This region is named after the town of Kayenta, Arizona, and includes the territory west of the Lukachukai-Chuska Mountains and Canyon de Chelly, south of the Colorado and San Juan rivers in Utah, and east of the Grand Canyon. The major Kayenta sites that may be visited are Betatakin and Keet Seel in the Navajo National Monument, Canyon de Chelly, and Tusayán at the Grand Canyon.

1

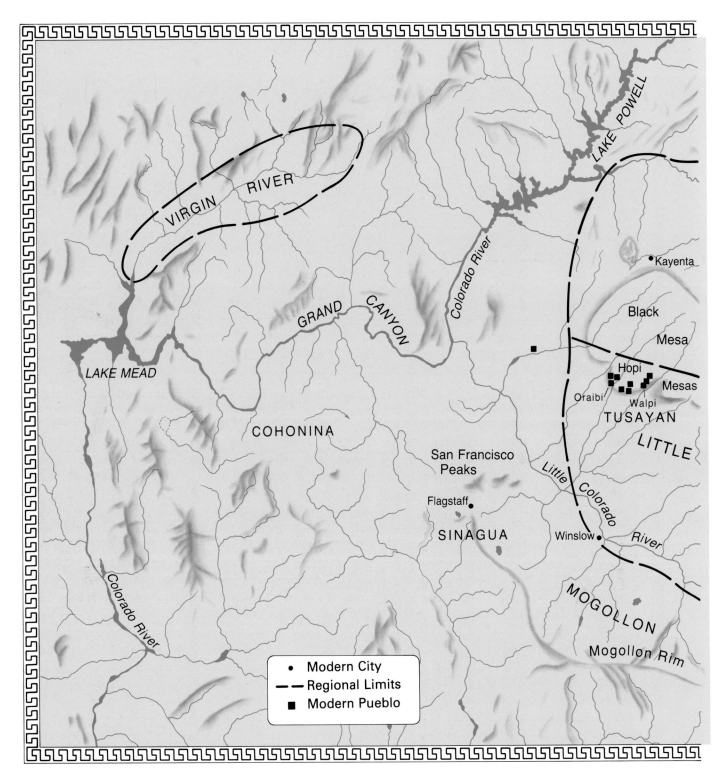

Anasaziland, the regions occupied by the Anasazi from
700 B.C. to the arrival of the Spaniards.

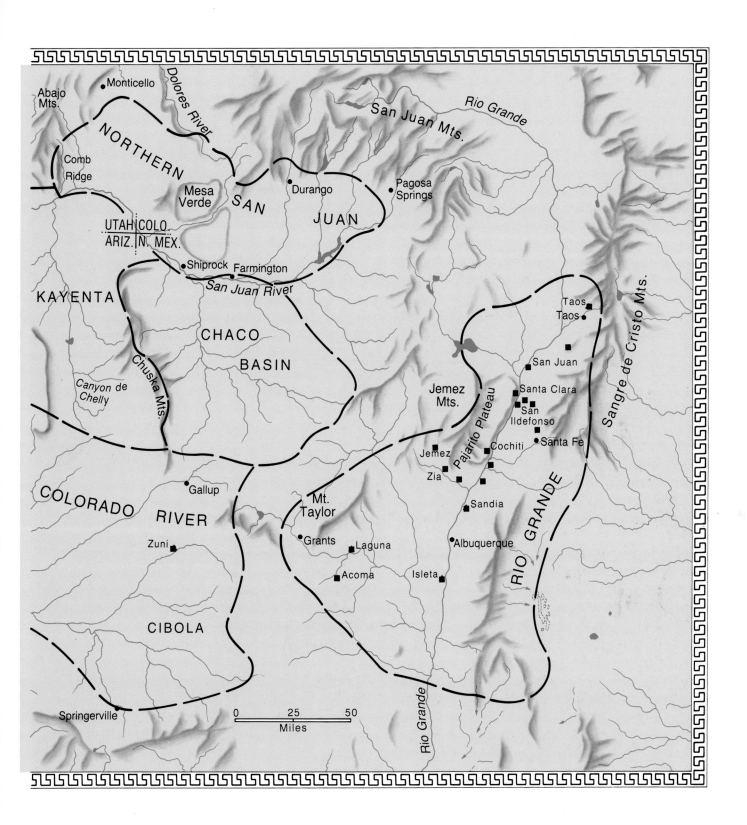

Abajo
Mts.
• Monticello
Dolores River
San Juan Mts.
Rio Grande

NORTHERN
Comb
Ridge
Mesa
Verde
• Durango
Pagosa
Springs

SAN

JUAN

UTAH COLO.
ARIZ. N. MEX.

KAYENTA
• Shiprock Farmington
San Juan River

CHACO

BASIN

Jemez
Mts.
Taos ■
Taos •

San Juan ■

Santa Clara ■
Canyon de
Chelly
Chuska Mts.
San
Ildefonso ■
Cochiti ■
Santa Fe •
Jemez ■
Pajarito Plateau

COLORADO
• Gallup
Zia ■
■

RIVER
Mt.
Taylor
Sandia ■

Sangre de Cristo Mts.

RIO GRANDE

Zuni ■
• Grants
Laguna ■
• Albuquerque

CIBOLA
■ Acoma
Isleta ■

Springerville •
0   25   50
Miles

Rio Grande

3

(4) Little Colorado–Zuni River valleys. The region includes the Zuni River valley beginning at the Continental Divide east of Zuni, New Mexico, to the junction of the Zuni River with the Little Colorado River near St. Johns, Arizona. From St. Johns, the Anasazi occupied the territory north and east of the Little Colorado River to its junction with the Colorado River at the Grand Canyon. In this region are the sites of Atsinna at El Morro and the Zuni Pueblo in the east, and the modern Hopi Mesa pueblos of Oraibi and Walpi in the west. The Little Colorado River–Zuni region joins the Chaco and Kayenta regions to the north. The Zuni territory is sometimes referred to as the "Cibola," and the Hopi Mesas territory is referred to as the "Tusayán."

By around A.D. 1300 the Anasazi had migrated from the Kayenta, Northern San Juan, and Chaco regions to the Zuni–Little Colorado River valleys and to the Rio Grande valley in New Mexico, ending the Pueblo III phase of Anasazi culture and beginning the Pueblo IV. The Pueblo IV Anasazi of the Rio Grande settled in two districts, one to the north and the other to the south of the modern city of Albuquerque. There were Anasazi in these areas before the end of Pueblo III, but the great migrations from Chaco Canyon and the Northern San Juan during the thirteenth century populated the Rio Grande valley from Taos to Socorro and emptied the northern regions.

Five cultural signatures enable archaeologists to determine what is Anasazi. First is the kiva—a generally circular, underground structure used for gatherings of kin groups. The kiva belongs to the Anasazi and is not found anywhere else. Second is

UNIT PUEBLO

The unit pueblo was the standard form for the construction of villages and pueblos from the mid-700s to after 1300. This modular household unit was composed of storage rooms, living rooms, a pithouse or kiva beneath the courtyard, and a trash dump, all aligned from north to south.

the unit pueblo. This building unit, made up of a room block of two to twelve rooms and a plaza or workspace containing a kiva, formed a modular unit of standardized design that was multiplied to form larger settlements—whether in the cliffs or in the open.

The third cultural signature was the orientation of kivas and unit pueblos facing toward the south and southeast. The fourth was the characteristic Anasazi gray-and-white pottery and the utility pottery with a corrugated exterior. They fired the pottery in a nonoxidizing atmosphere (a fire smothered to reduce available oxygen), producing the gray-and-white–colored ceramics. Many Anasazi pots were decorated with black paint producing the distinctive black-on-white pottery style.

Fifth, the Anasazi in all areas followed a characteristic pattern of burials. The bodies were buried with legs flexed against the chest, lying on the side with the heads oriented directionally—often toward the east—or parallel to the slope if the grave was on steep terrain.

These five characteristics are peculiarly Anasazi and were not shared by the other neighboring cultures. By matching these hallmarks to the discovered ruins it has been possible to delineate prehistoric Anasaziland for some 2,000 years.

A. V. Kidder adopted the name *Anasazi* from a Navajo term that translates into English as "enemy ancestors" but now has the generally accepted mean-

A masonry Pueblo III kiva showing a fire pit and a draft deflector. This kiva had a dome-shaped cribbed roof built upon the stone pilasters rising from the circular banquette. Entrance was gained by ladder through a hole in the roof. Step House, Mesa Verde.

Two distinctive styles of Anasazi pottery: a gray corrugated-surface cooking and storage jar, and two serving vessels with black geometric designs painted on polished white surfaces.

ing of "ancient people." The Anasazi were the ancestors of the modern-day Pueblo Indians of the Southwest. A chronological framework was agreed upon at the 1927 Pecos Conference which divided the history of the Anasazi into three Basket Maker stages and six Pueblo stages.

BASKET MAKER I. This is a postulated stage of nomadic hunter-gatherers estimated to cover some 3,000 years representing the latter stages of the Archaic Desert Culture to the beginnings of the Anasazi culture in the Four Corners area. The Oshara Tradition possibly represents the anticipated cultural remains for which the label *Basket Maker I* was intended. The Oshara Tradition represents a long-term development in the northern Southwest generally between about 5500 B.C. and A.D. 400, culminating in the Anasazi culture. These people were hunters and gatherers who utilized projectile points, chipped-stone implements, stone-grinding implements, and hearths. Excavations of the Desha Complex of the Oshara Tradition in south-central Utah and north-central Arizona revealed open twined sandals and one-rod foundation interlocking stitch basketry.

BASKET MAKER II. The Basket Maker II stage extends roughly from 700 B.C. to A.D. 400 or 450. These preceramic people take their name from the large quantity of baskets found at sites of ancient occupation in the area of the Four Corners. They tended to live under rock overhangs, but in some areas they did build circular pithouses.

These people combined game hunting and gathering wild seeds with farming of maize and squash. They made atlatls (spear throwers) and darts using carefully chipped points, knives, and drills of stone, and baskets and other woven artifacts, such as sandals, aprons, bags, and robes. The Basket Maker II stage is also sometimes referred to simply as "Basket Maker" because of the lack of any recognized evidence for a Basket Maker I.

The stages of Anasazi cultural development did not run concurrently in all areas, but for the sake of simplicity we consider the Basket Maker II stage to have begun by 700 B.C. and phased into Basket Maker III after about 1,000 years.

BASKET MAKER III. This stage is also referred to in the literature as Modified Basket Maker and extends from about A.D. 450 to 750. Although characterized as "basket maker" the remains of this stage in the development of Anasazi culture reveal a widespread use of pottery.

Basket Maker III sites are found all over the Anasazi area and embody these elements: pithouse villages, ceramics, the bow and arrow replacing the atlatl and dart, domesticated turkeys, a developing agriculture, and some large structures that are the prototypes of the later great kivas. Prototypes of

Late Pueblo II burial from the Ewing Site, Yellow Jacket district, Montezuma Valley.

Anasazi Chronology

	Revised (this book) Pecos Classification	Roberts's Terminology
1900	Pueblo VI	
1800		Historic Pueblo
1700	Pueblo V	
1600		
1540		
1500	Pueblo IV	Regressive Pueblo
1400		
1300		
1200	Pueblo III	Great Pueblo
1100		
1000	Pueblo II	Developmental Pueblo
900		
800	Pueblo I	
700		
600	Basket Maker III	Modified Basket Maker
500		
400		
300		
200		Basket Maker
100		
A.D.		
0		
B.C.		
100	Basket Maker II	
200		
300		
400		
500		
600		
700		
800		
	Oshara (Basket Maker I ?)	

small kivas that developed from the pithouses are not found until Pueblo I, and true kivas do not appear until Pueblo II times.

The Basket Maker III Anasazi appear to have been more sedentary than their predecessors. In addition to the wild plant foods (pinyon nuts, juniper berries, yucca fruit, rice grass, pigweed, acorns, and sunflower seeds), they grew corn, beans, and squash. Trade items from as far away as northern Mexico and the Pacific Coast were found at their living sites—pottery, marine shells, and turquoise pendants. This stage phases into Pueblo I about A.D. 700 to 750.

PUEBLO I. *Pueblo* is the name given to the village Indians by the Spaniards, a word in Spanish meaning "town" or "village." When Coronado arrived in 1540, the inhabitants of the Pueblos in Arizona and New Mexico were the descendants of the ancient Anasazi who developed the Pueblo culture.

The 1927 Pecos Conference divided the early Pueblo history into Pueblo I (A.D. 700 to 900) and Pueblo II (A.D. 900 to 1100). In 1935 Frank Roberts combined these two stages into one which he designated "Developmental Pueblo."

The eighth century was a dynamic period for the Anasazi, a time of a blending of peoples and cultural patterns. Pithouses continued to be built, but now jacal or wattle-and-daub houses were built on top of the ground, particularly in the open areas. These were structures with walls built of poles laced together with brush and faced with adobe.

The key element in the Pueblo I development, however, is the construction of aboveground rectangular rooms that were, at first, designed for storage while the Anasazi continued to live in the pithouses. As time passed during Pueblo I, the pithouse, which was primarily a dwelling, began to be used more consistently as a kiva, a ceremonial chamber, a workshop, and a gathering place. Richard B. Woodbury points out that the kiva was a perpetuation of the traditional form for the traditional activities, just as Gothic churches are still built in the midst of our modern dwellings. While the aboveground rows of single-storied rooms provided both storage and living quarters, these aboveground rooms were outgrowths of the formalized storage bins and ramadas arranged in rows and arcs to the north or northwest of the Basket Maker III pithouses.

Both painted and unpainted pottery were made and traded (painted pottery was produced as early as A.D. 600). The Indians relied increasingly on agriculture, and the more enterprising of them worked on improving production by developing reservoirs, dams, terracing, and irrigation.

PUEBLO II (A.D. 900 to 1100). It is during Pueblo II times that the architecture and site arrangement we see in the restored ruins today developed. Rectangular masonry houses with contiguous rooms were common in the Four Corners area. The unit pueblo consisted of a combination of a multi-roomed masonry building fronted on the south by a kiva and a trash dump. The Anasazi placed their garbage, broken pottery, worn out stone tools, and other dispensable things in a pile to the south of their work plaza. These deposits are called "trash dumps" by the archaeologists. The cliff-dwelling-unit–type construction was usually built against the back wall of a rock alcove with one or more kivas in front. Each block of ten to twelve rooms, one kiva, and associated refuse constituted a modular unit, a unit pueblo, of Puebloan village arrangement.

The kiva is the centerpiece of the Anasazi culture. During this stage it developed from the earlier pithouse into the cultural center of the unit pueblo. It became a fully subterranean chamber with a banquette around its circumference, a central fire pit, a ventilator, an air deflector, and a sipapu hole. The sipapu was a hole a few inches in diameter in the floor of the kiva representing the opening in the earth from whence their ancestors were believed to have reached the surface of the earth. The kivas were used by kin, lineage, or clan groups. Prototypes of great kivas were known as early as Basket Maker III, and true great kivas were in use by Pueblo I and continued into Pueblo III.

The Anasazi had no system of writing and therefore could leave no written records. So the only way we can hypothesize about their social system is to assume that the social order of the ancient Anasazi was similar to that of the Pueblo Indians of the historic period. Certainly this is conjecture, but by dovetailing modern Indian traits with prehistoric social systems of primitive peoples worldwide we are able to make an educated guess concerning how the Anasazi lived at the end of Pueblo II. By that time, the people were probably divided into descent groups or clans known by the name of some plant, animal, or object such as corn, bear, or flute. The members of the clan or lineage segment were the presumed descendants of a common ancestor, most likely female.

As in the case of modern Pueblos, we can as-sume that each of the ancient towns, together with their surrounding habitations, was politically and ceremonially self-sufficient. We might also postulate, based upon the architectural division of many of the later Pueblo III towns, that then as now there was a duality of social administration, something akin to the Winter and Summer People of the modern Pueblos.

Houses traditionally belonged to the women. Husbands came from another clan. Many ethnographers argue that the society was as egalitarian as it was in the hunting-gathering era, except that the men did the hunting and farming and the women did the gathering and took care of the children. Others suggest that as farming became more productive and the population increased, leisure and wealth became possible, at least for some, and an elite class developed.

The Chaco Canyon Anasazi offer the strongest argument for an elite class. The Chacoans produced a system resembling a hub culture with outlying towns connected to Chaco Canyon by a series of roads and a communication network. The architecture and irrigation works they built are impressive, but the culture flowered and waned in a very short period of time—only about sixty years from A.D. 1070 to 1130. If there was an elite class superimposed upon the existing society, it didn't endure and the Chaco Phenomenon died. Chaco and other Anasazi areas have no evidence of elite quarters. There are burials with jewelry, ceramics, and other artifacts but none with the essential symbolism that tells us that this deceased person was a ruler, a noble, an elite person of a special class. The Anasazi seem to have been egalitarian people.

During Pueblo II several other developments contributed to the flowering of the Anasazi culture. Baskets were frequently replaced with more versatile pottery, especially coiled pottery made by rolling the purified and tempered clay into thin ropes that were then coiled into various shapes and sizes. Smooth finishes were possible through the use of slips of clay in liquid form applied to the surface of the pot, which was then decorated with black painted designs. Cooking pots were not smoothed but left rough on the outside and were often crimped with the fingers to produce a corrugated surface.

A new plant, cotton, had been introduced, probably from Mexico during early Pueblo I. The turkey, which had been domesticated in Basket Maker III times, became a source of food during late Pueblo II.

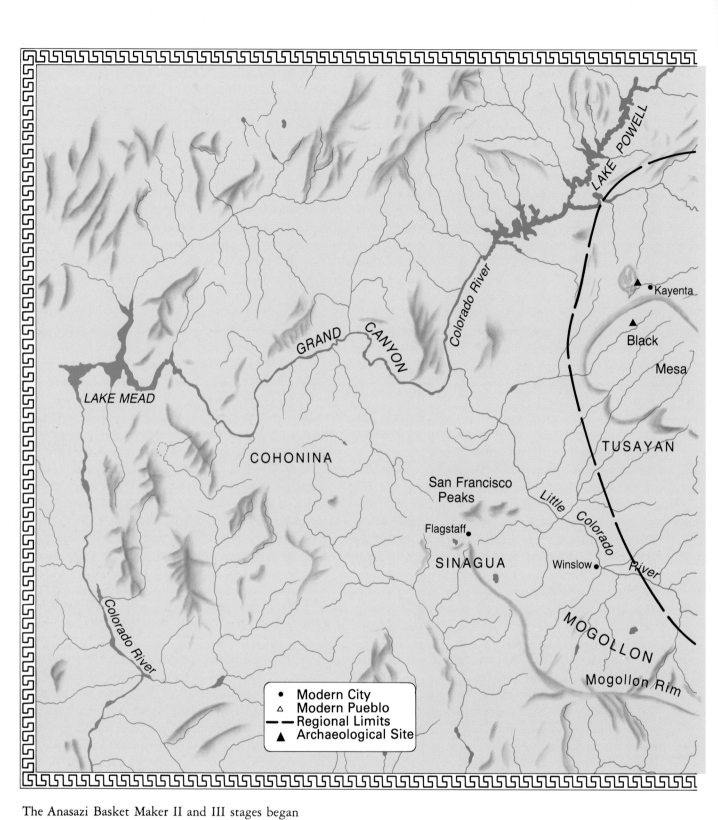

The Anasazi Basket Maker II and III stages began
around 700 B.C. and lasted for more than 1,000 years.
Relatively few of these very ancient sites have been
found. About the only excavated ones open to visitors
may be seen at Mesa Verde National Park.

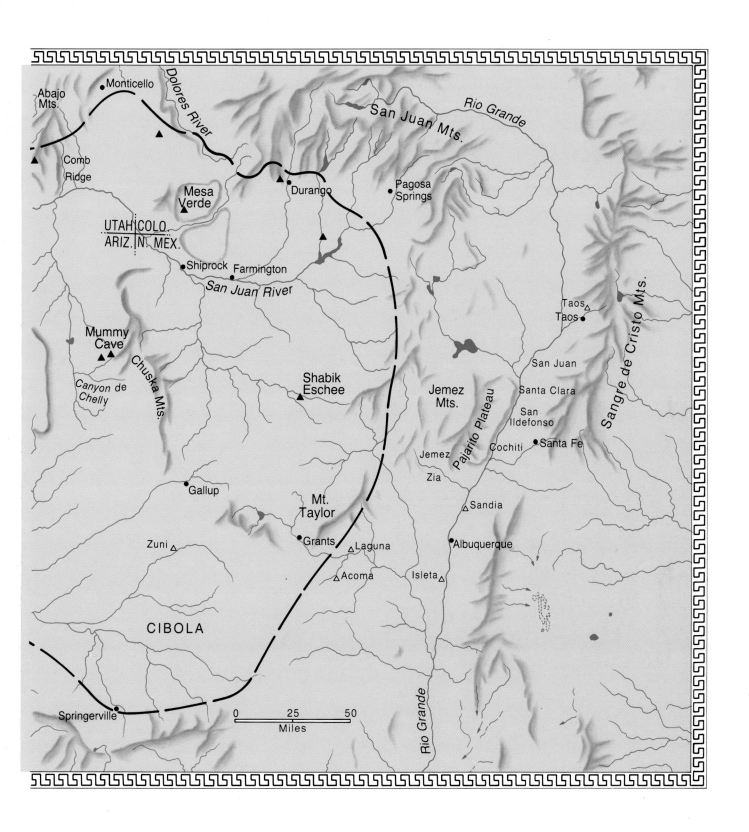

Abajo
Mts.

• Monticello

Dolores River

San Juan Mts.

Rio Grande

Comb
Ridge

Mesa
Verde

• Durango

Pagosa
Springs

UTAH COLO.
ARIZ. N. MEX.

• Shiprock   Farmington

San Juan River

Taos
Taos

Mummy
Cave

Chuska Mts.

San Juan

Santa Clara

Canyon de
Chelly

Shabik
Eschee

Jemez
Mts.

San
Ildefonso

Pajarito Plateau

Sangre de Cristo Mts.

Cochiti   • Santa Fe

Jemez

Zia

• Gallup

Mt.
Taylor

Sandia

Zuni

• Grants

Laguna

• Albuquerque

Acoma

Isleta

CIBOLA

0   25   50
Miles

Springerville

Rio Grande

9

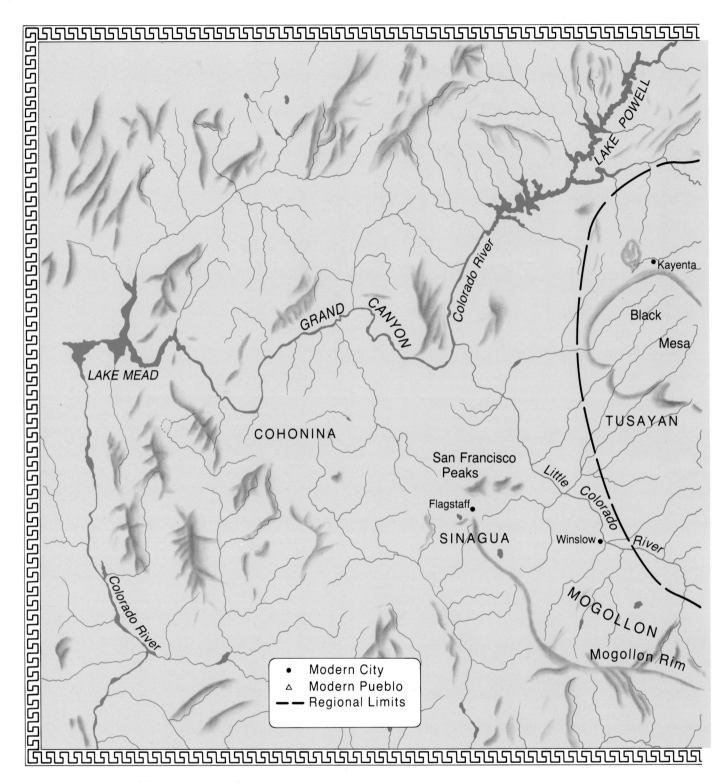

The regions occupied by the Anasazi during Pueblo I
(700–750 to 900). The only sites open to public
visitation are located at Mesa Verde National Park.

10

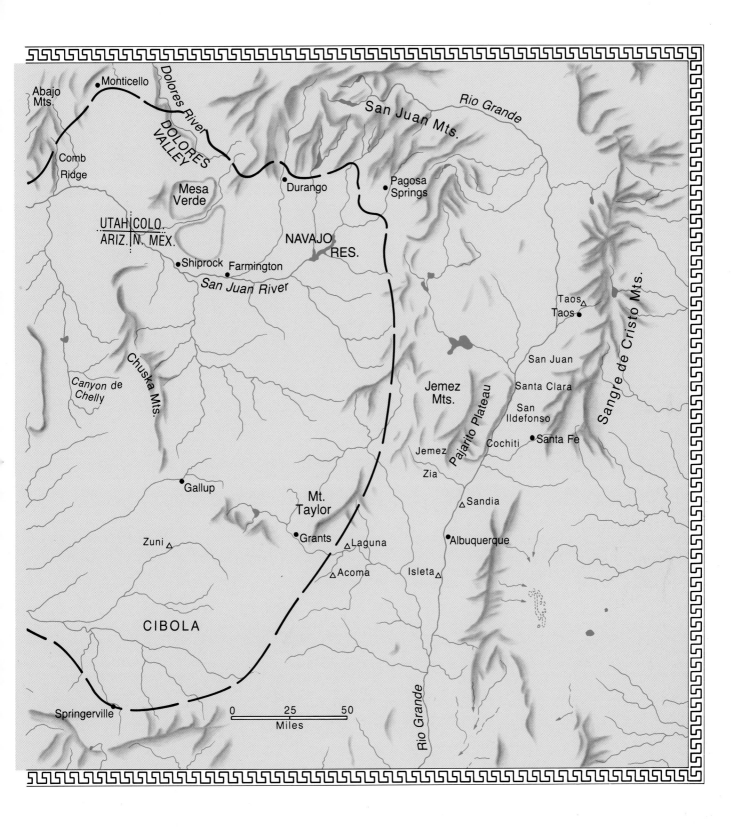

Abajo Mts.

Monticello

Dolores River

DOLORES VALLEY

San Juan Mts.

Rio Grande

Comb Ridge

Mesa Verde

Durango

Pagosa Springs

UTAH | COLO.
ARIZ. | N. MEX.

Shiprock   Farmington

NAVAJO RES.

San Juan River

Taos
Taos

Sangre de Cristo Mts.

San Juan

Chuska Mts.

Canyon de Chelly

Jemez Mts.

Pajarito Plateau

Santa Clara

San Ildefonso

Cochiti

Santa Fe

Jemez

Zia

Gallup

Sandia

Mt. Taylor

Zuni

Grants

Laguna

Albuquerque

Acoma

Isleta

CIBOLA

Rio Grande

Springerville

0   25   50
Miles

11

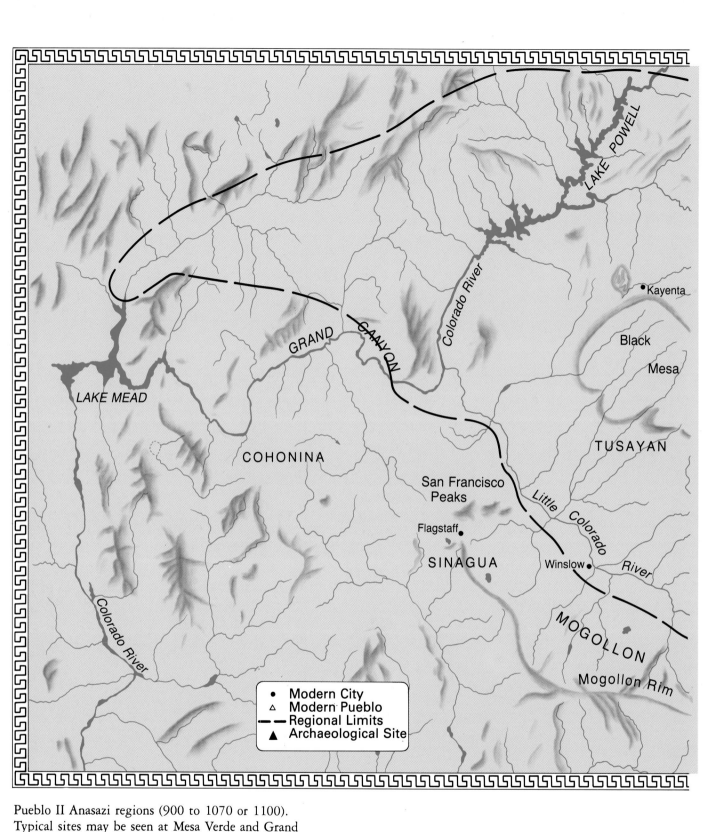

Pueblo II Anasazi regions (900 to 1070 or 1100).
Typical sites may be seen at Mesa Verde and Grand
Canyon national parks.

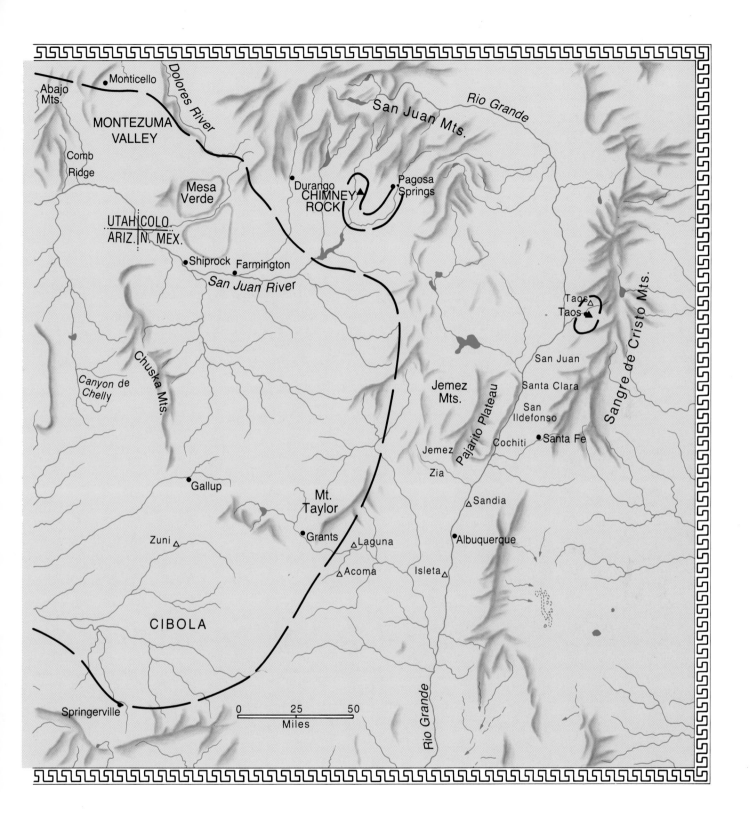

Abajo Mts.
• Monticello
MONTEZUMA VALLEY
Dolores River
San Juan Mts.
Rio Grande
Comb Ridge
Mesa Verde
• Durango
CHIMNEY ROCK
• Pagosa Springs
UTAH COLO.
ARIZ. N. MEX.
• Shiprock Farmington
San Juan River
Taos
Taos
Sangre de Cristo Mts.
Chuska Mts.
Canyon de Chelly
Jemez Mts.
San Juan
Santa Clara
San Ildefonso
Pajarito Plateau
Cochiti
• Santa Fe
Jemez
Zia
• Gallup
Mt. Taylor
△ Sandia
Zuni △
• Grants
△ Laguna
• Albuquerque
△ Acoma
Isleta △
CIBOLA
Rio Grande
0   25   50
Miles
• Springerville

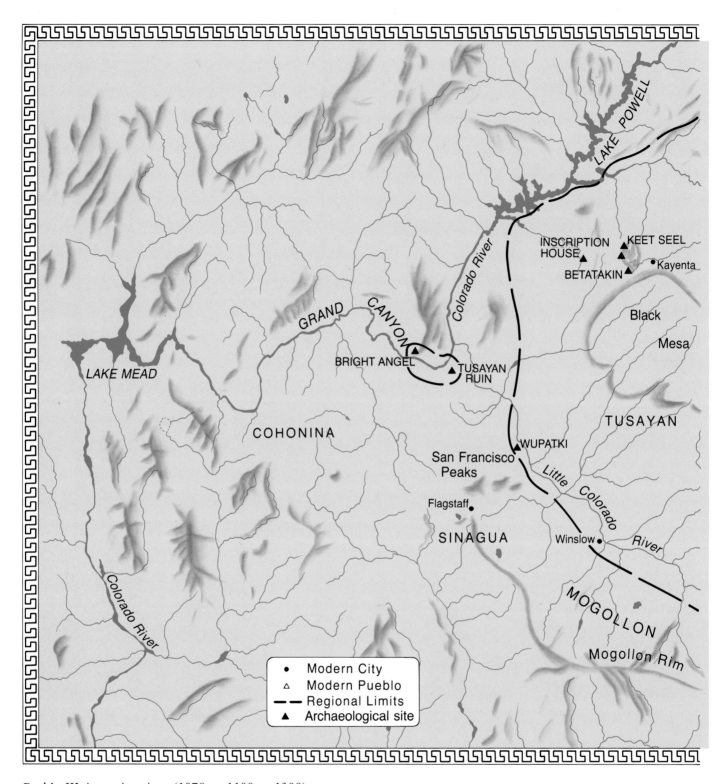

Pueblo III Anasazi regions (1070 or 1100 to 1300).
Most sites throughout Anasaziland open to the public
belong to the Pueblo III stage.

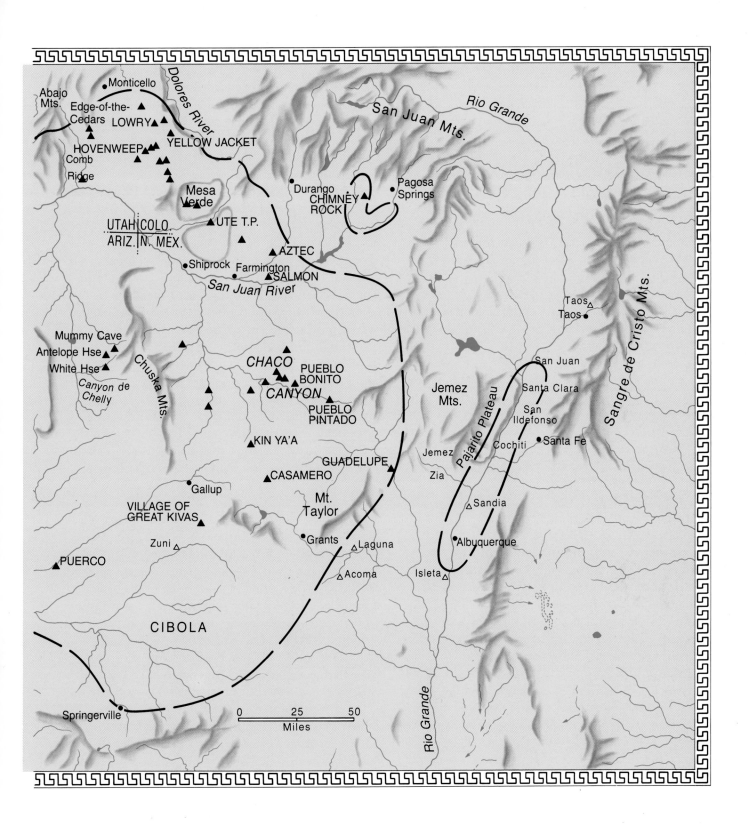

Abajo
Mts.
• Monticello
Edge-of-the-
Cedars ▲ LOWRY ▲ ▲
HOVENWEEP ▲ ▲ ▲ ▲ YELLOW JACKET
Comb ▲ ▲ ▲
Ridge ▲

Dolores River

San Juan Mts.

Rio Grande

Mesa
Verde
▲ UTE T.P.
• Durango CHIMNEY ▲ • Pagosa
ROCK Springs

UTAH|COLO.
ARIZ.|N. MEX.

▲ AZTEC
• Shiprock Farmington
▲ SALMON
San Juan River

Taos △
Taos •

Mummy Cave ▲
Antelope Hse ▲ ▲
White Hse ▲
Canyon de
Chelly

Chuska Mts.

CHACO ▲
▲ ▲ PUEBLO
▲ BONITO
▲ CANYON ▲
PUEBLO
PINTADO

Jemez
Mts.

San Juan •

Santa Clara

San
Ildefonso

Pajarito Plateau

Sangre de Cristo Mts.

▲ KIN YA'A

GUADELUPE
▲
• Gallup
▲ CASAMERO

Mt.
Taylor

Jemez
Zia

Cochiti
• Santa Fe

VILLAGE OF
GREAT KIVAS ▲

Zuni △

• Grants
△ Laguna

△ Sandia

▲ PUERCO

△ Acoma

• Albuquerque

Isleta △

CIBOLA

Rio Grande

• Springerville

0   25   50
Miles

15

The Little Colorado River region has not been investigated to the same extent as the other Anasazi regions, but the evidence indicates that it was a large population center in classic Anasazi times. Chaco is particularly interesting because it reaches its climax during the transition between Pueblo II and Pueblo III (A.D. 1100). Of all the major centers, it may have been the earliest example of Pueblo III, but early in Pueblo III times, Chaco ceased to be influential.

PUEBLO III (A.D. 1100 to 1300). Central to the Pueblo III stage were the great centers of population and influence: Mesa Verde and the Montezuma Valley in southwestern Colorado, Chaco Canyon in northwestern New Mexico, Kayenta (Betatakin, Keet Seel, and Canyon de Chelly) in northeastern Arizona, and the area along the Little Colorado River in east-central Arizona.

As a part of the Mesa Verde center we also include the pueblos of the Montezuma Valley near the Colorado city of Cortez, which included the unexcavated ruins of Mud Springs, Yucca House, Yellow Jacket, Sand Canyon, Goodman Point, and the partially stabilized site of Lowry. In northern New Mexico, the Aztec Ruin is a Mesa Verde–type site with a small Chacoan population, who constructed some Chacoan style rooms and kivas, while the Salmon Ruin is a Chacoan outlier.

The classic pueblo stage was characterized by settlements of large, multiroom, multistory stone masonry pueblos with many kivas, built in open valleys, at canyon heads, or in natural rock shelters. The largest settlements probably held 2,000–2,500 people and focused on a great kiva or a tri-wall structure. The Anasazi had developed water management systems that delivered and stored water for domestic and irrigation uses. Domesticated turkeys were eaten and their bones used in the tool kit. Most other aspects of material culture undergo further style changes. By the end of this stage the San Juan drainage, Chaco Basin, and Kayenta were abandoned. Essentially, Pueblo III Anasazi times are marked by three elements: population increase, architectural development of masonry apartment houselike structures, and migration from and abandonment of the Four Corners. We are most familiar with this stage because of the ruins of cliff dwellings, valley pueblos, and ceremonial great kivas, towers, and tri-wall structures that remain.

The major ruins at Chaco Canyon may have been abandoned by A.D. 1150. The final known tree-ring date at Mesa Verde is A.D. 1278, and it is assumed that the area was abandoned by 1300. These people left the northern area and moved southeastward to reestablish their culture along the Rio Grande. The Kayenta region in northeastern Arizona, which included the Canyon de Chelly, held on slightly longer. The 1270s and 1280s were the expansion years at Keel Seel and Betatakin (Kayenta) and at Canyon de Chelly, but they, too, were abandoned shortly after A.D. 1300.

At this juncture in the history of the Anasazi two questions arise: where did they go and why did they leave? The Mesa Verde and San Juan River peoples ultimately moved to and settled in the Rio Grande valley, while the western peoples moved south and west into what is now the Hopi settlement area. The Chacoans may have moved to the Zuni region or preceded the Mesa Verdeans to the Rio Grande. What precipitated the migrations is neither simple nor straightforward. In the first place, there was no sudden mass exodus. The evidence suggests they drifted away in smaller or larger groups for a period of more than a hundred years. Archaeologists suggest several reasons, none of which have unanimous agreement. The only fact agreed upon is that the great pueblos were abandoned by about A.D. 1300, which brought the Pueblo III stage to a close.

Among the suggested causes for the abandonment are: the great drought (1276 to 1299), climatic changes that caused arroyo-cutting which destroyed the tillable land, continued attacks by the Athapaskan Navajo and Apache and Shoshonean Indians, internecine warfare (one group of Anasazi against another), disease, and the shortening of the growing season because of a drop in the mean temperature resulting in sharply reduced production of food.

PUEBLO IV. This stage takes the Anasazi from A.D. 1300 to 1540, the beginning of the historic period after the arrival of the Spaniards. The principal centers of culture during Pueblo IV and Pueblo V times were located in the Rio Grande valley, the Zuni (or Cibola) region, and the Hopi Mesas (or Tusayán) region. There were other zones where the Pueblo IV and V Indians lived after the migrations early in the 1300s, but these three regions contain the principal extant ruins.

Among the Pueblo IV sites in the Rio Grande valley of New Mexico are the Pajarito Plateau sites of Puyé and Bandelier; the Galisteo Basin ruins; the Salinas Group sites located near Mountainair—Gran Quivira, Quarai, and Abó; Acoma and Kuaua, near Albuquerque; and Pecos, east of Santa Fe.

The Zuni Pueblos (Hawikuk and Halona), Atsinna, and Pueblo de los Muertos are located south of Gallup. The three Hopi Mesas and Antelope Mesa

Aztec Ruins National Monument ruin from southeast to northwest with the Hubbard Site tri-wall structure built by the Mesa Verdeans in the background. The excavated West Ruin shows some Chacoan influence. The restored great kiva is in the center of the plaza.

To the east is the large unexcavated portion of the pueblo. The pueblo was abandoned by A.D. 1300. (Photograph taken with the assistance of John Q. Royce.)

located southeast of Tuba City, Arizona, contain several Pueblo IV and V ruins: Awatovi, Kawaika, Kokopnyama, Sikyatki, Old Walpi, and Old Oraibi. And near Winslow is Homolovi.

Pueblo Indians today can trace their ancestry from Pueblo IV times in the 1300s through the Pueblo V stage (1540 to 1850), during which time they were subjugated by the Spaniards, Mexicans, and early New Mexicans. The last stage, Pueblo VI, beginning about 1850, brings the descendants of the Anasazi to the present time.

Text continued on page 20

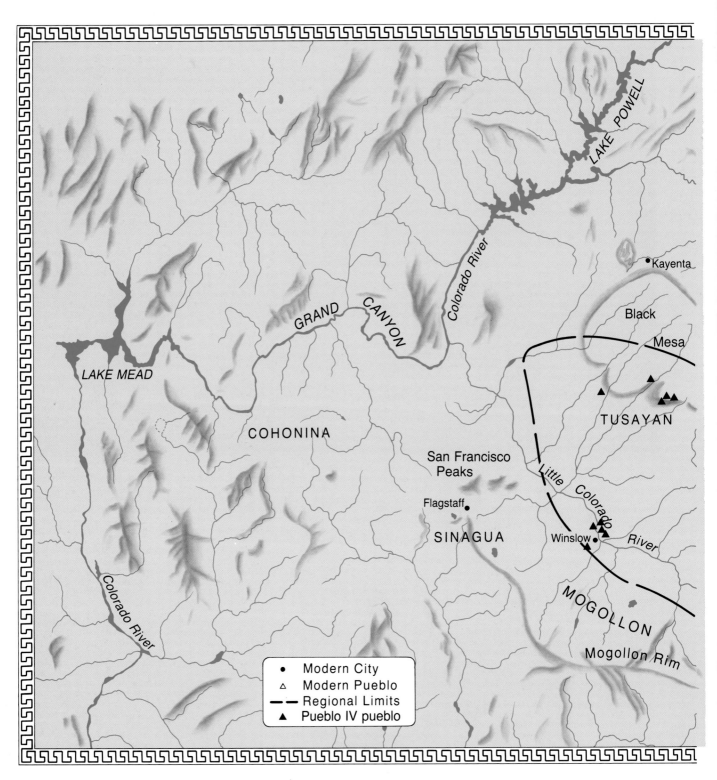

Pueblo IV Anasazi regions after the Great Migration of
ca. 1300 to the arrival of the Spaniards in 1540.
Modern pueblos grew out of these late prehistoric
population centers.

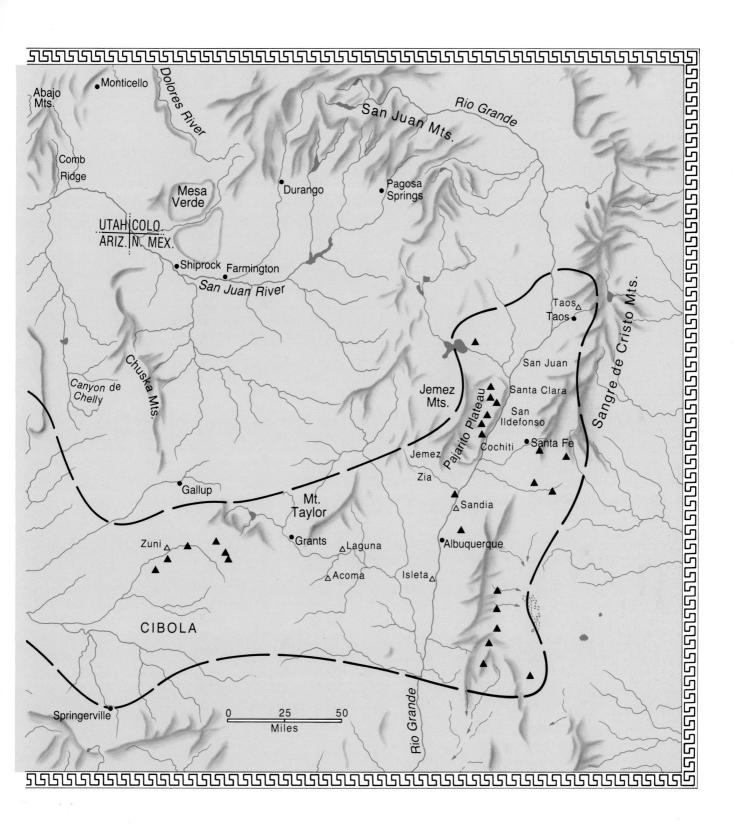

Abajo
Mts.

• Monticello

Dolores River

San Juan Mts.

Rio Grande

Comb
Ridge

Mesa
Verde

• Durango

Pagosa
Springs

UTAH|COLO.
ARIZ.|N. MEX.

• Shiprock   Farmington

San Juan River

San Juan Mts.

Rio Grande

Sangre de Cristo Mts.

Canyon de
Chelly

Chuska Mts.

Jemez
Mts.

Pajarito Plateau

Taos △
Taos •

San Juan

Santa Clara

San
Ildefonso

Cochiti

• Santa Fe

Jemez

Zia

Gallup

Mt.
Taylor

△ Sandia

Zuni △

• Grants

△ Laguna

• Albuquerque

△ Acoma

Isleta △

CIBOLA

Rio Grande

Springerville •

0   25   50
Miles

19

Physical Appearance

The ancient Anasazi resembled the Pueblo Indians of today; this we know because of the many withered bodies preserved by the dryness of the caves where they were buried. Their skin was dark brown. Their features show some Asiatic characteristics. The skeletal structure of their heads was rather long and narrow, and their faces were of medium length, with high cheek bones. The natural long-headedness was artificially deformed to round-headedness starting in the Pueblo I stage by the use of wooden cradleboards. We assume that they had brown eyes and smooth and relatively hairless faces and bodies.

The scores of skeletons found in the San Juan area show the men to have averaged about five feet four inches tall (some were six feet tall), and the women were somewhat shorter than the men. These skeletons also reveal that the Anasazi Indians had shovel-shaped upper incisor teeth, a physical characteristic found frequently in Asiatics.

It can be inferred from the skeletons that they were moderately sturdy people, perhaps even stocky. Generally speaking, change in physical appearance is slow to occur unless there is an infusion of different genetic types. Therefore, the ancient Anasazi probably looked significantly like the Pueblo Indians today.

Food, Clothing, and Shelter

Habits of the Anasazi relating to food, clothing, and shelter had their origins far beyond the recognizable beginnings of Anasazi prehistory. The earliest human migrants to North America derived their necessities from hunting large game animals such as mammoths, mastodons, large big-horned bison, tapirs, sloths, camels, and horses, all of which are now extinct.

These Paleo-Indians had first followed herds of these animals across the now submerged Bering land bridge more than 15,000 years ago. Meat predominated in their diet, but when a mammoth was unavailable—and it might have been weeks or months between kills—they ate small game, lizards, seeds, and insects. Animal skins provided both clothing and rudimentary shelter.

With the demise of most of the big game animals at the end of the Pleistocene Ice Age around 8000 B.C., North America's inhabitants turned to other food sources, especially plants. In the desert West, nomadic bands survived by harvesting a wide range of plant products that could be gathered while

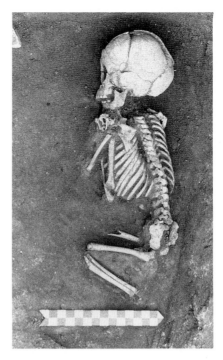

Burial of a child showing deformation of the back of the head, Ewing Site, Yellow Jacket district, Montezuma Valley.

hunting small animals as a meat source. In the process, these desert dwellers became immensely familiar with every detail in their environment—for example, where and when to find pinyon nuts, cactus buds, yucca fruits, grass seeds, berries, and pigweed seeds and greens. All of these wild plant products continued to be collected in later times by the Anasazi farmer.

The source of Anasazi agriculture can be traced back not only to the desert dwellers of the Southwest, but to their cultural cousins in Mexico. While the ancient Mexicans relied primarily on gathering wild plant foods, they steadily domesticated a growing number of plants. Among many others were the three the Anasazi later came to depend on for the vast majority of their food—squash (about 6000 B.C.), Indian corn or maize (about 5000 B.C.), and common beans (about 2000 B.C.). Corn and squash first appeared in the Southwest by perhaps 3000 B.C., but nearly 3,000 years passed before they had a major impact on the diet of the early Anasazi (Basket Maker II stage). Beans did not arrive until around A.D. 500–600 when they became an important protein replacement for declining meat supplies.

As the Basket Maker II peoples slowly evolved from their Desert Culture beginnings, they contin-

20

ued to hunt small game such as deer, rabbits, wood rats, squirrels, raccoons, and turkeys. In some places, like the Animas River valley of Colorado, they also snared water fowl. Less commonly, elk, mountain sheep, grouse, and other land birds were taken. As agriculture became more and more important, hunting decreased. By A.D. 600, turkeys had been domesticated for their feathers; four hundred years later turkey meat became common fare.

Thus, by the time Puebloan culture was well established in Pueblo III, the Anasazi raised the great bulk of their food—corn, squash, beans, and turkeys—but continued to gather the traditional wild nuts, seeds, berries, and greens, and to augment their meat supply by hunting primarily rabbits and deer. This subsistence pattern remained unchanged until the Spaniards introduced sheep, goats, wheat, melons, fruits, and a host of new crops. Despite this, however, the modern Pueblos still rely heavily on their traditional foodstuffs.

Men and women divided economic tasks along fairly fixed lines. Men hunted the animals for meat, frequently relying on hunting charms representing nature's successful predators such as the puma, bear, eagle, and badger. Hunting equipment included the bow and arrow, which had supplemented the older atlatl and dart by A.D. 600. Curved wooden throwing sticks designed for stunning rabbits also doubled as clubs. Small game were generally taken in traps or net snares.

Men also performed most of the farming tasks—working ground, planting, cultivating, watering—although women and children usually assisted in harvesting. Both sexes braided ears of corn together, cut squash into strips, tied bean plants into bundles, and dried all of them for storage. The women usually gathered wild plant foods, and they had the onerous task of preparing and cooking meals. The daily grinding of corn kernels and other seeds into meal and flour constituted a wearing and never-ending burden in every woman's life. They would have to kneel behind a tilted sandstone metate, often set in a bin, and draw the smaller handstone or mano back and forth across it for hours at a time. The resulting meal was added to the ever-present stew or made into cakes cooked on flat stones.

Standard fare at mealtime, besides the corn cakes, was a stew kept simmering in a pot over hot coals. A basic stock contained chunks of meat, sometimes even whole small animals, pieces of vegetables such as squash or beans, flavorings derived from wild fruits and berries, and a host of other items to provide variety. In the days before pottery, the ingredients were placed in tightly woven baskets sealed

A corn plant petroglyph from San Cristobal, Galisteo region, south of Santa Fe, New Mexico.

The three staples of the Anasazi diet: corn, beans, and squash. These staples produced by farming plus meat from wild game fed the Anasazi for more than 2,000 years.

A grinding room at Gran Quivira and grinding bins at Betatakin. These side-by-side metates allowed three women to grind corn at the same time, thus making a social event out of the daily, tedious, back-breaking task of making corn meal.

with pinyon pitch and brought to a boil by adding hot stones, as the basket could not be exposed directly to the fire.

Whole corn kernels were often parched in a basket with hot coals; whole ears of corn were roasted within their green husks in coals; meats were sometimes roasted directly over the fire; some wild nuts and berries were eaten raw.

Anasazi tastes are equally evident in the items they chose not to eat as well as those they did eat. Fish, reptiles, and amphibians (frogs and turtles) are absent from their food refuse, even though these resources abound in their environment. Water-fowl—ducks and geese—were taken only by a few of the earlier Basket Makers. Despite these aversions, detailed studies of human feces from Mug House at Mesa Verde revealed they frequently ate cactus fruit without removing the short spines and consumed small rodents, bones, hair, and all.

Like their food, the Anasazi derived most of their clothing styles from their Desert Culture beginnings. Most items of apparel were made from plant fibers, but animal skins were also used. The amount of clothes the Anasazi wore depended upon the season. As standard garb the women wore sandals and an apron and the men sandals and a breechcloth. For winter additional items were needed because there was little heat and the weather could be very cold—sometimes below zero. The daytime sun was warm, even in winter, but high-altitude nights were cold. Basket Maker peoples manufactured warm robes by wrapping strips of rabbit fur around yucca cords and twining them together. Some made deerskin robes and occasionally robes from elk hides and mountain sheep. The hides were sewn together with yucca twine, and some have been found fastened with human or dog hair.

After turkeys had been domesticated, the late Basket Maker III (A.D. 700) and subsequent Pueblo Indians made feather-cloth blankets that were light, fluffy, and very warm. They wrapped split brown and white turkey down feathers instead of rabbit fur with twisted strings of yucca to make a fluffy cord. These cords were then loosely twined into a blanket. Lighter garments were made of deerskins tanned into soft leather. Cotton became available in Pueblo I (A.D. 750) for belts, sashes, and robes to be worn next to the skin. To protect the feet and legs in cold weather, the Indians wore warm calf-length socks made of feather-wrapped cordage or winter grass or juniper bark tied to the lower legs by the sandal lacings.

The men sometimes wore buckskin jackets and short leggings, although generally the people preferred loose-fitting garments. Based upon the number of garments found, the Anasazi preferred robes of feather-wrapped yucca cords followed by rabbit fur wrapped cords, and, in a descending order of preference, they wore deerhide, cotton, and mountain sheepskin.

These robes were worn over the shoulders and around the waist and tied with sashes made of cotton or woven yucca fibers. Twined weaving with a narrow loom attached to the weaver's waist was used as early as Basket Maker II times to make aprons and sashes. Sometimes the robes were slit and worn like a poncho. The nearest thing to a tailored garment was a sleeveless leather jacket.

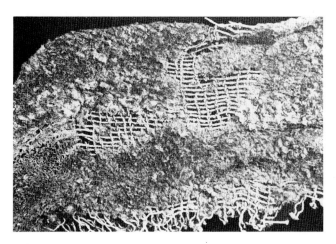

Anasazi robe. Turkey down feathers or rabbit fur were wrapped around cords held together by spaced, twined wefts.

aprons were also made from juniper bark fibers.

Sandals were the most important item of clothing. They were made of strips split from yucca leaves or twined, twisted yucca cords. The Basket Maker sandals were flat, squared across the toe, and rounded at the heel. They were held in place by a toe-loop and a heel-loop with a string passing through the loops and around the ankle. Basket Maker III (A.D. 450–750) sandals were decorated with woven geometric figures. The later Pueblo Indians wore undecorated split yucca leaves twilled into the shape of the foot.

The Anasazi wore jewelry, but not as much as has been popularly imagined. It was made from bird wing bones (turkey, eagle, and Canada goose), snail shells, lignite, shale, and turquoise. The various items included necklaces, pendants, and buttons.

From Basket Maker times onward the Anasazi wore beads of stone of various colors which were ground, polished, and bored for stringing. There were also beads of olivella and abalone shell, traded from the Pacific Coast, and beads of locally obtainable land-snail shells. Necklaces were made of bright seeds or polished bone cut into short tubes and polished and sometimes engraved. A number of chokers

Aprons worn by the women were made of dozens of yucca cords that hung down in front and were tied to a belt worn around the waist. The yucca strings were usually woven at the top. The cords were long enough to pass between the legs and loop over a string belt and hang down in the back. Similar

A yucca-fiber apron and juniper bark menstrual pad worn by an Anasazi woman in Pueblo I times during the ninth century A.D. A fiber skirt or breech cloth and sandals were the standard attire for both men and women. Feather and animal-skin robes were added in winter. Items found in Big Cave in Canyon del Muerto, Canyon de Chelly National Monument.

Basket Maker II yucca-fiber sandal from Mummy Cave, Canyon de Chelly National Monument. The big toe was inserted in the loop and the cord was tied behind the heel. Prior to the introduction of cotton, all Anasazi clothes were made from natural plant fibers, wild animal skins, and feathers. Sheep and goats (for wool) were unknown prior to the arrival of the Spaniards in the 1600s.

have been found made of leather or fiber cord with some large beads in the middle. These were held on by a loop on one end and a knot or toggle on the other. Bright feathers mounted on pins of wood or bone were worn attached to fur robes or in the hair.

Turquoise appeared late in Basket Maker III (A.D. 700), and with it the technique of mosaic work. Some pendants were made by attaching bits of turquoise with pitch to a thin flat slab of wood. By Pueblo III turquoise work became more refined. A necklace made of sky blue turquoise found at Pueblo Bonito in Chaco Canyon contained twenty-five hundred beads and four pendants. All the stones were shaped and polished by hand using only stone tools.

The development of Anasazi dress for the hundreds of years from Basket Maker II through Pueblo III can be traced from the bits and pieces found in dry caves and from the many excavated burials. Each find can be placed in its chronological niche by the various archaeological dating techniques. The sum of the evidence produces a record of the change over the centuries.

Some archaeologists have suggested that increased economic security beginning about A.D. 600 produced more leisure time and with it more refined garments. The aprons worn by the women were

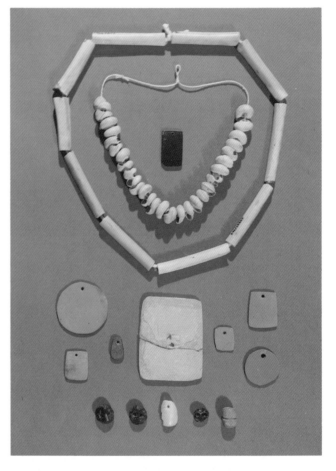

Anasazi jewelry from Mug House, Mesa Verde National Park. The beads were made from land snail shells and the wing bones of golden eagles and Canada geese; pendants were of red shale and black jet; and the three buttons in the bottom row were made from jet. The pendant in the center of the bottom row came from a *Conus* shell, a Pacific Ocean shellfish.

sometimes woven and painted. The fur robes were replaced by the much lighter and warmer feathered robes. Yet this leaves unexplained why later clothing often declined in quality and decoration. Clothing in Basket Maker III times was better and more artistically made than the later Pueblo apparel, with the exception of cotton garments. Cotton woven on an upright loom began during Pueblo I allowing men to wear kilts or breechcloths and women to wear dresses and shawls, or mantas, all made of woven cotton.

We really have no idea what form of shelter the pre-Anasazi Desert Culture people occupied. Some of their campsite rubbish has been found in natural rock shelters and caves, but most sites are in the open. Presumably they constructed simple huts or lean-tos of brush much like the historic Paiutes of the Great Basin.

The oldest known Anasazi of Basket Maker II were already building substantial houses, dug partially into the ground surface, even though they continued to move seasonally following food sources. Perhaps of greater significance, though, was the attention given to structures in which to store food for the lean months of the year. Well-built stone slab-lined storage cists not only accompanied the houses, but also have been found in rock shelters where the Basket Maker peoples must have camped. Basket Maker II houses actually resembled large versions of the storage cists, but usually with a fire pit added.

The attention shown to storage marks the important shift from a nomadic way of life to a sedentary one. As the evolving Basket Makers devoted more time and energy to agricultural pursuits, they could reside in one place all year round, occasionally foraging out on hunting and gathering expeditions.

By A.D. 600, Basket Maker III peoples lived in small villages of pithouses—substantial, circular, roofed pit-rooms with attached or nearby storage chambers. Above ground were storage rooms and ramadas (a carport-like roofed work area). Already a building pattern had developed. Each pithouse faced south, with storehouses and ramadas set immediately to the north. Rubbish was scattered to the south. Even though construction materials and architectural design changed dramatically through time, the unit construction pattern can be traced from Basket Maker III into Pueblo IV, just prior to the arrival of the Spaniards. The pattern unit consisted of storage rooms, ramada, pithouse, and trash on a north-south axis.

By Pueblo II and III, pithouses became kivas,

the place of much Anasazi ritual activity. A growing penchant for closeness brought increasing numbers of the aboveground rooms into physical contact with one another, forming multiunit, multistoried, apartment-like residences all built according to the pattern unit. By A.D. 1100, the Pueblo III Anasazi had congregated into large towns of up to 2,500 people. Anasazi pueblos never grew beyond about 3,000 people—which is true of modern pueblos—probably because larger numbers created problems of an urban society that the Anasazi were unable or unwilling to assume. Their egalitarian way of life could not readily adapt to a concentration of more than 3,000.

Each residence unit housed a kin group or lineage segment of related individuals. Within each unit, blocks or suites of rooms contained small family households. Within each suite, all rooms were mutually accessible, yet a single outside entrance provided relative privacy. The adjacent kiva and the courtyard formed by its roof served both practical and spiritual needs of the kin-group residents. These kivas were the lineage or clan gathering places that were comfortable in cold or hot weather. Archaeologists no longer believe that women and children were excluded from these kivas except during secret rituals.

This pattern of construction was more or less followed by the Anasazi whether the buildings were located on the flatlands or in the cliffs. Although we speak of suites and houses, these small masonry rooms were not used as living rooms in the modern sense. Many of the Mesa Verde rooms were no more than six feet square, and the ceiling was so low that an adult could not stand upright. The Pueblo Indians did not live in their houses; they lived out of doors as much as possible, and they convened in the kivas.

The living rooms were heated either with a hearth or by coals carried in from a fireplace outside and placed in a depression in the earthen floor of the room; this reduced the risk of fire. The parents probably slept in the larger of the rooms and the children in the smaller ones. During the cold months the pueblos were certainly not comfortable by modern standards, but by comparison with the crude shelters of their forebears the Pueblo III Indians had made great strides in housing.

Architecture

The most significant aspect of the Anasazi culture was their architecture. Anasazi architecture was

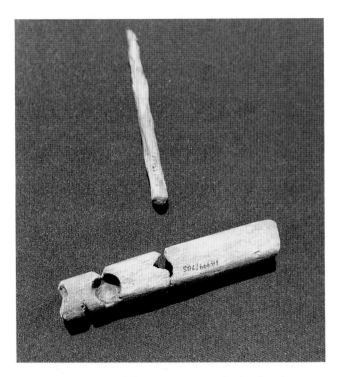

The Anasazi started fires with the aid of a fire drill—a hard stick twirled between the hands in a notch cut (and worn) in a stick of soft wood. Ultimately, the friction would create a spark that could be placed in tinder to break into flame.

utilitarian; its houses, storage units, and religious structures all developed with a very distinctive style.

Pithouses

The early Basket Maker II (700 B.C.–A.D. 450) pithouse shelters were set partially below ground level and built up with timber, branches, and mud. The floor was excavated about a foot or so into the ground, and then sandstone slabs were set upright to line the sides of the roughly circular pit. The side walls were then built up by cribbing horizontal logs forming a dome-shaped roof; sometimes upright sidewall poles were leaned against a central vertical post. Smaller sticks, bark, and mud plastered over the logs provided weatherproof shelter.

A series of about ten such houses is well preserved in Mummy Cave at Canyon de Chelly National Monument. The houses are oval shaped, about nine or ten feet across. Sandstone slabs up to three feet tall had been mudded to the sloping bedrock beneath the cliff overhang. Logs, branches, and reeds held together with mud formed a beehive-like superstructure above the stone slabs. The slanting bedrock floors required that benches be leveled by hacking out the bedrock or built up with logs and mud. Several of these houses contained internal storage cists and shelves, and one had a hearth. These early dwellings probably had holes in their roofs to allow smoke to escape and as a means for their occupants to enter via a ladder or notched log. They were barely tall enough for a person to stand up inside, and their floors were generally quite uneven.

From such rudimentary beginnings, Basket Maker III people developed the substantial semi-subterranean earth-covered lodge or pithouse. This lodge tended to be larger than the earlier Basket Maker II pithouses. It was up to twenty-five feet across, and its clay-paved floor was also dug below the ground surface. Upright sandstone slabs occasionally lined the excavated pit, and its shape tended to be from circular to squarish with rounded corners. A second, smaller room, or antechamber, served as a ground-level entry and provided additional storage.

Both the roof and sidewalls of the pithouse were supported by four upright posts set in the floor. Four horizontal logs laid on top of these posts formed a square on which the roof timbers rested. Sloping poles, footed either on the ground surface or on a very shallow ledge (banquette), leaned against the square central construction and constituted the sidewalls. Successive layers of sticks laid at right angles to the timbers, juniper bark, or brush were sealed with earth to complete the pithouse, making it weatherproof and giving it the general appearance from outside of a flat-topped earthen mound. A stranger would soon recognize it for what it really was by observing smoke rise through the hole in the center of the roof or people entering through an opening in the antechamber or emerging through the smokehole on a ladder, or seeing people sitting

The excavated remains of a Basket Maker II house from northern Black Mesa in northeastern Arizona.

on the roof grinding corn on metates or performing other household tasks.

Inside the pithouse were several clearly defined features. A clay-lined fire pit occupied the center of the floor. A stone slab or set of poles plastered with mud stood between the fire pit and the antechamber passageway to deflect drafts of air away from the fire. Low partitions or wing walls of stone slabs, poles, and mud linked the two southern roof-support posts with the sidewalls. Together with the deflector, situated between those same two posts, the wing walls effectively partitioned off the southern one-fourth of the floor space. This space was used for preparing food and storing bulky household items behind the wing walls. One could easily step over the wing walls to reach this space. Storage bins were created by tunneling through the lower earthen side-walls, by constructing a double set of wing walls, or by walling off spaces on the ledge or banquette on which the sloping wall poles rested. Small circular depressions in the smooth clay floor, often filled with sand, provided places to set round-bottomed pots so they would not fall over. One small circular hole between the fire pit and the north wall in many pithouses represented the earliest expression of the symbolic entry into the spirit world, called "sipapu" by the Hopi.

A classic example of a Basket Maker III pithouse may be seen in Mesa Verde National Park. Site 117, Earth Lodge B on the Ruins Road which

will be described later, exhibits almost all the standard features. Tree-ring dates place construction of Earth Lodge B around A.D. 600. Elsewhere in Mesa Verde, at Step House Cave, the stabilized remains of four other pithouses of the same age may be visited. These four demonstrate individual variability in this type of structure, yet all differ from the typical pattern by having a short ventilating tunnel in place of the antechamber. Entry must have been through the roof hatchway. One has been partially restored to illustrate how the roof and upper walls were constructed.

The basic elements of pithouse construction have remained the same from Anasazi times to the modern day. Even though building forms changed drastically and new materials and techniques were added, these original concepts were never completely abandoned. Roof construction has continued unchanged, with support provided by timber, masonry walls, or stone columns. In fact, the distinctive modern-day architecture of Santa Fe and Albuquerque is derived from the Puebloan style, especially in ceiling and roof construction. The practice of constructing walls of vertical poles laced with sticks and mud, often incorporting sandstone slabs in the base, continued for 700 years, even after stone-masonry walls came into vogue. The use of clay to plaster floors and walls and to line features such as fire pits has continued to the present day. Orientation of the house along an axis, running from the sipapu on the

This pithouse, reconstructed in Step House Cave on Wetherill Mesa in Mesa Verde National Park, was based upon the remains of Mesa Verde Basket Maker III pithouses. The dwelling was partially subterranean with access through a hole in the roof, which also served as a vent for smoke from the fire pit just below. During the hundreds of years following Basket Maker III (A.D. 600–750) the pithouse developed into the kiva—one of the hallmarks of the Anasazi Culture.

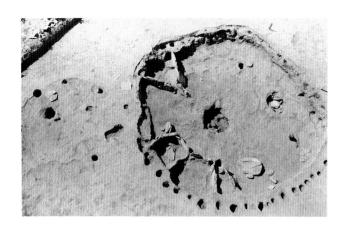

Archaeological excavations of this Basket Maker III (A.D. 600s) pithouse from the Yellow Jacket district of the Montezuma Valley reveal the ground plan of antechamber, main room with hearth and storage bins, and the pattern of potholes where wooden posts supported sidewalls and roof. Because this house burned, a full record was preserved of the materials used to construct the pithouse.

Jacal (wattle-and-daub) wall construction preceded the masonry walls of the later Anasazi pueblos. A framework of posts and limbs was plastered with mud. At Kayenta jacal walls were used along with masonry during Pueblo III. This is the wall of a living room at Keet Seel.

north through the fire pit, ash-holding pit, and the deflector to the antechamber or ventilator tunnel on the south became a rigid pattern reflected in all Anasazi architecture.

Pithouse architecture evolved considerably through time. By 700 in late Basket Maker III, pithouse floors were dug more deeply into the ground—up to three or four feet. This necessitated a distinct banquette on which to rest the now shorter sloping sidewall poles. Antechambers were nearly completely replaced by longer ventilator tunnels. Occupants had to enter through the roof hatchway. Internal storage bins were more consistently replaced by free-standing exterior storehouses.

The Deep Pithouses (Site 101) along the Ruins Road at Mesa Verde exemplify these changes. There are actually two pithouses at this site. The earlier was built just prior to 700, apparently with an antechamber. After it burned, the later house with a ventilator was built just after 700 by enlarging the older antechamber. A stone slab wall held back the loose fill of the older house's main chamber.

By 800, Pueblo I pithouses had become almost totally subterranean with only slightly domed roofs to shed water. The standard shape varies from round to square, but virtually all other features were retained: four-post roof support, wing walls, sipapu, central fire pit, ash pit, deflector, ventilator tunnel, and north-south orientation. An example of this pit-

house style may be seen at Twin Trees on Ruins Road at Mesa Verde (see page 78).

As Pueblo I culture evolved into Pueblo II, the Anasazi lived less in the pithouses and more in newly developing aboveground room blocks. They retained the pithouses, however, for places to conduct a growing number of religious rituals. Thus, by 900, these structures became readily recognizable as the specialized underground ceremonial chambers labeled "kivas" by the Hopi.

Kivas

The evolution of kiva architecture is a remarkable story in itself. The kiva changed through time, developed various styles representative of the Anasazi of different regions, and evolved into a structure that served both kinship groups and whole communities. Kivas have become one of the clearest hallmarks of Puebloan culture.

Development of the smaller kin-group kiva is most completely documented from studies at Mesa Verde. Ruins Roads Site 16 and Twin Trees show how the old pithouse four roof-support posts were first set in the front edge of the banquette around 900, then replaced by four short stone masonry columns or pilasters footed on the banquette around A.D. 1000, and finally increased to six tall masonry pilasters by 1100. The shift from four to six pilasters signaled a shift to a cribbed log, dome-shaped roof construction not unlike the old Basket Maker II cribbed log construction for pithouses, except that the area around the dome was filled to make a level courtyard at ground level.

While the kiva roof-support system was changing, so were other features. Stone masonry lining began to replace the old clay-plastered earth sides of the pit. At first, this masonry merely shored up weak spots of loose earth on the front of the banquette, but by 1100 it lined the entire structure. The Anasazi then applied coats of clay plaster over the face of the masonry. By the 1200s, painted murals appeared on kiva wall plaster, although the actual beginnings of this practice may date back considerably earlier. By the time of the Spanish conquest in 1540, kiva mural painting had reached a very sophisticated state, as exemplified at Kawaika on the Hopi Mesas, at Kuaua in Coronado State Monument near Bernalillo, New Mexico, and at Awatovi on Antelope Mesa in Arizona.

The interior alignment of the sipapu, fire pit, deflector, and ventilator on a north-to-south axis remained quite standard in almost all Anasazi kivas

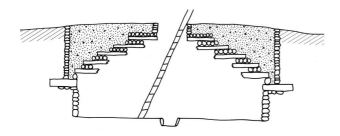

The cribbed roofs of kivas were constructed of horizontally laid logs built up to form a dome with an access hole. Earth fill leveled the roof's top and made the kiva completely below ground (after National Park Service pamphlet).

into Pueblo III (1100–1300). Mesa Verde–style kivas added new features to this axis. With the advent of stone masonry linings, small storage niches were frequently built into the masonry facing. Quite commonly one of these niches fell on the axis directly opposite the ventilator opening. When six roof-supporting pilasters became common, the space between the two southernmost pilasters and directly above the ventilator tunnel was deepened to form a recess at banquette level. A bird's-eye view of one of these kivas without its roof would reveal a keyhole shape.

Keyhole-shaped kivas with six masonry pilasters and ventilator tunnels entering at floor level are the style characteristic of the Pueblo III Anasazi at Mesa Verde and neighboring Northern San Juan districts such as the Montezuma Valley. Similar distinctive styles may also be recognized for Pueblo III Chaco and Kayenta Anasazi. Chacoan kivas tend to be larger than their Mesa Verde–style counterparts: their ventilators enter the chamber below floor level opening adjacent to the fire pit, thereby obviating the need for a separate deflector. They have a shallow southern recess at floor level—really more an offset in the wall—and they most commonly have eight low pilasters to support the cribbed roof. Chacoan-style pilasters consist of a short log embedded in the kiva wall with thin masonry veneers on each side; the logs of the cribbed roof rest on these short logs. Caches of turquoise have been found in pockets on the top surface of many such log pilasters in Pueblo Bonito kivas.

Chacoan kiva fire pits tend to be stone lined. Many have one or more long vaults set into the floor—used for storage or as foot drums. The typical Chacoan masonry style of small, closely fitting sandstone blocks sets this kiva style apart from the Mesa Verde style, where larger stones and some upright slabs above banquette level were set in thick mud mortar.

Kivas in the Kayenta region tend to be small, and somewhat squarish with rounded corners; they have four roof-support posts set into the corners and lack banquettes and recesses. Some are actually quite rectangular in shape, foreshadowing the historic Hopi rectangular kivas. A number of kivas in the southern Cibola region have a full D shape with a southern recess and floor-level ventilator tunnel on the straight side.

Of course not all kivas exactly fit these standards. Within a single settlement, no two are exactly alike. This probably reflects not only individual builders' variations, but also specific needs of the kin-group rituals and the setting where a kiva was built. Bedrock cave floors forced many kivas to be constructed above ground, where their builders sur-

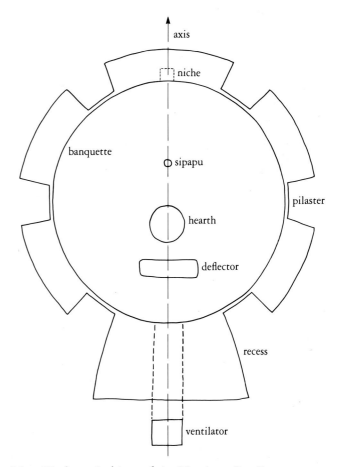

Mesa Verde–style kivas of the Northern San Juan exhibited very distinctive characteristics. The banquette-level recess on the south side of the circular kiva produced a distinctive keyhole-shape outline.

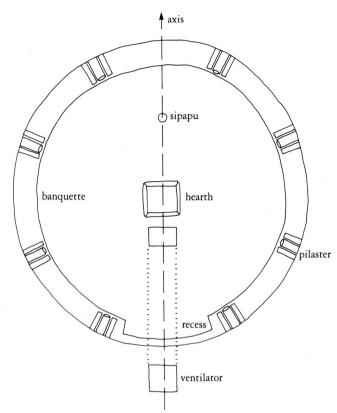

A typical Chacoan kiva was masonry lined with a banquette around the circular wall upon which stone and log pilasters supported a cribbed roof. The ventilation system entered from below floor level.

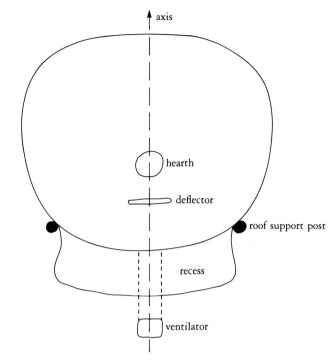

Kivas in the Kayenta region display more variability than do Chaco or Mesa Verde–style kivas. Wooden posts set in the masonry wall often replace pilasters as roof supports. While most have a circular outline, others were clearly rectangular.

rounded them with rubble held in place by walls to create an underground atmosphere. Kivas built within caves and rock shelters required ventilators to lead to the cave opening, whatever the direction, although many shrewd architects angled the tunnel toward the traditional kiva orientation once at the mouth of the cave.

Residents of upper stories had access to kivas set in the room blocks of the lower stories so as to provide access from an upper-story plaza and yet create the subsurface impression. The third-story resident could go out his door onto the plaza and down into the kin kiva in the same way his ancestors did when the kiva was dug in the pueblo courtyard.

Not all kivas were round; several Mesa Verde kivas were actually square. The numbers of pilasters varied from none (roofs resting directly on walls) to as many as ten. Deflectors were constructed of stone slabs, poles and mud, masonry wall stubs, arcs of masonry, and movable stone slabs. Some kivas even lacked a sipapu while others had two or more. Other features found in kivas include loom anchors, wall pegs set in pilaster faces, horizontal pole shelves

between pilasters, and stone anvils set in the floor. The loom anchors and stone anvils indicate that the kivas were used as a men's workshop or craft center as well as a gathering place for kin groups. Tunnels connected with other kivas, with rooms, or with towers.

The tower kivas of Chacoan sites such as Chetro Ketl and Salmon were built on the second story on top of a rubble platform and surrounded by walled-in rubble. Their central position in the sites where they occur suggests a specific community-wide function rather than a kin-group one.

Pueblo III marked the epitome of kin-kiva construction and use by the Anasazi. Probably every kin group had its own kiva for both ceremonial and domestic use. Following the Great Migration of the late 1200s kin kivas became less numerous. There were more people yet fewer kivas, especially in the Rio Grande valley. Typical kiva features continued to be incorporated into many Pueblo IV kivas, but a new style also developed. The Anasazi of the Pajarito Plateau west of Santa Fe built many of their houses and kivas against the bases of vertical cliffs of soft volcanic tuff. They burrowed many rooms and kivas into the cliffs themselves. Such cave kivas

On the Pajarito Plateau, including Bandelier National Monument, Pueblo IV Anasazi kivas were sometimes located in caves. This kiva with rock art decorations is located in Ancho Canyon.

tend to be ovoid with fire pits and side entries. Roof supports were not needed. Sipapus were only occasionally present. Side entries provided ventilation. Rows of loom anchors occur commonly. Because of the Spanish attempts to suppress Pueblo Indian religion, kin-group-style kivas are found today only in Taos and in the Hopi pueblos.

Great Kivas

The so-called great kivas had a separate path of development from the kin-group kivas. They are distinguished primarily by their large size—more than forty-five feet across—by the presence of masonry fire boxes and floor vaults, and by the rooms attached to the main chamber. Like the others, great kivas evolved from pithouses, but from a kind of pithouse that stood apart from others by virtue of its unusually large size. Several Basket Maker III villages have contained one such large structure. At Shabik'eshchee Village at Chaco Canyon, archaeologist Frank H. H. Roberts interpreted this distinctively large pithouse as a community-wide ceremonial building serving the inhabitants of two successive villages of nine pithouses each. He suggested that this large pithouse was a forerunner of the later great kivas found at Chaco Canyon sites.

Other such large pithouse structures have been identified at several sites north of the San Juan River, even though their complete village context has not been investigated. Between the Earth Lodge B settlement (600s) and the Twin Trees Settlement (700s) at Mesa Verde a large pithouse was partially excavated. It can no longer be seen, as the archaeologists filled in the excavation. Each of these two settlements contained eight pithouses, and although they were about a hundred years apart in time, each of the settlements may have used the large pithouse as a community center. The others occur at the Badger House Community on Wetherill Mesa and at Yellow Jacket and Alkali Ridge in the Montezuma Valley. Architecturally, these large Basket Maker III pithouses differ from the smaller ones only in size. Some features such as storage bins may be lacking.

Unfortunately, no definitive link has been demonstrated between the large Basket Maker III pithouses and the classic Pueblo III great kivas. Several prototype great kivas are known from Pueblo I contexts in the Northern San Juan, but only a few have been studied.

We know very little about the architecture of these Pueblo I great kivas. They were circular with central hearths and floor vaults, and mostly earth lined. No great kivas have been dated to the Pueblo II stage (900–1100), although many of the later Pueblo III structures may well have been remodeled from older Pueblo II versions.

A typical great kiva of Pueblo III was circular, forty-five to seventy feet in diameter, and dug partially into the ground. Stone masonry lined the pit and carried the walls above ground level. Chacoan-style masonry characterizes the great kivas of Chaco Canyon and its outliers, while those north of the San Juan River have Mesa Verde-style masonry. A set of four columns footed on sets of large sandstone disks supported the flat roof. These columns, usually square, consisted of alternating layers of stone masonry and horizontal poles. Large logs linked the columns to one another and to the side walls, forming the bottom layer of a typical Anasazi layered roof of successively smaller wooden elements covered with bark and earth. In the center of the floor stood a raised, rectangular masonry fire box. Similarly raised, oblong masonry vaults stretched between roof-support columns on the east and west sides. One, sometimes two low masonry benches—presumably where spectators sat—encircled the floor area.

Entry usually could be made down staircases

from the south and north sides. The north staircase normally led to a ground-level masonry room, attached to the circular kiva wall, in which an altar-like platform usually stood. The Aztec Ruin great kiva had a set of masonry rooms completely encircling the structure's exterior. Each room could be entered through an exterior door or from inside the kiva by climbing a ladder of short sticks set in the interior wall. Many great kivas lacked this circle of rooms but instead had a row of niches in the inside circular wall; others, such as Casa Rinconada in Chaco Canyon, had a tunnel leading from the north altar room beneath the floor to an opening near the center of the floor. Archaeologists speculate that masked performers could emerge from the opening of this tunnel as from out of the earth during a ceremony reenacting the Anasazi origin myth. As in the kin-group kivas, great kivas were oriented along a north-south axis from a north altar room through the north entry, firebox, and sipapu, to the south entry, with other features arranged symmetrically on either side.

Not all great kivas were circular. At Mesa Verde, two such structures were built in a rectangular form beneath cliff overhangs. One, Fire Temple, may be seen from an overlook in Fewkes Canyon; the other occupies a central position in Long House on Wetherill Mesa. Despite their rectangular shape, these buildings exhibit typical great-kiva features, including masonry fire box and floor vaults, low benches, a north altar room, and wall niches.

Wherever they are found, the great kivas seem to have served as places where community ceremonies were held. Each Pueblo III town or other central settlement had a great kiva or similar structure. After the Great Migration, while the smaller kiva styles were becoming less common during Pueblo IV, great kivas continued to function as community ceremonial structures, together with open plazas. Except at Taos where kin kivas survive, kivas in the historic Rio Grande pueblos are descendants of the prehistoric Anasazi great kivas.

Living and Storage Units

The Anasazi of Basket Maker II and III (700 B.C.–A.D. 750) lived in pithouses containing some

This great kiva at Pueblo Bonito in Chaco Canyon was used as a community center by many people of the canyon. It was roofed originally like the restored great kiva at Aztec Ruin. The great kivas built between 1000 and 1300 are the Anasazi counterpart of the Gothic cathedrals of Europe built at about the same time.

The Fire Temple at Mesa Verde served as a great kiva for the Cliff-Fewkes Canyon community of cliff dwellings at Mesa Verde National Park. It was probably not roofed.

Great kivas occurred at many of the large pueblos at Chaco Canyon and in the Montezuma Valley. This great kiva is located in the courtyard of Chetro Ketl.

Visible are the large round stones that served as footings for the columns that supported the roof. The rectangular pits were probably foot drums.

storage bins. They constructed additional detached storehouses to the north of the pithouses by lining slightly tapering pits with stone slabs, and constructing low domed covers of stones, sticks, and mud. Groups of isolated stone-lined cists have also been found in rock shelters near Kayenta and in southern Utah. By the 600s, Basket Maker peoples built additional aboveground granaries of upright poles woven into a latticework with branches and sticks and covered with mud. Archaeologists call this style of construction "jacal." At the same time, the Anasazi began to build simple roofs resting on four posts to shade themselves from the hot summer sun while working out-of-doors. These "ramadas" were arranged in rows in front of the storerooms to the north of the pithouses.

Once this pattern became established, it required few modifications to turn these structures into the first typical pueblo houses. Jacal walls added to the rows of ramadas created enclosed living spaces. Stone slabs helped reinforce the bases of the wattle and daub wall construction, and small hearths provided warmth. Smaller jacal store rooms attached to the north (back) side replaced many of the old separate granaries. Shaded outdoor work space was produced by attaching ramadas to the south (front) side of the rooms forming a sort of portico. Such a combination of buildings typified the Pueblo I transition from living in pithouses to living in aboveground room blocks. Each household would occupy one or two living rooms with attached storerooms and por-tico space; all were constructed using stone slabs, wood, branches, and mud.

The earliest stone masonry appears during the 800s in late Pueblo I. Roughly shaped sandstone blocks or cobblestones were laid in uneven horizontal courses in thick mud mortar. Initially, such elemental masonry appeared in the storeroom walls, but soon it spread to the back and side walls of the living rooms. Front walls, in which doorways had to be framed, continued to be built of jacal. The flat roofs of logs, sticks, bark, and mud rested directly on wall corner posts, sometimes supplemented by additional posts set in the floor inside the room corners. Those roofs were strong enough for people to stand or sit on while working outdoors.

The pace at which stone masonry walls supplanted jacal walls varied greatly from one place to the next. Some Anasazi built their entire housing and storage room blocks out of masonry by the early 900s, while others persisted in using jacal for their houses into the mid-1000s. Single walls of jacal have been found in late Pueblo III (1200s) cliff dwellings of the Mesa Verde and Keet Seel in Tsegi Canyon.

Early stone masonry employed large amounts of mud mortar. The wall was one stone thick, and both the inside and outside were smoothed. Neither this thin masonry nor the jacal construction could support more than one story in building height. However, by the late 1000s in Chaco Canyon, multiple-stone thick walls permitted rooms to be stacked atop one another from two to three stories. Several Chacoan buildings, such as Pueblo Bonito, reached five stories by the early 1100s. For this height, the curved back wall of Pueblo Bonito tapered from a

One of the earliest examples of Anasazi construction was the slab-lined cist used to store grain. Anthropologists believe these Basket Maker II Indians (before A.D. 400) built these receptacles to protect harvested grain while they continued as nomadic hunters. These cists are evidence of the transitional stage between hunters and gatherers and sedentary farmers.

The slab-based jacal walls were developed in Pueblo I. These were found, along with rudimentary masonry walls, at the Duckfoot Site in the Montezuma Valley.

Chacoan regular masonry walls, such as these at Pueblo Pintado, were constructed with carefully laid flat stones, two stones thick, bound together with mud mortar.

Chacoan masonry is Anasaziland's most sophisticated form. Here pictured is a wall from Wijiji displaying banded masonry: courses of large stones interspersed with closely fitted tablet-size smaller stones.

Mesa Verde–style masonry was as substantial as that of Chaco but not so refined. These double-coursed walls are part of Hovenweep House.

basal thickness of more than four feet to about one foot thick on top.

Stone masonry construction flourished in the Chaco Canyon during the time of greatest building activity from 1070 to 1130. The masons quarried tabular blocks and small slabs of sandstone, dressed their faces to a smoother surface by pecking away undesired bumps, and laid them in even courses with only small amounts of mud mortar. The close fit of the stone building blocks has allowed Chacoan walls to withstand the ravages of erosion, and many walls are still standing.

Chacoan wall builders expressed considerable artistic individuality in their work. Some used relatively uniform sizes of stones, be it large or small, in a single wall. Others alternated one course of larger stones with several courses of small stones to produce a banded effect. Individual tastes and skill may even be seen in different banding patterns. Still other masons persisted in using a much higher proportion of mud mortar to building stone, or they

employed masonry veneers on both sides of a core of rubble and earth. Neither of these last two styles produced walls as strong as the solid stone masonry.

Multistory construction appeared somewhat later, after 1100, in the Northern San Juan and Kayenta regions. Mesa Verde–style masonry employed walls from one to three stones thick, with faces pecked or ground smooth. Relatively uniform size building stones were placed in a single wall. Larger stones faced a wall's exterior with smaller stones on the interior face. Mortared spaces between stones were chinked with small sandstone spalls and

Kayenta masonry was generally one stone thick and used large quantities of mud mortar. These walls are found at Big Cave in Canyon del Muerto, Canyon de Chelly National Monument.

Many Anasazi painted the inside walls of their living rooms in two colors: pinkish red around the bottom third and white above. These rooms may be seen in Spruce Tree House at Mesa Verde National Park.

occasionally with potsherds and even corn cobs. Kayenta builders used larger proportions of mud mortar between thinner stones with wedge-shaped edges, filling the spaces with dense chinking. Those same masonry styles also occurred in kivas, but usually without any chinking.

Despite the individual artistry shown in masonry wall construction around Anasaziland, most wall faces were covered with coats of mud plaster, especially on the inside. Interior plastered walls were frequently painted a reddish basal color topped by a white or cream. Both geometric and life figures occasionally appear. It was common to place a row of red dots just above the red-white junction or to extend the red zone upward as a series of triangles, presenting the impression of mountains on the horizon. Mural decorations in living rooms never exceeded two colors, although a tan sometimes substituted for the red or white figures that were painted against a dark gray background.

Throughout all the changes in wall construction, the roofs were built the same way—successive layers of smaller and smaller poles, branches, and twigs set at right angles to one another and covered with bark and mud, all resting on one or more main beams built into the tops of the walls. The mud covering of one room's roof provided the floor for the room above. Basic construction of these rooms remained the same whether the houses were built in the open on valley floors and mesa tops or in rock shelters as cliff dwellings. Beneath the cliff overhangs, the cliff itself sometimes provided a wall or ceiling for a room.

Doorways through masonry walls required positioning of a lintel across the top of the opening

Flat roofs were constructed by laying poles across the tops of room walls. Smaller poles were laid on top of the large poles and then covered with split twigs, juniper bark, and mud. This is an original roof from Keet Seel.

and a sill across the bottom. Long, thick stone blocks or sets of short poles made strong lintels; smooth flat stones provided sills, sometimes projecting slightly from the wall face. Where rectangular stone slabs served as doors, wooden door stops in the form of twigs were mudded into the sides and top of the doorway and a shallow groove in the top of the door sill held the doorslab in place. The door could even be locked from the outside by sliding a pole through two loops on either side. Other doorways were closed by hanging a woven mat in front of the opening (as in Aztec Ruin).

Most doorways were rectangular with raised sills and low lintels, requiring someone passing

Room doorways were often designed with stops at the top and sides to support a stone slab door to close the opening. This doorway is in a cliff dwelling in Johnson Canyon in the Ute Tribal Park, Colorado.

through to crouch and squeeze. The high sill blocked out cold drafts, and the small size accommodated smaller, more readily handled doors. Chacoan doorways were consistently larger than those in Northern San Juan and Kayenta sites. Some doorways in Chaco and the Northern San Juan have been constricted on both sides above the sill producing a generalized T shape. Access to many living rooms in Keet Seel near Kayenta is through jacal front walls at floor level, then over a low wall deflector on the inside.

Inside the living rooms, small hearths lined with clay or stones lay in a corner or along one wall; small openings at floor level provided fresh air; and openings in the roof or at roof level carried away smoke. Wooden pegs projecting from the wall and short beams across the corners just below the roof allowed the tenants to hang their possessions. Twig loops set in the walls provided attachments for string or ropes, and small valued possessions could be placed in wall niches. Smaller rooms without hearths and with poorly faced and unplastered walls were the storerooms. Some rooms contained batteries of grinding bins, while others were built to house the domestic turkeys. People performed many daily activities outdoors on rooftops and in courtyards where hearths and grinding bins are customarily found. Additional outdoor space was gained by constructing narrow balconies on roof beams extended through the walls.

Yet another stylistic difference sets Chacoan rooms—at least those in the big pueblos of the Chaco

Doorways were rectangular and sometimes T-shaped. The small square-shaped opening was a ventilator. This wall may be seen at Pueblo del Arroyo in Chaco Canyon.

Canyon—apart from those elsewhere in Anasaziland. Chacoan living rooms were decidedly larger, by factors of two to three times, and taller than those of Mesa Verde and Kayenta. Except in these Chacoan rooms, the average Anasazi Indian could not stand up straight in the rooms. Once inside, people would sit or lie down on woven mats spread across the earthen floors. We have already seen how indoor spaces provided room primarily for storage and for sleeping, while most other household tasks took place outdoors.

Not even the Great Migration at the close of the thirteenth century seriously disrupted average domestic architecture. The biggest changes resulted from the different nature of building materials available in the Rio Grande valley. Hopi and Zuni architecture at the time of Spanish contact remained essentially the same as that of their Pueblo III ances-

Access to rooms built above the first floor was often obtained by a narrow balcony built upon the extensions of the interior roof poles. This balcony is part of Balcony House at Mesa Verde National Park.

tors. The evenly bedded sandstones of the Colorado Plateau did not occur in the Rio Grande valley. Rio Grande Pueblo IV Anasazi used lava boulders, blocks of volcanic tuff (consolidated ash), and sun-dried adobe bricks to build multistoried pueblos either in the open, as at Kuaua, or against cliffs, as at Bandelier. The relatively soft tuff cliffs of the Pajarito Plateau west of Santa Fe allowed the Anasazi to carve niches and roof-beam sockets out of the cliff face, to smooth portions of the cliff for room walls, and even to carve entire rooms (cavates) entirely inside the cliff. Yet even with these changes, Anasazi housing style continued directly into the historic architecture of Pecos Pueblo and Gran Quivira.

Unit Pueblos

Any discussion of Anasazi architecture must go beyond a description of the pueblo style. The way various buildings are arranged in relation to one another reflects an organizational design in the minds of the builders. The most significant such design has been called the "unit pueblo" concept. It was a standardized pattern of building. We have already noted a regular row-like placement of the store-houses, ramadas, and living rooms along the north side of pithouses during Basket Maker III–Pueblo I (450–900). This north-south location constitutes the basic element in the unit pueblo concept. All the buildings faced south.

Prior to 900, rows of storage units were arrayed along the north side of an east-west row of ramadas or living rooms. Immediately southward a plaza, including the roof of the subterranean pithouse, constituted an outdoor work space. To the south of this outdoor work space rubbish was discarded. Even when storage and living rooms were arranged in masonry-walled blocks and kivas replaced pithouses in Pueblo II and III, this layout design is recognizable. The large Pueblo III pueblos of Chaco Canyon and the Northern San Juan preserve this pattern simply by attaching the standardized units to one another in east-west rows that are terraced or grouped to emphasize the southern exposure. In a typical unit pueblo settlement are a block of six to fifteen living and storage rooms, one kin-group kiva (whose roof provides courtyard work space), and a rubbish dump, all aligned from north to south. This architectural unit reflects the residence of a standardized social unit centered around kinship ties.

The unit pueblo concept became less recognizable after the Great Migration. Still the southern orientation, north-south kiva orientation, disposition of rubbish southward, and placement of storerooms behind living rooms persisted. Beginning in Pueblo IV and by historic times the southern orientation finally gave way to orientation inward around a central plaza. Thus, the unit pueblo concept allows us to understand an organizational principle of Anasazi society.

Village Layout

Yet another significant principle of organization can be seen in the layout of villages or settlements. Throughout Anasazi prehistory, buildings were found in clusters; rarely does a single structure constitute a prehistoric community. Basket Maker II and III (700 B.C. to A.D. 750) settlements consisted of groups of three to a dozen pithouses with associated storage units, ramadas, outdoor hearths, and other features. Single houses are occasionally found, but often within an hour's walking distance of a village. The standardized housing units with their southern orientation were generally arranged in east-west rows fronting on an open space toward the southeast. Along the northern edge of Anasaziland, wooden post stockades surrounded all or por-

The soft volcanic tuff enabled the Anasazi of Frijoles Canyon at Bandelier National Monument to dig rooms out of the cliff face. Additional masonry rooms were built in cliff-dwelling fashion in front of these cavates.

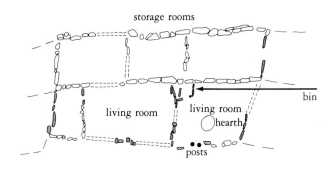

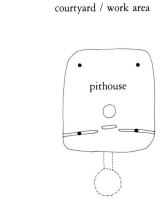

A Pueblo I (A.D. 750–900) unit pueblo—the central unit from the Duckfoot Site in the Montezuma Valley. Each of the two living rooms has its adjacent storage rooms. The two households shared the outside courtyard work space and the pithouse in which some ceremonies probably took place. A rubbish dump lies south of the pithouse.

tions of some Basket Maker III villages. The largest of these villages probably housed around 100 to 150 persons. Proto–great kivas, serving community needs at several villages, generally stood outside the village itself.

With the shift to Pueblo I in the 700s and 800s, village size began to grow dramatically. The standardized housing and storage units were still laid out in east-west rows, quite often abutting one another directly. The southern or southeastern village orientation remained strong. Populations of the largest villages doubled, and smaller outlying settlements sprang up. In the Northern San Juan, at least, great kivas provided for community ceremonialism at many of the larger villages.

Complete settlement plans of Pueblo I and Pueblo II villages have not really been fully investigated except in a few rudimentary cases. About all we can note in Pueblo II villages is the continued growth in population of the largest villages and further differentiation in sizes of outlying smaller settlements. We do have evidence of the construction of reservoirs to supply water for community use (Mummy Lake at Far View on Mesa Verde).

By Pueblo III, the larger towns of the Montezuma Valley, Mesa Verde, the San Juan River valley, Chaco Canyon, and the Little Colorado River valley, had grown to house thousands of people. The standardized housing units (unit pueblos) continued to face southward in east-west rows, while streets and plazas focused traffic flow among them. Artificial reservoirs and other devices promoted a steady water supply for the community. Each of the larger settlements contained a great kiva or a similarly functioning concentric wall structure as a kind of ceremonial center not only for the town itself, but also for surrounding smaller villages and hamlets.

Both the large towns, such as Lowry, and smaller villages, such as Mug House, reflected a two-part physical division—at Lowry the house blocks were divided by the water; at Mug House it was a wall. Settlements of all sizes faced south.

Except for Chaco Canyon, the largest Anasazi towns housed up to around 2,500 people. In Chaco Canyon there was a large, densely arranged group of large towns with a total population of four to six thousand—enough people to make up a city or urban area. The Chaco Basin roadway network involving outlying communities seems to support such an evolution, but the urbanization failed. Chaco Canyon collapsed after about two generations, and the population of pueblos in the rest of Anasaziland remained at 2,500 to 3,000.

Modern pueblos follow the single pueblo organization: each pueblo stands autonomous in government and society with maximum populations of 2,500 to 3,000. They have housing units arranged along streets or around plazas. Kivas provide ceremonial places. Many, such as Zuni, have outlying villages whose occupants always return to the pueblo on ceremonial occasions. Pueblo organization and size have changed little in the 700 years since Pueblo III times.

Concentric Wall Structures, Towers, and Shrines

Pueblo III settlements contain several features about which we know far too little. A series of walled buildings stand apart from others by having two or three walls trace concentric paths around a central circular space. This central space usually contains the basic elements of a kiva, while the surrounding spaces between walls were subdivided by cross walls into compartments, many of which had no apparent means of access. Overall ground plans are either circular or in the general shape of a D.

These concentric wall structures occur almost exclusively north of the San Juan River. The Hubbard Ruin at Aztec Ruin has three circular walls around an aboveground kiva with a second subterranean kiva on its south side. The Sun Temple on the point between Cliff and Fewkes canyons at Mesa Verde has three concentric walls arranged in a D-shape around three ground-level kivas. A circular tower stands slightly apart from the main building. The Hovenweep villages in the Montezuma Valley each contain a D-shaped building with two walls around an aboveground kiva. Those structures have been called horseshoe houses. The only tri-wall circular structure south of the San Juan River may be visited behind Pueblo del Arroyo in Chaco Canyon; it represents what the archaeologists refer to as the "McElmo influence"—that is, it was probably constructed by people from the Mesa Verde–Northern San Juan region. The McElmo people lived side by side with the Chacoans.

Because of their positions in the larger towns and villages, concentric wall structures probably provided community ceremonial activities in much the same manner as great kivas. They seem to reflect a characteristic unique to the Northern San Juan and limited to Pueblo III in that region. We know nothing of possible antecedent structures prior to 1100, nor what happened to these features after abandonment of the San Juan drainage around 1300.

Another structure found almost exclusively north

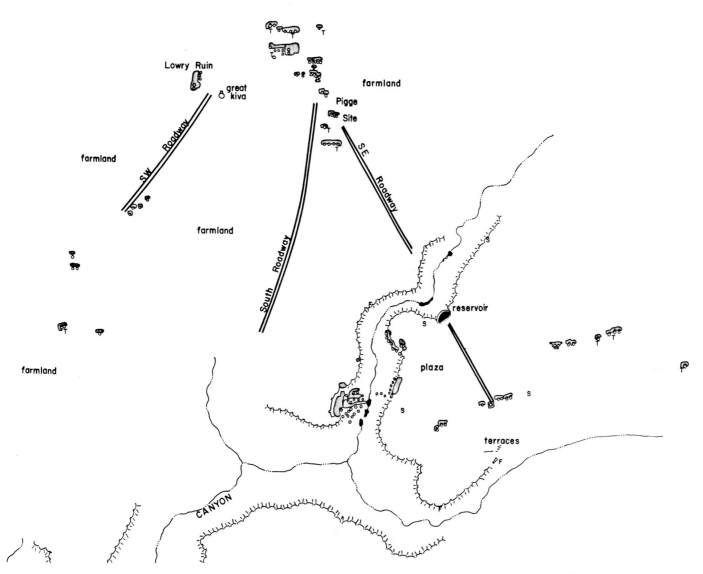

farmland

Lowry Ruin

great
kiva

farmland

S.W. Roadway

farmland

South Roadway

farmland

farmland

Pigge
Site

farmland

S.E. Roadway

reservoir

plaza

terraces

CANYON

Ground plan of the Lowry Town in the Montezuma Valley during Pueblo III (1100–1300). Probably 1,800 people inhabited the various buildings sharing use of the central water supply and the surrounding farmlands while attending ceremonies held at the great kiva or in the two plazas. Several streets connect various parts of the town and lead away to the neighboring smaller communities.

The Hubbard Site (right) at Aztec Ruin, and a building at Pueblo del Arroyo (above) in Chaco Canyon, are two of several known Anasazi tri-wall structures. Originally the central kiva at Hubbard Site was surrounded by a tower made up of three circular walls.

of the San Juan River is the round tower. Circular masonry walls stand one to two stories high within settlements, or in isolated settings usually on the ends of ridges. When in villages, towers usually stand adjacent to the southeast or southwest side of kivas to which they are often linked by an underground tunnel. Tower masonry contains unusually well-dressed stones without chinking, a style common in kivas but not in domestic buildings. For these reasons the round towers have been interpreted as ceremonial buildings rather than watchtowers. The isolated tower at Cedar Tree Tower at Mesa Verde was not only joined by a tunnel to a kiva, but it also had a sipapu laboriously pecked into its bedrock sandstone floor. Towers generally appear around 1100 and cease to be built after 1300. Towers have also been reported from the Gallina District in extreme northern New Mexico.

The kiva-tower combination set apart in some settlements may have functioned as the community ceremonial building. For example, Far View Tower at Mesa Verde, built on the ruins of an ancestor's house, probably served the whole early Pueblo III (1100–1200) Far View community. Isolated kiva-towers occupy settings in nature similar to typical locations of shrines—in isolated areas on mesas or in canyons, often with striking vistas, which were of special significance to the Anasazi.

Like their modern pueblo descendants, the Anasazi constructed a variety of shrines. None have been clearly dated before 1100, but good examples do occur in Pueblo III and IV (1100–1540) contexts. Besides the kiva-towers and some isolated tower-like structures, many shrines take the form of rectangular boxes, U shapes, or alcoves. The boxes are formed by stone slabs set in the ground or by low masonry walls without mud mortar set on the ground surface. Occasionally an old building stone or piles of small sandstone spalls fill the interior. U-shaped shrines resemble dry masonry wall boxes with only three walls and sometimes rounded corners. These U-shaped shrines often open toward a cardinal direction or a prominent feature on the horizon. Alcove shrines were formed by building a dry masonry wall stub with a niche or alcove in it.

An unusual stone enclosure shrine was built on a mesa west of the Bandelier visitor center during Pueblo IV and is used today by the modern Pueblo

The kiva and tower combination, such as this one at Far View in Mesa Verde National Park, was a ceremonial or religious complex. The tower was not built as a defensive structure but to serve a function as yet unknown in association with kivas.

Indians. A crude circle about thirty feet in diameter of large stones encloses a space in which a pair of crouching mountain lions have been sculpted on two low boulders. These two stone lions occupy the southwest portion of the enclosure, and a large stone-lined passage leads due south from its southeast corner.

Probably much of the rock art in Anasaziland marks shrine locations. Concentrations of rock art, such as the numerous places labeled "newspaper rock," often exist well apart from settlements. Painted Cave in Capulin Canyon at Bandelier National Monument contains a dazzling array of paintings with ancient Pueblo pictographs mingled with recent ones done by the Cochiti Indians.

Many Anasazi and modern Pueblo shrines consist of a small masonry box, U-shaped arc, or alcove such as this one from Mesa Verde. They apparently served as receptacles for ritual offerings or objects.

Settlement Locations

Anasazi settlements grew in a variety of different settings—open valley floors, mesa top ridges, rims of canyons, vertical cliffs, or rock shelters beneath cliff overhangs. While all of these locations were in use throughout Anasazi history, several patterns distinguish different cultural stages. For example, cliff dwellings were more common during Pueblo III, although rock shelter locations were also relatively popular in Basket Maker II. Canyon rim locations were also widely used during Pueblo III and IV. The selection of valley bottom settings or mesa top ridges varied more according to local topography.

Throughout Anasaziland are cliff wall shrines etched with rock art symbols. Here pictured is Newspaper Rock at Canyonlands National Park, Utah. Some of the figures, the horseman with a bow and arrow and others, were not incised by the Anasazi but were done by later Indians, indicating that the sacred nature of the shrine continued after Canyonlands was abandoned by the Anasazi.

Which was more important to the villagers: access to water or access to their fields? At Mesa Verde during Pueblo II, it is apparent that the villages built along Ruins Road on the mesa top were as much as a mile from water; they chose to live near the fields. Later at Mesa Verde in Pueblo III, when the people moved off the mesas into the cliffs, they selected sites near springs; these people chose access to water. On balance, most Anasazi settlements and villages were located near a reliable source of domestic water.

Water Management

The ancient Anasazi culture developed in the semiarid Southwest, and each of its settlements was placed to provide access to water. One of the central accomplishments of the Anasazi was the management of water for the household and for crops. Anasazi villages and towns were generally, but not always, located near a water source. The Anasazi had four options: to build on a permanent stream as did the residents of Aztec, Salmon, or Kuaua; to use seasonal streams or washes as did the residents of Tsegi Canyon (Keet Seel), Canyon de Chelly, Chaco Canyon, or Bandelier; to use canyon heads watered by a strong spring as they did at Spruce Tree House at Mesa Verde and most of the Hovenweep settlements; or to impound runoff rainwater as they did at Far View on Mesa Verde.

Generally, springs were produced by rainwater percolating down through porous sandstone to an impervious layer of shale along which it flowed until it came out at the canyon wall. Such a spring comes out beneath the overhang at Long House at Mesa Verde. The Anasazi understood the nature of these springs. They built check dams over the water course above the springs to prevent runoff after rains in order to enhance the spring by holding the water and forcing it to percolate downward.

At Mesa Verde, before they moved into the cliffs, the Anasazi lived on the mesa tops, near the farmland. These locations required them to carry water for washing, drinking, cooking, and pottery making from the water source in the canyon. In late

The Anasazi often built pueblos in canyon heads containing a spring. In many cases they built dams on the cliff tops to prevent runoff and cause the water to trickle down through the sandstone and enhance the flow of the spring below. (Drawing by Joan Foth.)

The Pueblo IV (1300–1540) Anasazi from Bandelier and the Pajarito Plateau farmed on both the plateau top and natural benches in the White Rock Canyon cut by the Rio Grande. The sloping ground prompted the farmers to build stone-walled terraces such as these to hold rainwater and in some cases irrigation water.

The Anasazi built shelters and storerooms near their fields. This field house in White Rock Canyon utilizes a natural cavity beneath a large boulder upon which the Anasazi inscribed an undulating feathered serpent.

Garden plots were created by building masonry walls in dry waterways to collect and hold sediment and moisture. These dams were built near Cedar Tree Tower at Mesa Verde National Park.

Rock art in White Rock Canyon at the east edge of the Pajarito Plateau depicts a horned serpent, a kokopelli, a kachina mask, and bird symbols. These figures were chiseled on a granite boulder located near a Pueblo IV corn field.

Pueblo III, the Mesa Verde people built the cliff dwellings that were nearer to water but farther from the fields.

The Anasazi universally watered their gardens and crops, in some cases by overflow irrigation from the streams or washes, by building check dams in the waterways, or by impounding and diverting run-off rainwater into canals or ditches. Chaco irrigation engineering included floodwater irrigation of the fields along the wash, stone check dams across small washes to hold the soil and moisture, and large earthen dams and storage reservoirs designed to catch and hold runoff rainwater combined with canals and ditches to carry the water to headgates for distribution to terraced or gridded garden plots. Similar irrigation methods were employed at other Anasazi sites. One such irrigation ditch snakes its way down White Rock canyon near Los Alamos.

Ceramics

The Anasazi developed pottery manufacture to provide storage containers and cooking and eating utensils. The production of simple earthenware requires such technological skill and talent that many scholars believe pottery making was more frequently learned from neighboring tribes than independently invented. Archaeologists now believe the pottery-making process spread northward out of central Mexico to the Hohokam and Mogollon of the southern Southwest and thence to the Anasazi. A well-made highly fired pottery was being produced by Basket Maker III Anasazi by the later 500s, and possibly earlier. Unfortunately, the archaeological record is extremely sparse for the period from 300 to 600.

The early Anasazi potters were distinctive and founded a 1,400-year tradition of outstanding ceramic artistry. Gray and white coloring produced by firing the vessels with the reduced oxygen of a smothered fire became a hallmark of the tradition along with the decoration of many vessels with geometric designs executed in black paint against a white background. The painted wares served much as our dinnerware would—for eating and drinking vessels—while unpainted vessels, some with corrugated surfaces, were employed for cooking and storage.

We assume most, or all, Anasazi potters were women because women made most of the pottery in historic pueblos. Ceramic making requires the potter first to find a source of suitable clay, collect it, and clean it. Sometimes a soft shale needed to be ground on a metate and winnowed. Then, to keep the pot from cracking while the clay dried, a coarse tempering material had to be added. This temper might be sand or crushed rock. In later periods old potsherds were crushed for use in tempering the painted pottery.

The potter built up the vessel's shape by rolling ropes of moist clay and coiling them up the sidewalls. She then bonded the coils together by smearing and scraping the surfaces. Between 900 and 1350 potters made distinctive corrugated cooking pots by bonding only on the interiors of the vessels and finger crimping the exteriors. If vessels were to be decorated with paints, their surfaces were polished with a small pebble and usually coated with a slip of fine clay to produce the white background. Paint pigments were derived from either an organic substance like boiled beeweed or an iron oxide powder.

While most painted decorations were geometric, the intricate combinations of figures, the balance of black versus white, the symmetry, layout, and overall patterning bespeak numerous talented artists. Occasionally, stylized humanoid and animal figures were depicted, and some stylized effigy vessels were modeled. These decorations went far beyond the mere function of the pottery vessels. Some figures may have been symbols, although we do not understand their significance. Most decoration, however, seems to be just ornamentation—an aesthetic expression.

Completed pots were first dried in the shade to prevent cracking from rapid shrinkage; then they were ready for the final step—firing. Modern Pueblo potters fire their pots in open fires by piling fuel in a mound around them. We assume the ancient Anasazi fired their pottery in the open; archaeologists, however, have recently discovered a group of kilns that may have been used by the Anasazi.

The undecorated gray and corrugated vessels served primarily as standard cooking pots, although larger ones were also used as storage containers and smaller ones accompanied the dead into an anticipated afterlife. These utility jars generally had a globular shape with wide mouths allowing easy access to their contents. Storage jars were sealed with stone lids held in place with clay. Large globular jars (ollas) with narrow vertical necks and strong handles held water for both transport and storage. Smaller containers held liquids for travelers.

Water was scooped with dippers from spring to pot, from pot to pot, and from pot to mouth. Drinking vessels took the form of handled mugs, some of which resemble pitchers. A very common shape was a bowl with a curved bottom and sides, like a soccer ball cut in half, from which food was eaten and which also served as a general container. Some smaller jars—seed jars, effigy jars, kiva jars, and oblong ceramic boxes—held valuable items such as feathers, charms, scarce raw materials, and pollen for safe keeping.

Each separate locality, village, and social group had its own style of manufacture, form, and decoration, just as different manufacturers and different regions in our own time produce distinctive styles. The Anasazi followed fads and changing styles through

These two Pueblo III gray and corrugated cooking vessels were found and are now displayed at Keet Seel in Navajo National Monument, Arizona.

A group of Pueblo I (A.D. 750–900) potsherds from Big Cave in Canyon del Muerto at Canyon de Chelly National Monument. The four painted sherds represent Kana'a black-on-white; the two dark gray pieces show neck banding typical of Pueblo I cooking pots; the lower right fragment is part of a sun-dried mud platter showing the impression of a basket.

48

This large olla or water jar from the Ewing Site near Yellow Jacket shows how a vessel may look when first uncovered and later, following reconstruction.

time, thus providing a means for recognizing where a pot was made, when, and by whom. A skilled archaeologist can examine the broken fragments of pottery vessels scattered across a rubbish deposit and read the probable ages of occupation, the regional affiliation of the residents, whether there was more than one occupation, and possible trade connections. The brittle ceramics broke frequently and were replaced with new ones, thus giving the archaeologist a running record of the pottery made in the community.

Some of the changes through time are well chronicled across Anasaziland by the utility wares. The earliest Basket Maker III cooking pots were a plain gray tempered mostly with sand, except in the Northern San Juan where the temper was crushed igneous rocks. These early vessels were medium size, and many jars had no necks (like *tecomates* of Mesoamerica).

Pueblo I cooking vessels had tall straight necks, many of which exhibited bands formed by not obliterating the construction coils on the exterior surface. True corrugation—finger indenting unobliterated coils—appears by 900 and marks the Pueblo II and III stages. Fine details in the way corrugations were treated, in vessel shapes, and in tempering materials herald both regional and time differences. By the fourteenth century in Pueblo IV, corrugation rapidly dies out and is replaced by very large, thick, plain gray cooking pots.

The design and shape of painted wares were sensitive to both the passage of time and regional styles. During Pueblo III, densely painted zones with patches of underlying white slip showing through

the black paint as a negative design were popular in the Kayenta region, especially Tsegi Canyon and Long House Valley. Designs carried by figures filled by fine line hatching and bordered by heavier black lines signaled a Chaco Basin origin. Symmetrical and interlocking band designs on thick-walled bowls and on distinctive mugs marked the Montezuma Valley and Mesa Verde.

Other features of pottery also contribute to this stylistic story. Kayenta potters almost always painted

These Pueblo I (800s) gray utility pots came from the Duckfoot Site in the Montezuma Valley.

49

Mesa Verde–style black-on-white pottery vessels from Mug House illustrate several shapes for different uses—clockwise from upper left: a food bowl, a canteen, a large water carrying and storage jar, a dipper, a small jar for storing valuables, and a drinking mug.

The distinguishing feature of Kayenta black-on-white pottery may be seen in the extensive areas of black paint allowing the underlying white surface to show through in a sort of "negative" design. Food bowls, canteens, dippers, and large jars are common, but mugs do not occur. Many orange-red polychrome vessels also accompany the black-on-white pots in Kayenta sites, and they were widely traded throughout Anasaziland.

Chaco-style painted pottery was decorated in broad line figures filled in by close straight parallel line "hatching" to create a half-tone effect against a white background. Distinctive shapes include food bowls, cylindrical vases, and tall mugs with expanded bases.

with organic pigments, while Chaco and Little Colorado artisans used mineral pigments. North of the San Juan River, potters used both, but once popular mineral paints gave way to organic paints between 1050 and 1150.

Red pottery, often painted, first appears in the western Montezuma Valley by 700, then becomes

popular in the Kayenta region and dies out north of the San Juan by 950. The three-colored vessels produced by Kayenta potters meanwhile became treasured objects of trade between 1000 and 1250 all over Anasaziland. A separate invention of red pottery occurred in the Little Colorado River region by Pueblo II and ultimately led to the protohistoric and historic polychromes, some of which used glaze paints, of the Rio Grande valley. Shortly after 1300, ancestral Hopi potters began to fire their pots using coal as a fuel. This method produced a background orange or yellow coloring that identifies Hopi pottery to this day.

While many more examples can be cited, the value of Anasazi pottery can be seen as a tool for recording both history and point of origin. The obvious trends are easy to comprehend, but it takes a great deal of knowledge and study to read the finer details.

Basketry

Baskets were made and used by the Anasazi throughout their entire history. In fact the fine-quality baskets with multicolor decorations produced by the earliest Anasazi have led to use of the name "Basket Maker" for those earliest cultural stages. Unlike pottery, baskets do not break frequently, and thus are not quite so susceptible to fashion changes.

A very utilitarian shallow bowl basket was made by plaiting (over one, under one) or twilling (over two, under two) a mat with split yucca leaves, then

Throughout their history, the Anasazi produced baskets of many shapes by plaiting and by coiling. This coiled basket tray was made by Basket Maker II people almost 2,000 years ago in the Falls Creek locality north of Durango, Colorado. The earliest pottery appeared several centuries later.

attaching the mat to a willow ring about ten inches in diameter and tying off the cut ends. Such ring baskets became standard household items and never changed in style from the earliest Basket Maker times to the present.

Numerous shapes of baskets were made by coiling reed and grass bundles, much like the pottery clay ropes were coiled, and then fixing the coils together by closely set stitches of rabbitbrush and sumac bark. Different colored stitches produced designs of both geometric and natural figures. Trays, bowls, globular jars with no necks, and conical burden baskets were all produced. As pottery became steadily more popular during Pueblo I, many of these shapes were abandoned, leaving only trays and shallow bowls. Many of the painted designs of early Basket Maker III pottery actually mimicked the stitched designs of the coiled basketry.

The modern Pueblo Indians, especially the Hopi, still manufacture ring baskets and coiled trays, bowls, and plaques. The Hopi have added stiff wicker (a variety of twining) baskets of similar shapes. They decorate these baskets with both life forms and mythical figures and use them during rituals and special occasions.

Stone and Bone Tools

Each Anasazi family produced its own food, clothing, and shelter. Because there were no craftsmen who specialized in building or tool making,

each family also produced all of its own tools for farming, hunting, building, garment making, and cooking. Some evidence indicates a division of labor between men and women, and there may have been some semispecialized pottery makers, basket makers, or weavers. However, on balance, each family produced the necessary items to be self-sufficient.

To perform the required tasks the Pueblo III Anasazi made stone-grinding tools, hammers, axes, cutting knives, scrapers, saws, drills, and arrow points. The knives, scrapers, saws, and points were chipped or flaked, and the cutting edges of the axes were ground. Scrapers, reamers, awls, weaving tools, and needles were made from animal and bird bones.

Anasazi tools evolved over thousands of years. The Paleo-Indians developed chipped-stone spear points, leaf-shaped knives, and palm-sized scrapers. By Basket Maker times mauls, hammers, and axes were notched for hafting, and by early Pueblo times the edges were ground.

Worldwide, ground and polished stone implements are a hallmark of the Neolithic (New Stone) Age. The change from the Old Stone Age to the New Stone Age is said to take place when a culture produces its own food through agriculture and animal domestication and is sedentary, and when many chipped-stone forms are replaced with ground and polished stone implements. Thus it can be said that by Basket Maker III, the Anasazi had become Neolithic people.

Life in the Mug House Cliff Dwelling

Because of its fine state of preservation, little complicated by extensive remodeling, Mug House provides an excellent case for illustrating how the Mesa Verde cliff dwellers lived. The hundred or so inhabitants of Mug House belonged to about twenty households, each occupying a cluster of rooms (apartment or suite). A central living room with hearth and small ventilator was surrounded by smaller rooms for storage and sleeping and by an outdoor courtyard space, where general household work, including cooking, usually took place.

Several households shared outdoor space in one courtyard, usually atop the roof of one subterranean kiva. Such households may have been related through common descent to form a sort of lineage or clan group. Traces of Puebloan duality may be seen in the separation of the northern two-thirds of the site from the southern third by a row of six rooms, which prevented access between the two sectors, by a round tower at each end of the site, and by marked dif-

Mug House, Mesa Verde National Park, a cliff dwelling, contained over ninety living and storage rooms, eight kivas, two round towers, and a turkey pen. About 100 Anasazi lived here during the 1200s raising crops on the mesa top above and burying their dead along the steep slope below. Trails led out of this small village along the base of the cliff, toward their water supply to the right, and to a trail leading to the mesa top to the left.

ferences in kiva construction between the two parts.

The inhabitants of Mug House cultivated corn, beans, and squash on the mesa top reached by two trails, one on the north side of the pueblo, the other on the south. Stone-walled terraces in nearby ravines and on the steep slope below the site augmented the mesa-top farmland. Stone axe heads mounted on short wooden handles were used to clear land for farming, while sharpened hardwood sticks served to loosen the ground for planting (hence the use of hills rather than rows) and to remove weeds.

Most of the corn was ground into a meal or flour with sandstone manos and metates, usually set in stone-lined bins. The meal was then cooked in rough-surfaced (corrugated) jars to form a gruel or stew flavored with meats, berries, or wild plants such as yucca and cactus fruits. Pinyon nuts, greens, and seeds were also gathered. Meat could be obtained by butchering domestic turkeys or hunting for deer, rabbits, rock squirrels, and wood rats. The turkeys were kept penned in a large room in the south part of the site or were allowed to roam about while tethered to stone weights. Curiously, these people ate no fish, reptiles, or wild game birds. Runoff rainwater from the mesa top was impounded in a small reservoir about fifty yards south of the village. Large painted water jars, filled with the aid of painted

ladles, were used to carry the water to the households.

When someone died, the body was buried in a shallow oval grave in the small cave north of Mug House or along the steep, sloping talus below the cliff face. The corpse was dressed in ordinary clothing, wrapped in a turkey-feather robe or woven mat, and given offerings to assist in an afterlife. Often a decorated food bowl and drinking mug contained sustenance, while a small corrugated jar might contain useful possessions such as a charmstone, paint pigment, or stone arrowheads. One man took two stone axes and a bone weaving-tool kit into his afterlife.

The people wore only simple clothing of a breechcloth or apron and sandals on the feet, but they added woven feather robes and leggings or socks during cold weather. They sat and slept on matting placed directly on the floors. Personal possessions included tools for working sandstone into building blocks and grinding implements, tools for cutting firewood and roofing timbers, and tools for working both wood and fibers into many items such as cradles, bows, weaving sticks, cordage, and textiles. Other implements made from the bones of turkeys, deer, and other animals were used to weave baskets and cloth and to serve as general household utensils.

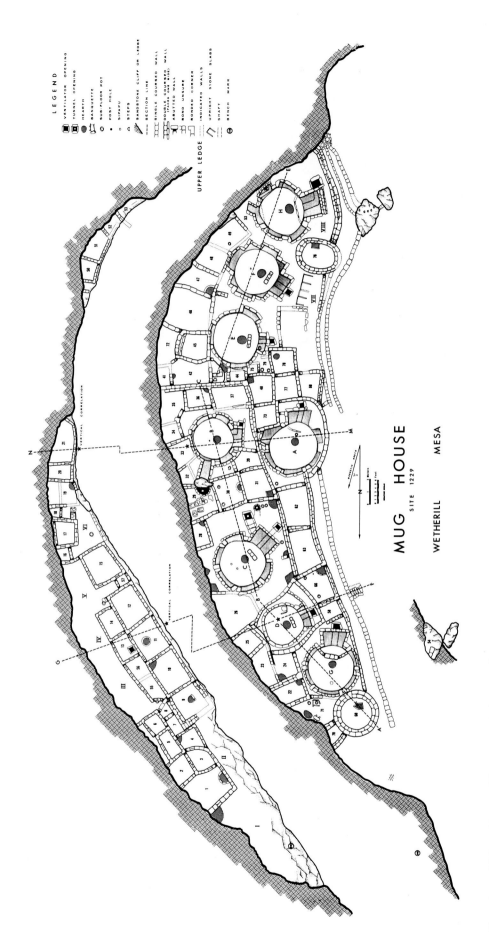

Site plan of Mug House. The upper ledge has been set back from directly above the lower rooms to clarify the horizontal relationship.

53

Well-preserved living and storage rooms one and two stories high on the upper ledge of Mug House. The nearly complete walls allowed the plotting of interconnections into suites of rooms occupied by separate households, each with one larger living room, several smaller storerooms, and outdoor work space.

Jewelry consisted of pendants, beads, and buttons made from attractive stone materials, from bone, and even from rare pieces of shell traded all the way from the Pacific Coast. The people of Mug House were frugal. They saved short lengths of twine, knotting them together into longer lengths; they repaired pottery, baskets, sandals, and textiles; and they reused broken tools for new functions.

These people were always subject to the caprices of nature. Inadequate rainfall not only threatened their crops, but often caused their nearby reservoir to dry up, necessitating the carrying of water from springs located a mile and a half away. Consequently, religious practices seemed to focus on aspects of nature. Well-preserved murals in one kiva suggest a symbolic horizon line of mountains and other features. Several kivas seem to have been dedicated to animals such as the turkey and cottontail rabbit. A mass of corn tassels suggests the collection of pollen to use in rituals.

Much religious activity took place in the kivas, out of sight of the rest of the community. At this time in Anasazi history, kiva ritual probably most strongly related to the clan or lineage group living around the courtyard formed in part by the kiva roof. Perhaps some public portions of ceremonies were held in the open courtyards, but most likely the residents of Mug House attended (perhaps also participated in) larger rituals with both public and secret events held at Long House with its rectangular great kiva. Long House lies only one mile to the south and must have functioned as the ritual nucleus for all the cliff dwellers of Wetherill Mesa and neighboring Long and Wildhorse Mesas.

Many other activities were also performed in the kivas. After all, these buildings were the best-made and most comfortable enclosed spaces in the entire village. Here, the men manufactured their ceremonial costumes, headdresses, prayer plumes, and other sacred objects. Here, too, we find evidence for the weaving of textiles, the knapping of stone tools, and other craft activities associated with males. Around the fire in the central hearth, young men and boys undoubtedly learned from their elders all the history and lore of these people. If we can assume that these Pueblo III Anasazi had customs similar to those of the modern Pueblo people, it is likely that the sons of the family were instructed in the kivas of the mother's kin group, by her brothers, rather than by the boys' father, since kiva society was most likely organized by kin groups in the female line. While men were most active there, the kivas were not closed to women, and we can picture all members of several families clustered around the kiva fire during inclement weather.

The Anasazi abandoned Mug House sometime near 1300. They left behind a large portion of their material belongings, and from this evidence we have been able to reconstruct the way they lived.

Government and Society

Since the prehistoric Anasazi left no written records, it is impossible to reconstruct their social organization with certainty. They were, however, the ancestors of the historic Pueblo Indians—Indians of, among others, the Taos, Acoma, Jemez, San Ildefonso, Zia, Zuni, and Hopi pueblos—whose basic customs have changed little since the arrival of the Spaniards. Pueblo society was, and is, egalitarian. The Spaniards were surprised and frustrated to find that the Pueblo Indians had no identified individual leaders, no chiefs.

The modern Pueblo people govern themselves basically through their social customs and ritual practices. Administrators are chosen to serve on a temporary basis by the residents of the community. Any member of the pueblo who actively seeks power, influence, or wealth is ostracized by the remainder of society. Leadership seems to be vested in those who are reluctant to exercise it—those who do not seek to press their views on others and, oftentimes, those on the lowest economic scale. These leaders direct the rituals and make other necessary decisions.

The historic Pueblos evince several levels of social organization: households, kinship groups, communities, and Summer and Winter People.

The husband, wife, children, and occasionally another relative such as an uncle or grandparent make up the household unit. They share living space and basic subsistence activities such as food preparation. They also give mutual economic support.

The kinship group, sometimes referred to as a lineage segment, is composed of several households related one to the other, generally through the female line. That is, all members of the kinship group trace their lineage to a common female ancestor.

Mug House was reportedly named for a group of painted mugs found tied together with string through their handles. (Drawing by Joan Foth.)

Marriages are made outside the kinship group so that the mother and children are from one kinship group and the father from another. As a consequence, the sons are generally instructed by an uncle within the matrilineal kinship group rather than by the father, who belongs to another. The Hopis refer to these kinship groups as clans. Marriage and some ritual customs are controlled by membership in the kinship group.

The people of the pueblo (community or village) recognize a special relationship with each other by virtue of living together, and the pueblo is the unit by which they govern themselves and perform religious ceremonies. The pueblo owns land and hunting territories, allocating them to kinship groups who, in turn, allocate them to individual households.

The eastern historic Pueblo communities are divided into two parts, producing a duality of social and religious organization within the pueblo. Among the western Hopi and Zuni, the duality affects only religious behavior. These are called the Summer People and Winter People. The Winter People are responsible for ritual and ceremonial activities during the winter and provide pueblo leadership during this period, and the Summer People have the same obligations during their tenure.

55

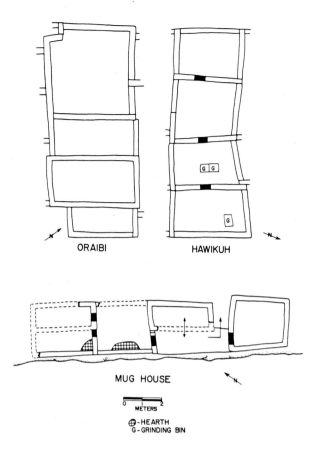

ORAIBI   HAWIKUH

MUG HOUSE

0   1   2
METERS
⊕ - HEARTH
G - GRINDING BIN

Plan of a typical suite of living and storage rooms from Mug House compared with similar units from Pueblo IV–V Hawikuh (Zuni) and from historic-modern Oraibi (Hopi). The striking similarities suggest the basic Puebloan social unit of the household has existed with little or no change for at least 700 years.

Ritual activities involve teaching and reemphasizing the traditions, customs, and myths of the pueblo. Each child is taught his obligations to society and his relationship to his kin group, not only by formal rituals but by storytelling. In earlier times during the winter evenings the elders would tell stories around the fire where the kin group would be gathered (probably in the kin-group kiva). From them the children would learn about their expected behavior and about actual and legendary events of the past.

One example of the legends is the history of the creation of the Pueblo peoples. The ancestors of the Indians lived in a spirit world far below the surface of the earth, and through a number of generations these ancestors emerged to successively higher levels of existence by passing up through holes in the ground. The point of emergence is recognized as having been through a "sipap" or "sipapu" and is

symbolized by a small hole in the floor of kivas and other ceremonial structures.

The primary sanction for antisocial behavior was ostracism by other members of the community. The offender would be ignored, not spoken to, and omitted from group activities. Since Pueblo society was and is founded on communal sharing, to become an outcast was a very severe punishment.

Historically Pueblo society fit this egalitarian and, superficially at least, relaxed manner of living at the time of the arrival of the Spaniards. Thus, it may safely be assumed that it represented the social organization of the Pueblo IV stage that began after the Great Migration around 1300. Evidence available from Pueblo III architecture and burials (1100 to 1300) indicates the Anasazi mode of living in the pueblos and cliff dwellings was not significantly different during this time from what it was later in Pueblo IV.

All the evidence points to an egalitarian society; there is no evidence of an elite class either in housing or personal possessions. The kivas and great kivas indicate kin groups, and communities used them in the same or similar way as the historic Pueblos. The sipapu has continued unchanged through time. At Balcony House and Mug House at Mesa Verde, Pueblo Bonito at Chaco, Betatakin and Keet Seel at Kayenta, and other Anasazi sites, the village was divided into two sections indicating the Summer and Winter People duality.

The kin-group kivas and the community great kivas both find their origins in Basket Maker times. The architecture and burials from before A.D. 700 reveal a classless society based on small villages of pithouses. The household units of the pithouses evolved during Pueblo I, II, and III stages into the later kin groups, while continually growing communities settled in villages and towns of cliff dwellings and pueblos.

Pueblo II–III times saw the beginnings of a potential fifth level of social organization linking several communities together. In such cases as Chaco Canyon and its outliers, Sun Temple and the Chapin Mesa settlements, Long House and the Wetherill Mesa settlements of Mesa Verde, and Yellow Jacket and other towns in the Montezuma Valley, one locality or town became the center for area-wide activity—a sort of budding ceremonial center concept.

This community organization of Pueblo III continued after the migrations to the Rio Grande valley and the Little Colorado River region to make up the Pueblo social structure that exists in the twentieth century.

Diet and Disease

The Precolumbian Indians of the New World did not suffer from many of the common Old World diseases such as measles, mumps, chickenpox, smallpox, scarlet fever, and venereal diseases. These were introduced by the Europeans. Nevertheless, the diet deficiency brought about by living on maize (corn), the crowded and unsanitary conditions of the pueblos, and the absence of health care resulted in a high disease and mortality rate, particularly among the young children.

Stomach and intestinal disorders, especially gastroenteritis, probably took a toll as high as 50 percent of children under three years old. If an Anasazi survived childhood, life expectancy extended into the early forties, and there were some who lived into their eighties.

The maize diet, with an insufficiency of meat, was high in carbohydrates and low in protein, resulting frequently in malnutrition, especially among the young children. The maize diet also led to dental problems: deterioration of the gums, caries, and excessive wear on the teeth because of the grit ground in with the cornmeal. The bones also suffered, resulting in osteoporosis at an early age, and so did the blood, probably with iron-deficiency anemia. The Anasazi had other health problems. Respiratory infections were common, resulting from living with the smoke of enclosed fires, and tuberculosis was exacerbated by the crowded living quarters and lack of sanitation. Parasites, especially lice and pinworms, were common.

The major threat to the adult Anasazi was the chronic disorder of degenerative arthritis. The adults were plagued with bad backs brought about by the lifting and carrying of heavy loads. It appeared in the women in the elbows and knees from the endless hours spent kneeling to grind corn. Nearly all middle-aged adults must have suffered from bad teeth, bad backs, and painful arthritis. They also suffered from fractures due to falls, a common occurrence among the cliff dwellers. Some were properly set and healed; others were not. There were compression fractures of the vertebrae from lifting, and fractures of the skull.

We know of these Anasazi maladies only from the skeletons and mummies and the effects of diet on the children of other primitive societies. Doubtlessly there were other health problems that can never be known. It is obvious that life was hard and often times very painful.

Spiritual Concepts and Rituals

The folklore of the Pueblo Indians features a combination of origin and migration myths handed down from generation to generation by the storytellers of the pueblo. The origin myth relates the upward migration of the Indians through different levels of the spirit world inside the earth until they reach the surface through a "sipap" from whence they start looking for a sacred spot to live. During the migration the spirits and kachinas came from the spirit world to guide and teach them. The supernatural kachinas left their masks with the people so that by using the masks and following the proper dances and rituals they could bring rain, produce crops, and do other good works. These folktales have doubtlessly been told during the Pueblos' fire-lit ceremonies for centuries.

Representations of the migrations appear in the Anasazi rock art at Pictograph Point at Mesa Verde where several Hopis, one group of descendants from the Anasazi, have traced a migration story from the petroglyph figures. Petroglyphs in Cow Canyon near Lowry show similar traces of the myth. Sets of human footprints as well as turkey, bird, and bear tracks probably mark this myth. There also may be kin-group, lineage, or clan symbols recording the movements of the group. A long, sinuous line wanders through various symbols on the rock face indicating the route of travel.

The Pueblo Indians, and likely the Anasazi, practiced animism, a concept in which animals and inanimate objects of nature all had souls and as spirits could do good or evil for men. Mankind is considered to be only one of several classes of beings

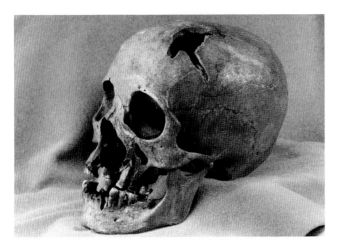

The skull of an Anasazi woman found in the Navajo Reservoir district of the Northern San Juan. Her face was eaten away by a serious disease before her death.

57

Anasazi rock art contains many expressions of legends recounting ancient migrations. The key element is usually a line wandering about among symbols for clans (lineages), for significant geographic features or events, and for supernatural beings. Such symbols may take the form of animals, birds, kachina figures and

masks, hand and foot prints, and geometric forms. This legend was pecked into the face of the cliff-house sandstone about a mile south of Spruce Tree House at Mesa Verde National Park. Perhaps some Anasazi sages recorded there the legends of their origins and migrations to their Mesa Verde homes.

that inhabit the earth and spirit world and is no more important or unique than any of the other classes. Their concept of the cosmos included an afterlife for humans. The burials indicate there was a "right way" to treat the dead as indicated by the position of the body and the inclusion of food and water vessels, tools, clothing, and jewelry in the grave to make provision for life after death.

The rock art of the Anasazi could tell us much about the culture if only we could understand it. Glimpses behind the veil come when a kachina figure in current ritual use can be identified as the same figure that appears in ancient rock art. One set of characteristics includes oval shapes with eyes or feathers sticking out of heads. On the Kachina Wall on the San Juan River are a number of rock art figures that can be equated with known kachinas. The Kokopelli (hunchback flute player) is found painted, pecked, and incised all over the Southwest. Who or what it represents is still unknown. Sometimes the figure is definitely male, sometimes female, and in other cases neuter; most kachinas are neuter. The placement of

the rock art also can furnish a clue. Representations of corn near the fields suggest the use of magic to induce good crops.

Hunting magic also appears in the small caves in Sandia Canyon near Bandelier. A hunter disguised as a deer is shown shooting a large bird with a bow and arrow, and another with an erection—or is he sitting on a limb—is shown fighting a bear with a club. A Pueblo II bowl displayed at the Mesa Verde museum depicts hunters and ducks. At Long House there is a kiva figure with a bow. These acted as talismans to give skill and luck to the hunter.

The Pueblo IV kiva murals at Kuaua, in the Coronado State Park north of Albuquerque, are beautifully painted scenes of kachinas and supernatural birds and animals. The ceremonies probably depict supplications for rain or fertility to crops. The Kuaua murals and the Stone Lions shrine at nearby Bandelier reveal the animistic concept of Pueblo religion. Many ancient shrines throughout Anasaziland suggest man's contact with and appreciation of nature. The Stone Lions shrine, still in use, focused

An ogre kachina from Puerco Indian Ruin, Petrified Forest National Park. To the Pueblos, kachinas carry messages from humans to the gods who control the forces of nature, thereby governing the growth of crops and the availability of wild food resources.

An Anasazi hunter disguised as a deer shoots a wild fowl with a bow and arrow. This rock art appears in a cave kiva at Sandia Canyon near Los Alamos, New Mexico.

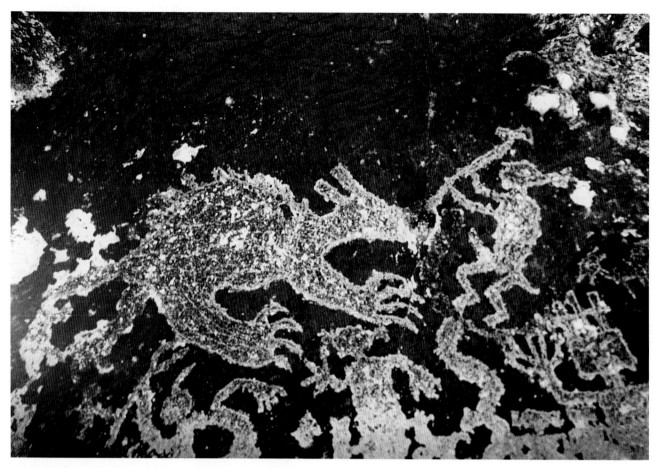

Sandia Canyon (near Bandelier National Monument) cave kiva art pictures a man fighting a bear with a club. The figures have been pecked through heavily smoke-blackened walls and ceiling.

Inside this Sandia Canyon cave kiva the Anasazi pecked a kokopelli (humpbacked flute player).

upon two prehistorically carved crouching mountain lions surrounded by a stone enclosure. On the trees above are gifts from Indians of feathers and seeds or pollen. Around the lions are stacks of bleached antlers and animal bones. Its location deep in the forest of Bandelier National Monument denotes a particularly significant natural setting that is shared by other Anasazi shrines at Chaco Canyon, Mesa Verde, and Lowry.

In the modern pueblos ceremonial responsibility is shared by the Summer People and the Winter People. Each segment of the pueblo is responsible for rituals and ceremonies during its tenure. Evidence of this social dichotomy appears in the Pueblo III sites of Pueblo Bonito at Chaco and Balcony House at Mesa Verde. Even earlier, at the Village of the Great Kivas near Zuni, the orientation of the burials indicates the bodies were aligned with the heads pointing either to the northeast or to the southeast, close to the angle at which the sun would rise at the summer and winter solstices.

Most rituals probably focused on those things necessary for preservation of life: water and crop fertility. In Basket Maker times when people were living in pithouses, rituals were performed there. The sipapu is the clue. Later on, the pithouses were succeeded by the small kin-group kivas, and rituals performed by the kin group took place there. During Pueblo IV the small kiva fell into disuse and was replaced by the small plaza, as evidenced by the plazas at Long House in Frijoles Canyon at Bandelier.

Community rituals probably began as early as Basket Maker times. The open spaces of the Basket Maker settlements surrounded by stockades may have been community ritual centers. Large pithouses such as at Shabik'eschee at Chaco Canyon served as the forerunners of the great kivas. Following these are the great kivas—the Anasazi equivalent of the Gothic cathedrals of Europe—the tri-wall structures, other concentric wall structures, and towers, all pointing to community-wide ceremonies. Plazas were also used in Pueblo III at Chaco Canyon, and at Yellow Jacket and Lowry in the Montezuma Valley.

All modern Pueblos have religious or kiva societies responsible for certain kinds of rituals. Their paraphernalia include feathers tied to prayer sticks connecting them with the macaw and other birds whose feathers have been found in prehistoric sites. These societies may have begun during late Pueblo III when some kivas were built without an association with specific room blocks. Previously each room block had an associated kiva, and it has been assumed that the kin group conducted the ceremonies. This change in architecture indicates that kiva societies may have begun to conduct rituals replacing the kin groups.

Celestial Observations

Each of the modern pueblos has a system for making solar observations for the purpose of determining the equinoxes and solstices and establishing a yearly calendar. Pueblo rituals for hundreds of years have been governed by the movements of the sun from winter to summer. Knowing that the Anasazi were outdoor people, we can assume they noticed that the sun rose and set farther and farther to the south after the solstice in June, and as it moved south the days grew shorter until it began its reverse journey in December.

The Anasazi were farmers who planted and harvested corn, beans, and squash in the same way their ancestors had done for hundreds of years. These farmers knew when to plant by the length of the days, the

Beautiful examples of kiva painting (Pueblo IV) cover the walls of a restored kiva at Kuaua, Coronado State Park, New Mexico. The eagle, the snake, and the kachina figure all promise bounty from nature.

A private ceremony practiced in a small (kin) kiva by
the ancient Anasazi. (Drawing by Lisa Ferguson.)

warmth of the weather, and where the sun rose on
the horizon. They didn't require a priest or shaman
to tell them that. The only reason for a precise
determination of the solstice would be for ceremonial
purposes, then as now.

There have been rather exhaustive observations
of the reflection of the sun through windows, doors,
and portholes in various structures throughout Anasaziland that seem to indicate a deliberate design to
mark either the solstices or equinoxes. These include
Wijiji, Peñasco Blanco, Pueblo Bonito, and Casa
Rinconada in Chaco Canyon; Hovenweep Castle,
Unit Type House, and Cajon at Hovenweep; and
buildings constructed by the Zuni and Hopi. But
in none of these buildings can it be demonstrated
that they were actually built for that purpose.

The Anasazi constructed solar observatories that
were demonstrably designed to mark solar movement. One is the Sun Dagger site on Fajada Butte
at Chaco Canyon and another is the Holly observatory at Hovenweep. The most publicized is the
Chaco Sun Dagger site. Here behind three roughly
vertical and parallel stone slabs are two spirals (one
large and one small) pecked into the rock. At mid-
day, shafts of light between the slabs mark the spring
equinox, the summer solstice, the fall equinox, and
the winter solstice. The other solar observatory consists of two pecked spirals and one series of concentric
circles under a rock overhang at Holly. Here a shaft
of light at sunrise marks the spring equinox, the
summer solstice, and the fall equinox. The sun does
not reach the markers in the winter.

Text continued on page 65

Dr. Arthur H. Rohn studying the solar spirals near Holly Ruin, Hovenweep National Monument. During the summer solstice, a thin horizontal shaft of sunlight splits the spirals and concentric circles just beneath the overhang ceiling.

Rock art figures at the Holly solar observatory in Hovenweep National Monument. Slivers of sunlight shine through the centers of the two spirals on the left and the concentric circle on the right at the summer solstice.

Near the top rim of Fajada Butte in Chaco Canyon are located the rock spirals known as the Sun Dagger.

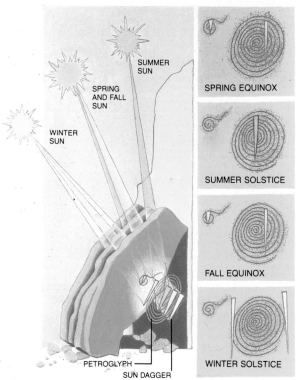

SUMMER SUN

SPRING AND FALL SUN

WINTER SUN

SPRING EQUINOX

SUMMER SOLSTICE

FALL EQUINOX

WINTER SOLSTICE

PETROGLYPH

SUN DAGGER

Diagram showing the position of the sun relative to the rock spirals. (National Geographic Society.)

The ancients could see the North Star as clearly as we can and it is no mystery that many of their buildings were aligned on a north-south axis.

The moon moves from north to south in a nineteen-year cycle known as a progression of nodes, and it has been suggested that the Anasazi had markers for this measurement, but such a function has yet to be demonstrated. There is also no evidence that the Anasazi were able to determine the movements of other celestial bodies.

By comparison, many of the historic and prehistoric Indians of the Great Plains are known to have observed not only the movements of the sun and moon but also the visible planets and many bright stars. The Pawnee and their ancestors recognized numerous constellations and bright stars as supernatural beings. They recorded in their artwork the activities of both evening and morning stars (Venus and Jupiter) and the heliacal risings of stars such as Aldebaran, Sirius, and Capella.

The Mesoamerican Connection and Barter

Corn (maize) was the central and most important element in the development of the Anasazi farming society in the Southwest. Corn, beans, and squash were the staples that fed the Anasazi, and they all came from Mesoamerica. The earliest corn known was found in dry caves in the Tehuacan Valley of central Mexico, dated about 5000 B.C. It took another two thousand years for corn to work its way to the American Southwest. By 1000–400 B.C. the basic trio of southwestern domestic food—corn, squash and beans—was in use in the southern Southwest.

The extent to which Mesoamerica influenced the Anasazi either directly or indirectly is the subject of much controversy. In addition to agricultural products and cotton, it is probable that ceramics (pottery), or at least the concept for making pottery, came to the Southwest from Mexico.

Prehistoric Mesoamerica is the term given to the area of Mexico and Central America beginning north of Mexico City and extending south beyond Guatemala and Belize into Honduras. Here developed the magnificent Olmec, Maya, Teotihuacan, Toltec, and Aztec civilizations beginning around 1500 B.C. and ending with the arrival of the Spaniards three thousand years later. Of these, the Toltec civilization (centered at Tula), which flourished from about A.D. 900 to 1150 on the north edge of the Valley of Mexico, seems to have had the greatest influence on the Anasazi. The Toltecs spread black plumbate pottery and metallurgy over all of Mesoamerica. The Tula-Toltecs are credited with long-distance trading activities to the north.

The area of northern Mexico north of Mesoamerica formed a frontier zone known as the Gran Chichimeca. The Toltecs expanded into the Gran Chichimeca about 900. It has been suggested that about 1050, Casas Grandes, in what is now northern Chihuahua, grew from a small village into a Mesoamerican trading center. The Aztec traders were called *pochtecas*, and perhaps so were the earlier Toltec merchants. Richard E. W. Adams says, "From this [Casas Grandes] and other centers such as Zape, *pochteca* made trips into the Hohokam and Anasazi areas of Arizona and New Mexico trading copper bells and other items for turquoise, slaves, peyote, salt, and other commodities that the southwesterners provided" (Adams 1977:235). Other trade items found in the Anasazi ruins indicating Mesoamerican contacts are stone palettes, cloisonné-decorated sandstone, pottery stamps, and macaw remains.

Anthropologists who see an Anasazi-Mesoamerican connection assume that cultural influences follow commerce. This Mesoamerican influence is seen by its proponents in the architecture of the Anasazi, particularly at Chaco Canyon, in the rubble-cored masonry and square columns used in colonnades.

Walls constructed of rubble and faced with masonry are certainly characteristic of Mesoamerica, while both round and square columns are particularly characteristic of Toltec architecture. Chetro Ketl at Chaco displays a long front wall originally built of masonry columns rising atop a low masonry wall, which once held horizontal timbers to support a roof over an open cloister-like porch. Robert Lister also suggests that the Anasazi architectural styles found in the circular structures in the form of tower kivas, tri-wall units, seating discs beneath roof support posts, and T-shaped doorways were inspired by the Mesoamericans. On the other hand, these architectural characteristics are found at Mesa Verde, Hovenweep, and Kayenta—regions not thought to have been subject to Mesoamerican influence.

He also suggests that "water control means such as dams, canals, and reservoirs, the roads and signal stations, and the alignments of architectural and other features for the purpose of observing and recording astronomical data, all of which have been noted in Chaco Canyon, are much more common in central Mexico" (Lister and Lister 1981:174). However, all of these elements, with the possible excep-

Rock art feathered serpents from
Tenabo Pueblo near Mountainair,
New Mexico. This Pueblo IV (1300–
1540) depiction represents contact
with central Mexico prior to arrival
of the Spaniards.

tion of the signal stations, are found elsewhere in
Anasaziland.

In summary, we can say that the Anasazi crops
of corn, squash, and beans came to them from the
Mesoamericans through the Desert Peoples of the
Southwest and that there is evidence of barter between the Southwest and Mexico. If there was a
social influence on the Anasazi by the Mexicans it
does not appear to have been of great significance.
The feathered serpent is a Mexican concept that came
into the Southwest and probably carried with it
religious connotations that are now impossible to

identify. The Pueblo III flowering of the culture
would have come about with or without the Mesoamerican connection.

There was internal exchange within the Anasazi
area from one village or town to the next. Pottery
vessels, not locally made, are found at nearly every
site. Whether the vessels were being exchanged for
themselves or their contents, such as salt or food,
is unknown. The presence of exotic vessels such as
Kayenta Polychrome in the Northern San Juan suggests trade for the vessels themselves. Turquoise and
obsidian may have been the subject of internal ex-

change as well as banded siltstone, petrified wood, and agates.

Trade outside of Anasaziland is evidenced by shells from the Pacific Ocean or the Gulf of California. Beads and pendants of olivella and glycymeris shells were made by the Hohokam and Casas Grandes peoples and traded northward to the Anasazi. Also, probably through Casas Grandes and the Hohokam, macaws, macaw feathers, and copper bells worked their way to the Anasazi. Other trade items were cotton textiles that came from Canyon de Chelly, the Hohokam, or the Salado peoples. Bones from mountain sheep, bison, and Canada geese came from mountain or plains people.

By the time the Spaniards arrived corn grown at the Taos and Pecos pueblos was being exchanged for meat from animals killed by the Apaches and Comanches from the plains. This same kind of trade may have occurred in other regions during earlier times. All the barter and trade was, however, conducted person to person. There were no traders, no markets, no itinerant peddlers. Each Anasazi household produced its own food, clothing, tools, and shelter, and with few exceptions the little barter that was done provided an occasional exotic item.

Scarlet macaws from tropical Mesoamerica were rare and prized trade items by the Chacoan Anasazi. According to Lyndon L. Hargrave's exhaustive study of these birds, they must have been brought in alive and were not bred by the Anasazi.

Warfare, Weapons, and Violence

The Pueblo peoples were more peaceful than their neighbors the Utes, Navajos, Apaches, and Comanches, but the historic Pueblo data indicate continual raiding, murder, and violence, and we can infer that their Anasazi ancestors behaved similarly.

In many cultures, warriors are aggrandized in art, literature, and folklore, but that is not the case in Anasazi rock art or the folklore of the modern Pueblos. Depiction of warriors or warfare is completely missing in the rock art or pottery vessels of the Anasazi, and the folk tales and myths of the modern Pueblos are singularly lacking in stories of war. But that is not to say their peaceful intentions guaranteed peace. The Pueblos had war chiefs, and we know that in historic times they fought losing battles against the Spaniards. In 1680 they banded together to drive the Spaniards out of New Mexico and Arizona. The Hopi took part in the 1680 revolt, and then in the winter of 1700–1701 (following reconquest by the Spaniards) some of the Hopis, probably from First Mesa, came over and destroyed

Awatovi because it had allowed the Spanish priests to reestablish the mission there.

In earlier times the defensive location of cliff dwellings and the fortified construction of many villages suggest that unrest occurred. Timber pali-

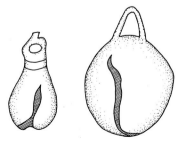

Cast copper bells (the only metal objects known to the Anasazi) were rare trade items from Mexico.

sades are known from as early as the seventh century at Basket Maker sites of north-central New Mexico, the Montezuma Valley, and Falls Creek near Durango, Colorado, but there is no certainty that these stockades were constructed for defense. They may have been merely to delimit the village space.

The Grass Mesa site in the Dolores Valley was a Pueblo I site built in a defensive situation on top of a vertical cliff with a very narrow ledge as the only means of access. Nancy Patterson Ruin and Sacred Mesa near Bluff, Utah, were defensively situated. The Chimney Rock Pueblo near Pagosa Springs, Colorado, and Guadalupe, near Albuquerque, were located on high ridges.

During Pueblo III and IV, pueblos were constructed with access limited to one narrow opening. Balcony House and other cliff dwellings at Mesa Verde, Keet Seel and Betatakin at Kayenta, Pueblo Bonito at Chaco, and Aztec Ruin are all Pueblo III examples of sites with defense-oriented access. Tyuonyi at Bandelier and the Pecos Pueblo were defensive sites built in Pueblo IV.

Coronado reported that the Zuni of western New Mexico fought with hammers, bows and arrows, and shields. The hammers were probably stone mauls or axes made by hafting a stone head onto a short wooden handle. An oval-shaped coiled basketry shield measuring thirty-six by thirty-one inches with a hardwood handle and coated with pitch was found at Aztec Ruin. The Spanish explorers reported the Indians of the Southwest used round shields made of buffalo or elk hide that were between twelve and twenty-six inches in diameter, and they wrapped pieces of elk or buffalo hide around the stomach as a sort of armor.

Prior to the bow and arrow, which appeared in the Southwest in general use between A.D. 500 and 700, the Ice Age mammal hunters developed a spear thrower called an atlatl in use 10,000 to 12,000 years ago. The effect of the atlatl is to lengthen the arm, enabling the thrower to propel the dart harder and farther. A hand-thrown spear has a maximum range of seventy-five feet, whereas an atlatl dart may be effective for three hundred feet. The atlatls found in the Southwest were made of a flattened stick about two feet long with a projecting spur on one end to fit the base of the dart and a double loop of hide on the other to fit two fingers. The dart was in two parts, the main shaft, four or five feet long, with a feathered end like an arrow and a six-inch foreshaft to which a stone point was usually attached. The foreshaft was fitted into the hollow end of the main-shaft. Bows and arrows, atlatls, stone axes, and clubs

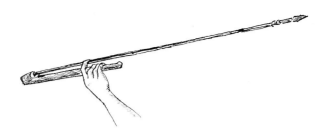

Basket Maker II Anasazi and their Archaic Desert Culture predecessors employed the atlatl (throwing stick) and dart for a hunting weapon. The atlatl was held in the hand to provide an extension to the arm which would then impart greater velocity when throwing the dart or spear. (Drawing by Joan Foth.)

were primarily used for hunting or woodcutting but doubled as weapons in times of war.

All violence may not have been connected with warfare. The primary evidence appears in human bodies that were not accorded proper burial. At the Crow Canyon Duckfoot Site two bodies were found on the floor of a burned pithouse. The bodies were sprawled as if they had been thrown in, not placed there for burial. This is evidenced by the absence of the careful positioning accorded the deceased in a normal burial. Skeletons, some dismembered, others with crushed skulls and not properly buried, have been found at other sites, indicating they died violently. Whether these deaths were the work of raiding parties from other tribes or other Anasazis, or were simply domestic crimes of passion can never be known.

The little evidence we have concerning the conduct of the Anasazi indicates that they were not as warlike as their neighbors although they did make war, perhaps more defensively than offensively. They were not as sanguinary as the Indians of Mesoamerica, particularly the Aztecs and the Maya, although they occasionally practiced cannibalism and often killed witches. Also they may have preferred to run rather than fight, for some believe that the Great Migration from the Northern San Juan and the Kayenta regions around 1300 was precipitated at least in part by the pressure of raiders from the north.

The Great Migration

The only thing known for certain about the Great Migration is that by 1300 the Kayenta, Chaco, and Northern San Juan regions had been abandoned by the Anasazi. First Chaco was abandoned in the early 1200s, and later in the century the people of Mesa Verde, the Montezuma Valley, Aztec, Salmon, Chimney Rock, Canyon de Chelly, and Kayenta all were gone. Anasazi sites had been abandoned before and there had been migrations, but this was a demographic cataclysm. In many ways this abandonment of a huge territory, leaving it devoid of people, is unique. So long as there have been people on earth, there have been migrations. People have moved out or have been forced out, but in all known cases except the Anasazi migration, at least some people remained—either a portion of the original population or the immigrants who forced out the indigenous people.

During Pueblo III there were probably 50,000 Anasazi living in the three regions. Either they all died at once or they migrated. The northeasterners (Northern San Juan and Chaco people) probably went into the Rio Grande valley, and the northwesterners (Canyon de Chelly and Kayenta) probably migrated to the Little Colorado River valley of northeastern Arizona. There is no proof of these movements other than the circumstantial evidence that the populations of these latter two regions increased sharply around 1300.

What happened? The most common answer is that the cause was environmental. Reduced to its basic elements the argument suggests a combination of too many people and too little food. During Pueblo III there was a population increase, and in the 1200s there were droughts and water shortages. The food

shortage may have been enhanced by nomadic or internecine raiders who destroyed crops and stole grain. The result was disease, starvation, and death.

During Pueblo III, as the population increased, people moved into larger and larger villages and towns. They became more dependent on farming and less on hunting, because as the population increased and became more concentrated, wild game and wild seeds became more difficult to come by. The diet deteriorated from lack of protein. To counter the population increase, food production was increased by farming more marginal land and by irrigation and water management. In good years there was adequate food, which in turn increased the population.

In earlier times when the crops failed, the people could return to hunting and gathering. They lived in small communities, and virgin land abounded. But by Pueblo III the people were clustered in large villages and towns living a more structured life. They were prime targets for raiders.

The argument continues that the society was egalitarian; there were no leaders. When things turned bad—crop failures, depletion of irrigation water, malnutrition and disease, a breakdown in intervillage exchange, and raids by outsiders—there were no leaders to address these calamities. Kin groups or clans became discouraged and felt the situation was hopeless, so they moved. Others did not want to see a breakdown in their way of life so they too migrated.

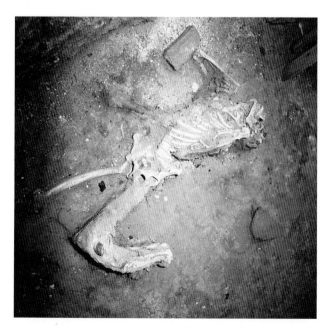

Evidence of violence or possible warfare found at the Duckfoot Site. These skeletons represent bodies thrown into a burning pithouse. Their sprawled position indicates that this was not a formal burial.

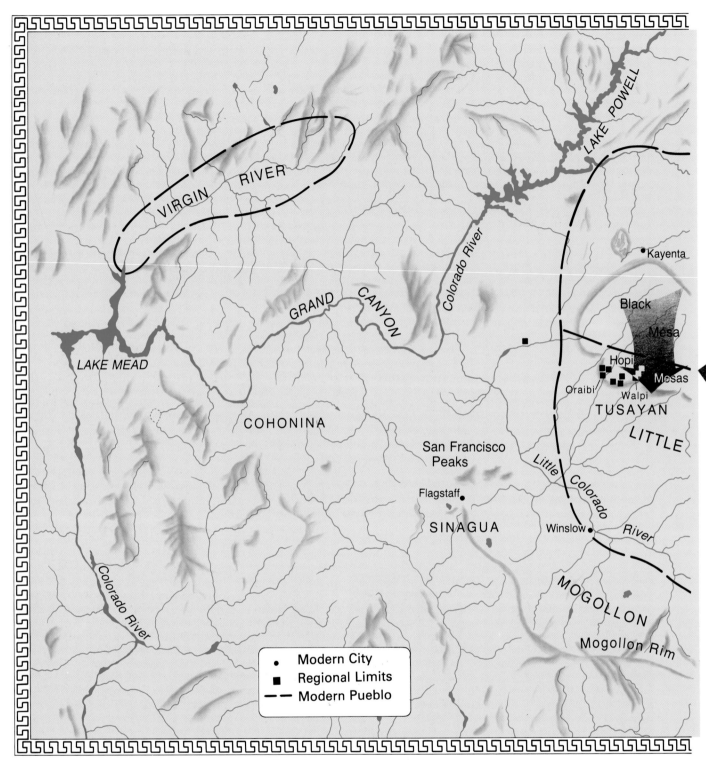

The Great Migration of ca. A.D. 1300 emptied the entire drainage of the San Juan River including the Montezuma Valley, Mesa Verde, Kayenta, and the Chaco Basin. Subsequent population centers concentrated in the Rio Grande valley, the Zuni region, and the Hopi Mesas.

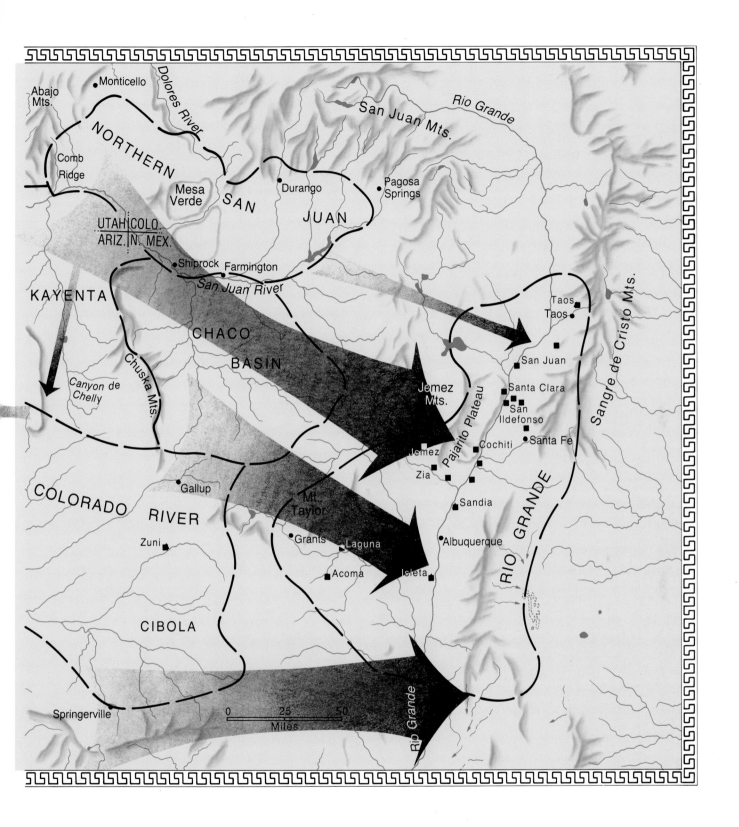

These suggested reasons for the Great Migration may apply to Chaco and Kayenta, but do not apply to the Montezuma Valley, the Animas and San Juan River valleys, the Zuni–Little Colorado River valleys, and the Canyon de Chelly. All of these regions were well watered and amenable to irrigation. Even at Kayenta, the Tsegi Canyon can now and could then have supported a sizeable population. Moreover, the destinations of the migrations—the Rio Grande valley, the Zuni River valley, and the Hopi Mesas—were not significantly more hospitable than much of the Northern San Juan region they left behind. It is as if the entire Anasazi population pulled back into core areas: the Chacoans and the people of the Northern San Juan into the Rio Grande valley, the Kayenta people to the Hopi Mesas, and the upper Little Colorado River valley people to Zuni.

The causes are an enigma, and the results fit no previously known pattern. This brings us back to the original proposition: all we know is that the Northern San Juan, Kayenta, and Chaco regions were abandoned by 1300.

Summary

In this section we have briefly examined the elements of the Anasazi culture and followed its development for nearly two thousand years. The Pueblo Indians are unique, or nearly so, among the surviving cultures of the world because of the amazing continuity of customs, attitudes, methods of government, language, religious beliefs, and architecture, from the Anasazi beginnings in Basket Maker II times (around 700 B.C.) to the twentieth-century Pueblos. These Indians have preserved the essential thread of their way of living despite centuries of environmental catastrophes and assaults on their lives and social organization by other Indians, Spaniards, and Anglos. Few, if any, peoples of this century can show such resistance to acculturation as have the Anasazi-Pueblo Indians of the Southwest.

Having seen that the Anasazi were flesh-and-blood people who struggled with hunger, cold, backaches, dry weather, raiders, and all the other vicissitudes that plague man, that they were not simply spectres occupying the ruins of ancient pueblos and cliff dwellings, we can now consider the tangible things they left behind. We will look at what remains—some of it restored and some not—of their towns and villages from the air and from the ground. From these buildings and other artifacts, we will reconstruct the culture of the ancient Anasazi.

Although we have tried to avoid it, occasionally we may slip into the jargon of the archaeologists. Several terms have special meaning to archaeologists. A "site," for example, means any remnant of the early culture—anything from a few rocks outlining a room to a huge cliff dwelling. The site may be "surveyed" (carefully checked over by looking at the surface) or "dug" or "excavated"—the covering trees, bushes, rubble, or soil removed to reveal the remains of the buildings. While digging a site, one may "trench" a portion of it, in which case he may dig a trench down through the various levels of occupation. Some sites were occupied from time to time for hundreds of years, each period of occupation by a different culture, by peoples with different ways of life. The trenches are usually dug down to bedrock or to "sterile soil," meaning that level below which there was no occupation.

Some Anasazi sites show evidence of several occupations from Basket Maker II through Pueblo III; each phase might be revealed in the trench by the stone tool fragments and pottery. Other sites may show only one or some of the phases.

The ancient "trash dumps" (areas near the village and usually on the south side) where the Anasazi discarded their "artifacts"—anything made or used by the ancient people—are particularly revealing of sequent occupations. Grave robbers, commonly known as "pot hunters," excavate the ancient graves, often found in trash heaps, to recover pottery vessels for sale to art collectors. In the process, they destroy all evidence of such successive occupations.

When Anasazi archaeological sites are excavated to become exhibits-in-place, they are either restored or stabilized. If left exposed with no treatment, the walls will deteriorate further into rubble. One alternative restores the ruin to its supposed original state with walls to their full height and roofs replaced. This kind of restoration should not be confused with an artist's restoration drawing to depict what archaeologists think the occupied building once looked like. The United States National Park Service prefers to stabilize ruins rather than to restore them. Stabilization involves rebuilding the top portions of standing walls with concrete to protect them against further deterioration. Occasionally portions of some walls must be restored to stabilize the foundations of other walls above them. Stabilization avoids speculation about the original building design.

Northern San Juan Region

The Northern San Juan is that part of Anasaziland lying north of the San Juan River and drained by streams flowing into it from the north. The region stretches from the upper San Juan valley around Pagosa Springs, Colorado; through the lower drainages of the Piedra, Pine, Florida, Animas, and La Plata rivers of southwestern Colorado and northwestern New Mexico; across the Mesa Verde and Montezuma Valley to the Abajo Mountains and Comb Ridge in southeastern Utah. Its frontiers shifted through time, sometimes to include the Cedar Mesa and Grand Gulch to the west and the Dolores River valley to the north. Following Pueblo I, the entire eastern portion—essentially east of the La Plata River—was abandoned by Anasazi except around Chimney Rock.

Introduction to Mesa Verde

From Mancos on U.S. 160 east of Cortez, the escarpment of the Mesa Verde ("green table") rises like the prow of a huge ship where the road into the park snakes upward from the east edge of the Montezuma Valley. The west edge of the mesa curves southwest from the park entrance and winds its way south across from the Sleeping Ute Mountain into New Mexico, where it ends at the San Juan River. Mesa Verde National Park makes up a relatively small portion of the northeast corner of the mesa; the balance is on the Ute Mountain Ute Indian Reservation.

The mesa covered by pinyon-juniper woodland is a magnificent place to visit any time of the year (the Wetherill Mesa is closed except in summer), but it is especially lovely in summer. The weather is mild and the accommodations excellent. Chapin Mesa with the stabilized ruins at Far View, park headquarters and the museum, Ruins Road sites, Sun Temple, Cliff Palace, and Balcony House can be visited year round. The Anasazi sites on the Mesa Verde and in the Montezuma Valley, which runs from Cortez to Monticello, Utah, make up the majority of the Northern San Juan Anasazi settlements.

Within the park nearly 3,900 sites have been located, including over 600 cliff dwellings. There are additional sites in the Ute Mountain Reservation. During Pueblo III times (1100 to 1300) probably more than 30,000 Anasazi lived in towns and villages in the Montezuma Valley northwest of Mesa Verde, ten times more than were living on the mesas and in the cliffs.

The Mesa Verde mesas and cliffs were occupied by the Anasazi for at least 700 years, from about 600 (the Basket Maker pithouses on Ruins Road and in Step House) to 1300, when the entire area was abandoned and the Anasazi migrated southeastward to the Rio Grande valley. The period of occupation encompassed several stages of cultural development: Basket Maker III (450 to 750), Pueblo I (750 to 900), Pueblo II (900 to 1100), and Pueblo III (1100 to 1300). The spectacular cliff dwellings were inhabited during the terminal phase of the Mesa Verde Anasazi occupation, during late Pueblo III times between 1200 and 1300, after which the Mesa Verde was abandoned.

B. K. Wetherill and his sons Richard, Alfred, John, Clayton, and Win were ranchers in the Mancos River valley to the east of Mesa Verde in the 1880s. They were friendly with the Ute Indians who allowed them to pasture cattle in the Mancos Canyon. In December 1888, Richard and Al Wetherill and their brother-in-law, Charlie Mason, rode up out of the canyon onto the mesa top where, on the opposite canyon wall filling the great cave overhang, they saw the ruin they named "Cliff Palace." Later the same day Richard Wetherill discovered Spruce Tree

House. In the following years the Wetherills explored some 180 Mesa Verde buildings, removing and selling artifacts that now rest in private collections and museums throughout the world. In 1891, with the help of the Wetherills, Gustaf Nordenskiöld of Sweden excavated several ruins both in the cliffs and on the mesa top on Wetherill and Chapin mesas. His collection is now in the National Museum in Helsinki, Finland, but he published the first scientific study "The Cliff Dwellers of the Mesa Verde" in 1893.

Mesa Verde became a national park in 1906, Jesse Walter Fewkes began systematic investigations two years later. His studies continued into the early 1920s when he was followed by Jesse L. Nusbaum. In the 1930s Earl Morris made repairs and stabilized Cliff Palace, Spruce Tree House, Balcony House, and Far View Ruin. In the 1950s and 1960s work was done on Wetherill Mesa by George S. Cattanach at Long House, Arthur H. Rohn at Mug House, and Robert Nichols at Step House. The National Park Service maintains and repairs the ruins in order to make them visitable by the public.

Ruins Road

Mesa Verde's Ruins Road displays a series of excavated and stabilized Basket Maker III and early Pueblo pithouses, kivas, and dwellings that enable visitors to see the evolution of Anasazi architecture from 600 to 1200. Nowhere else in Anasaziland are there excavated sites showing this progression.

Site 117 (Earth Lodge B) on Ruins Road is a typical Basket Maker III pithouse. Its tree-ring dates indicate construction in 595. The pithouse was constructed with a large room (twenty feet across) and a centrally located clay-lined fire pit. It was entered through an antechamber to the south that also served for ventilation and as storage space. A stone-slab draft deflector was installed in the passageway between the two rooms; another stone-slab draft deflector stood in front of the fire pit. Other features include low wing walls to set off the general living area from the corn-grinding area, storage cists in the walls and floor, and a sacred sipapu.

The roof was supported by four upright posts upon which were laid cross members that were covered with brush, juniper bark, and mud to form a solid roof except for the smoke hole directly above the fire pit. The side walls were formed by setting poles on the ground surface and leaning them against the square roof, following which they were covered with small brush and sealed with mud. The floor

was from twelve to fourteen inches below ground level.

Pithouses of this stage were built in clusters or villages. Around Earth Lodge B there were seven more pithouses. Each pithouse probably housed a small extended family including a father, mother, children, and possibly grandparents, or aunts and uncles, or the spouse of a married child. The Anasazi of all stages lived and worked outside their dwellings. There were fire pits and work spaces adjacent to the pithouses, and from Basket Maker times on they lived and worked on the roofs of their houses. In the Yellow Jacket district, northwest of Mesa Verde in the Montezuma Valley, Basket Maker sites have been excavated where outdoor ramadas, storage units, and hearths were found between and around the pithouses.

At Step House on Wetherill Mesa are four excavated and partially restored pithouses (there were two additional pithouses covered by the later cliff house). At this time, about 600, most of the Anasazi of the Mesa Verde lived on the mesa tops, but some, like the people who lived in Step House Cave, remained in the cliffs. The Step House pithouses were constructed somewhat differently from Earth Lodge B. The floors were dug deeper into the ground and the antechamber was absent. A tunnel replaced the antechamber for ventilation. The only access was the hole in the roof reached by a ladder. Also the sidewall poles were rested on a slightly elevated banquette or bench. These sides were constructed of wattle-and-daub (jacal)— that is, interwoven branches filled with mud.

A hundred years later around 700, Deep Pithouse (Site 101 at Twin Trees Village on Ruins Road) was constructed in the antechamber ruins of a slightly earlier pithouse. As at Step House, Deep Pithouse had no antechamber. Access was through the roof. The roof hatch could be covered with a stone slab for warmth or to keep out the rain. The floor was about twenty-four inches below ground level, and the room was surrounded by a banquette on which the wall poles rested. Otherwise the functional plan of the house was similar to Earth Lodge B. The most significant change that took place during that hundred years of building evolution was the tunnel ventilator. This concept of bringing fresh air into the pithouse through a tunnel on the south side of the structure evolved into the ventilator system found in almost all kivas constructed by the Anasazi.

A further development of the pithouse found at Mesa Verde can be seen at Twin Trees Village. Site 103, constructed during Pueblo I, has two deep,

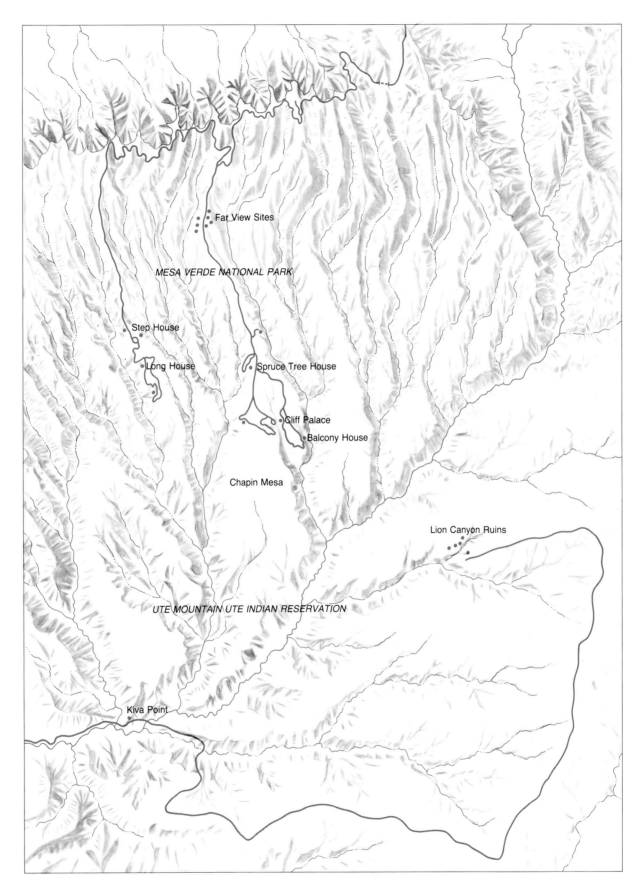

The Mesa Verde includes Mesa Verde National Park and Ute Tribal Park on the Ute Mountain Ute Indian Reservation. Ruins may be visited on Chapin and Wetherill mesas and in Mancos and Johnson canyons.

square-shaped pithouses dated about 850 (one has been backfilled for preservation). The fire pit, ventilator tunnel, stone-slab deflectors, wing walls, sipapu, and roof hatchway are basically unchanged from the first Basket Maker III pithouses. But the depth of six to seven feet below ground made these pithouses substantially subterranean so that the roofs were at about ground level. By 850 at Mesa Verde, the basic elements of the kiva had been developed.

As a part of Pueblo I architectural change, the Anasazi expanded the old aboveground storage rooms into both storage and living quarters; at first they were of jacal and later of masonry construction. These units were built in a single-story line to the north of the pithouses. During the Pueblo I stage (750 to 900) the Anasazi were living both in subterranean pithouses and in aboveground quarters located just to the north of the pithouses. The rooms were square and generally constructed two deep or sometimes three deep front to back. These aboveground structures were built of posts and adobe with upright stone slabs around the base. The living rooms had fireplaces in the corners, and there were smaller storage chambers behind. Sometimes they built porticos (ramadas) in front of the living rooms.

At Twin Trees Village, Sites 101, 103, and 102 are constructions superimposed one above the other. Site 101 (Deep Pithouse) was a Basket Maker III pithouse that was a part of a larger village dating from about 700. Site 103, dating from 850, was part of a Pueblo I village built over the Basket Maker pithouses. Site 102, which consists of one kiva and two small masonry rooms, dates from the 900s in Pueblo II times. The kiva (Site 102) was round and built in about the same way as the Site 103 pithouse except that the roof supports were fitted on top of stone pilasters located on the banquette that surrounded the room.

By this time the Pueblo residence organization was set in place from earlier Basket Maker beginnings. Aboveground dwellings and storerooms were positioned to the north of the pithouses or kivas with work areas in between. This was the beginning of the "unit pueblo" concept that consisted of the aboveground buildings, outdoor work spaces, the kiva, and a trash dump, arranged along a north-south axis. The unit pueblo may also be referred to as a "modular unit" because these units of construction later coalesced into larger pueblos and cliff dwellings.

Text continued on page 80

Earth Lodge B, a Basket Maker III dwelling built around A.D. 600. It and seven other similar partially subterranean houses with earth-covered brush walls and roofs made up a typical Basket Maker III village. This typical house had an antechamber on the south attached by a stepped passageway, a circular firepit, four holes for roof-support posts, and a storage cist built into the sidewall.

Deep Pithouse, Site 101, at Twin Trees on the Mesa Verde. Actually there are two pithouses here, the larger (below) built just prior to A. D. 700, and the smaller constructed in the ruins of the older one's antechamber just after A.D. 700.

A deep pithouse at Site 103 showing a squarish shape, ventilator tunnel, wing walls, central hearth, five post holes marking the position of a post and mud deflector, and four corner post holes where roof-support posts once stood.

Segment of four living rooms at Site 103, Twin Trees, Mesa Verde. Room floors were excavated slightly below ground level; wooden posts covered by mud formed walls and roofs; upright stone slabs support the bases of some walls. Many adjacent rooms have not been excavated. Pueblo I Anasazi lived here during the 830s.

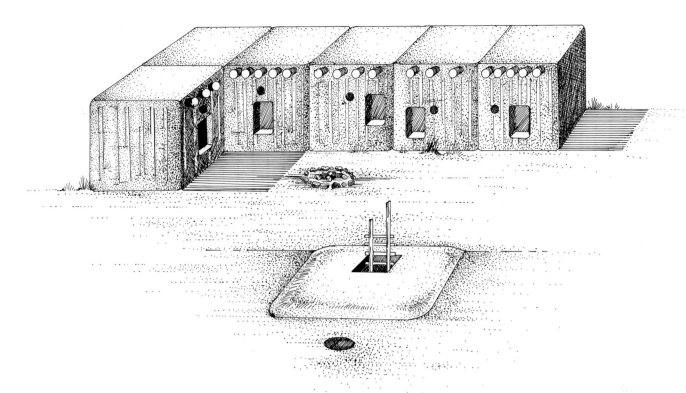

Artist's reconstruction of a single unit pueblo of the Pueblo I (A.D. 750–900) Anasazi showing the aboveground living and storage rooms, the underground pithouse, and the outdoor living and work space. (Drawing by Lisa Ferguson.)

Two small rooms built of crude stone masonry and a circular kiva mark early Pueblo II Site 102 at Twin Trees on Mesa Verde. This small pueblo, built in the mid-900s on the rubbish from Pueblo I Site 103, illustrates the beginning of stone masonry pueblo architecture.

Circular kiva at Site 102 marks an early stage in the development of kivas from earlier pithouses. The walls were earth lined, and the roof was held up by timbers resting on four low stone masonry pilasters rising above the earthen banquette. The sipapu, circular hearth, and ventilator tunnel all carried over from pithouse antecedents. Most likely, a movable sandstone slab served as a deflector.

Site 16 shows the remains of three separate superimposed structures: an early Pueblo II unit pueblo, a late Pueblo II unit pueblo, and a Pueblo III ceremonial platform with three towers and a kiva. Remains of yet earlier houses were noted by the excavators but were not stabilized as part of the exhibit. One of the most interesting features visible here at Site 16 is the stratification of earth fill in this earliest kiva. When the Anasazi residents of the second house (late Pueblo II) dug the pit for their kiva (the north one), they deposited their back dirt in the older kiva, in reverse order. Thus, the archaeologists encountered the whitish band of sterile caliche, that came from the bottom of the newer kiva, on top of the human rubbish left by Site 16's previous inhabitants.

The latest structures at Site 16 fit the Pueblo III stage around 1100. They consist of a rectangular space outlined by a low masonry wall, three round stone masonry towers, and the large kiva beneath the western shelter. The low rectangular wall may have outlined an earthen platform or stage for religious ceremonies.

Two tree-ring dates of 1074 from the large kiva suggest it was constructed in that year or slightly later. This masonry-lined kiva had eight stone pilasters to support its roof and a rectangular stone-lined fire pit. Two long rectangular vaults in the floor on either side of the fire pit may have functioned as foot drums or storage space.

This latest group of structures lacked any domestic living quarters or refuse. They more probably represent an early Pueblo III ceremonial unit consisting of the low-walled platform with its radiating walls, three towers, and the large kiva. It appears to have been built intentionally on top of the ruins of earlier houses. This site reflects a pattern of the Anasazi to build ceremonial buildings on the remains of ruined residences. Similar examples are found at Far View Tower, Site 1 near Twin Trees, and numerous other sites. These ceremonial buildings may have been constructed over the older residential structures to show respect and veneration for their ancestors.

Sun Point Pueblo located on Ruins Road consists of the remains of a block of twenty surface rooms arranged around a core of a kiva and tower that were connected to each other by a tunnel. The kiva is a typical Pueblo III masonry-lined kiva with six pilasters. There are no tree-ring dates available here. The pottery indicates an occupation in the 1100s or possibly early 1200s.

Site 16 displays partially restored structures from three phases of Anasazi history. The charred post stubs are all that remain of a wood and mud pueblo of early Pueblo II (900–1000), the block of rectangular masonry rooms at the left center represents a late Pueblo II (1000–1100) unit pueblo, while the circular tower and low walls to the right belong to an early Pueblo III (1100–1200) ceremonial platform. In 1984 the National Park Service built a protective structure over the excavated kivas.

The early Pueblo II kiva at Site 16. Its roof was held up by four wooden posts set in the front edge of an earthen banquette. This kiva was filled in by earth layers in reverse order excavated from the second kiva nearby. The base of an early Pueblo III round tower overlaps both kivas.

During Pueblo III this tower was constructed over the two earlier kivas. The tower was part of the complex of towers and low walls to the north and the large kiva under the shelter to the west.

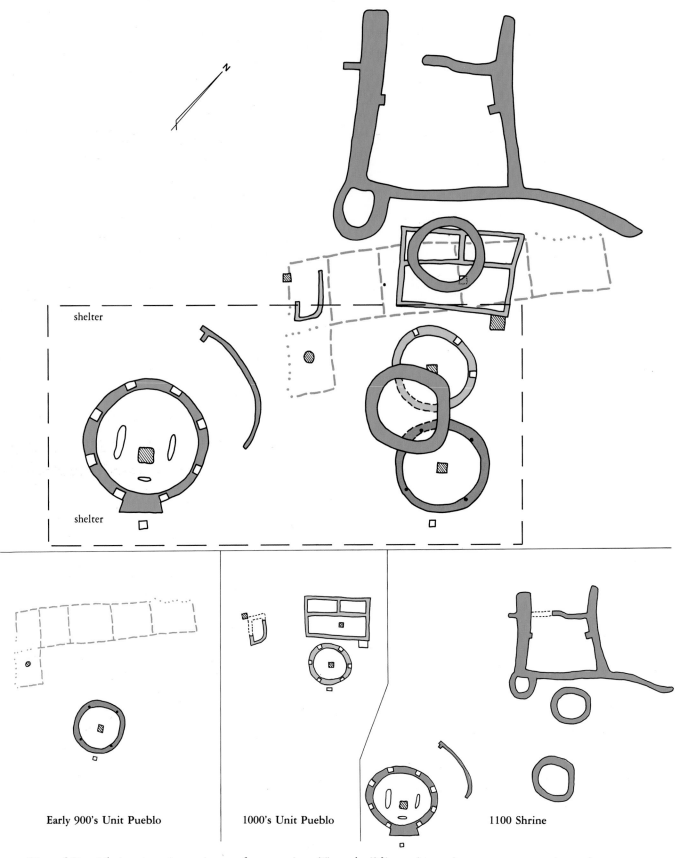

Plan of Site 16 showing three phases of occupation. Those buildings shown in *gray* represent the early Pueblo II house, *blue* marks the late Pueblo II house, and *green* shows the early Pueblo III ceremonial platform and towers.

shelter

shelter

Early 900's Unit Pueblo   1000's Unit Pueblo   1100 Shrine

Large kiva at Site 16 on Ruins Road at Mesa Verde, associated with the early Pueblo III (A.D. 1100s) ceremonial platform and towers. Eight masonry pilasters supported the roof and two elongated floor pits may have been foot drums. Tree-ring dates suggest construction in A.D. 1074.

Tower and kiva complex at Sun Point Pueblo, an early Pueblo III (1100s) unit pueblo on the Mesa Verde. A tunnel opening into the kiva wall leads directly to the circular tower.

The Anasazi left this mesa site and moved into the cliffs. Very little rubble remains because when the occupants moved out and into the canyons to the east, they apparently dismantled their houses and took the building stones with them. All that remains are the bottom courses of room walls, the stub of the tower, and the kiva.

Far View Locality

On the northern part of Chapin Mesa, beginning in early Pueblo II times (in the 900s) the Anasazi began the development of a farming community. A fan of ditches on the hill to the north collected rainfall and channeled it into Mummy Lake, primarily for domestic use. A diversion above Mummy Lake irrigated fields of corn, beans, and squash.

The water was carried further by a ditch constructed by the Anasazi in late Pueblo III times for several miles down the mesa. This was constructed after the Far View locality had been abandoned to provide water for the settlements down the mesa.

The Far View group consists of a cluster of individual sites. An early Pueblo II village was built at the time Mummy Lake was created. Later construction, in late Pueblo II times, overlay the early Pueblo II village and then the new masonry of Pueblo III was put on top of the late Pueblo II–style masonry. Far View House, Pipe Shrine House, Site 820,

Site 875, and Far View Tower represent the remains of the later construction around Mummy Lake.

The lake could have stored some half million gallons of water and thus provided domestic water for the inhabitants of successive villages around it. By early Pueblo III times (about 1100), the total community may have housed some 400 to 500 people in about 375 rooms, with thirty-two kivas located in eighteen sites.

Far View House was constructed with four kivas incorporated in the room block and one subterranean kiva outside. The roofs of the interior kivas served as courtyards for the second-story rooms located along the north, east, and west sides of the pueblo. The large central kiva stands apart from the other four kin-group kivas by having eight pilasters, oblong vaults in the floor, and a clearly larger size. Presumably it too served as a kin kiva, albeit with a special role. Another such large kiva with similar features characterizes the early Pueblo III ceremonial platform and tower component at Site 16. On the south side of the pueblo was a built-up terrace supported by a low masonry wall.

Text continued on page 88

Far View Settlement and water system near the head of Chapin Mesa were reconstructed by *National Geographic* artist Peter V. Bianchi, to approximate how it looked in the 1100s. Inhabitants of the scattered houses, including Far View and Pipe Shrine houses in the upper right, cooperated in building a rainwater-collection system (seen in upper left), the half-million gallon reservoir called Mummy Lake (next to canal fork), and an irrigation ditch leading to terraced fields in the lower left. This settlement of 400–500 people

also shared a common ceremonial center in Far View Tower (upper center). About 1200 these people moved into the cliff dwellings of Cliff and Fewkes canyons, about five miles farther south on Chapin Mesa and 1,000 feet lower in elevation. They took their water system with them by constructing a ditch from Mummy Lake around Far View and down the mesa for some six miles. (National Geographic Society.)

Five excavated ruins of upper Chapin Mesa belong to the Far View Community of the 1100s: Site 820 (lower left), Far View House (just right of center), Pipe Shrine House (far right), Far View Tower (just left of center), and Mummy Lake (white patch next to bend in road). Additional unexcavated sites lie among these. This settlement lies at about 7,700 feet elevation toward the upper end of Chapin Mesa, one of many finger mesas making up the sloping flat-topped Mesa Verde. Mesa Verde's undulating north rim extends across the top of the photograph beyond Soda Canyon. (Photograph taken with the assistance of L. A. Villarreal.)

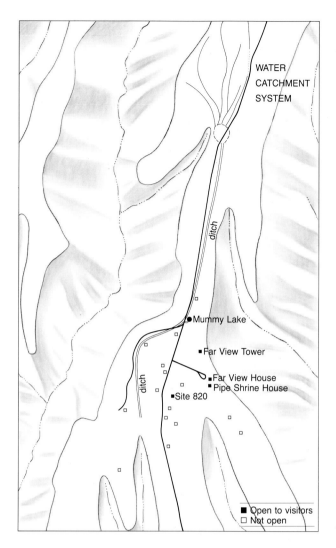

Mummy Lake stored water—up to half a million gallons—for the occupants of the Far View community. It was originally built around A.D. 900 and added to at least twice. Water was led into the stone-lined reservoir through an intake channel at the southwest corner where a 180-degree turn caused sediment to settle where it could be readily dredged out. A flight of steps in the south wall allowed access for water carriers. The water was only for domestic use as the lake had no outlet.

Map of the Far View early Pueblo III community.

Far View House with about fifty rooms and five kivas was built on a terrace formed by a low stone retaining wall. Several rooms stood three stories tall, and several walls show rubble-core and veneer construction. Four kivas are surrounded by rooms while the fifth lies outside the room block. The large central kiva has eight pilasters and oblong floor vaults.

The northernmost ten rooms of Pipe Shrine House in the Far View Community were built during the 1000s while the round tower and other rooms were added during the 1100s when the kiva was remodeled. Stone steps led down through the terrace retaining wall to a small shrine. When excavated, the shrine held a number of pipes for smoking; as a consequence, J. W. Fewkes named the pueblo "Pipe Shrine House."

Pipe Shrine House (late Pueblo II and early Pueblo III construction), so named by Jesse W. Fewkes, who dug the site in the 1920s and found a cache of tobacco pipes in a small shrine located to the south of the pueblo, contains twenty-two masonry dwelling and storage rooms, one kiva, and one tower. In Pipe Shrine House, the two rows of nine rooms on the north side were built in late Pueblo II of loaf-shaped stones in walls only one stone thick. The remaining masonry walls are two or more stones thick and made with sandstone blocks shaped by rough spalling and occasionally dressed by pecking. This unit pueblo is an example of the addition of Pueblo III construction to Pueblo II masonry.

Site 820 (located southwest of Pipe Shrine House next to the highway) contains five kivas and a round tower. All the kivas are incorporated into the room block. On the southwest corner of the building is a room containing six stone slab-lined grinding bins. This was a room set aside for the preparation of food. Within each bin a sandstone metate would have been fixed at an angle. The Pueblo women would kneel behind the bin where the higher end of the metate was fixed and lean forward to grind the corn into flour or meal using a stone mano. The flour or meal collected at the lower end of the metate could then be scooped out for use. The six bins in a row indicate that the grinding was often a women's group activity.

The kivas are circular, masonry-lined, and have ventilators, built-in stone-slab or masonry deflectors, hearths, sipapus, banquettes, southern keyhole recesses, wall niches, and usually six masonry pilasters supporting a cribbed roof. One kiva in Site 820 is a typical Mesa Verde keyhole-shaped kiva with six tall masonry pilasters that rise above the bench level for roof supports. There is a masonry wall deflector and a square fire pit. Two poles connect each pair of pilasters about midway up the column. The poles were not to support the roof but rather to serve as hangers. This is evidence that the banquettes were used for storage and not as benches. The occupants sat on mats on the floor.

Site 820 in the Far View Community consisted of five kin kivas enclosed within their associated blocks of rooms. Some of the back rooms were three stories tall. The round tower standing next to three kivas was not for defense or lookout purposes, but like other such towers in the Northern San Juan region, it functioned with the kivas in ceremonial activities. Low stone walls visible to the right and in front support an earthen terrace on which the site was built.

Across the highway to the west of Site 820 is Site 875. It is composed of fourteen rooms and one kiva and is an early Pueblo III (1100s) example of the unit pueblo. The three elements of the unit pueblo are a room block, a kiva, and a community trash dump, all aligned from north to south. During Pueblo III the kiva was incorporated into the room block as is the case in Far View House, Site 875, and Pipe Shrine House.

Far View Tower is a ceremonial structure superimposed on top of the rubble of older residential rooms and a kiva that were part of a late Pueblo II habitation. The excavation revealed two kivas. One was probably built contemporaneously with the tower and the other was remodeled from an already existing kiva.

Another ceremonial complex similar to the Far View Tower is Cedar Tree Tower, located near Soda Canyon on Chapin Mesa about three-fourths of a mile north of the entrance to Ruins Road. Here is an ovoid tower that originally was probably twice as tall as it now appears, built with double-coursed

Far View Tower, a circular tower with two kivas built for ritual use of the early Pueblo III (1100s) Far View Community. The tower stands on the ruins of an older late Pueblo II (1000s) house, and one kiva has been remodeled from an earlier kiva belonging to the older house.

Two views of Cedar Tree Tower, a probable religious complex, consisting of a tower, a kiva, and a subterranean room all connected by tunnels. Mesa Verde's Pueblo III (A.D. 1100–1300) peoples maintained shrines at natural places important to them. Cedar Tree Tower was constructed at the end of a ridge adjacent to the canyon rim.

masonry walls. Nearly every stone was dressed by pecking to fit the curvature of the walls. Inside is a sipapu carved out of the bedrock sandstone. A natural crack in the sandstone foundation of the tower leads to a tunnel that passes beneath the south wall. This tunnel divides once it gets beyond the wall of the tower, one portion leading into a low room walled-up beneath the sandstone ledge off to the west, the other portion opening out into a subterranean kiva. The tunnel comes in at banquette level alongside one of the pilasters. The kiva contained all the standard features of a Pueblo III kiva—ventilator, deflector, pecked-faced masonry, banquette, six pilasters, hearth, and wall niches—everything except the sipapu, which was located in the tower. A low retaining wall supported a plaza-like space over the kiva roof. There is no precise date on the Cedar Tree Tower structures. The architecture suggests Pueblo III.

Check dams were constructed all over the Mesa Verde. The restored check dams in a wash just south of Cedar Tree Tower, and accessible by trail, represent more than sixty dams constructed in that area. The dams formed small terraces by holding the soil and were used as farm plots (page 47).

Spruce Tree House

Located near the large spring at the head of Spruce Tree Canyon just across the canyon from the Mesa Verde National Park headquarters is one of the most visited Precolumbian ruins in the Americas: Spruce Tree House, mistakenly named by its discoverers Richard Wetherill and Charlie Mason for the Douglas firs growing in front of the ruin. It has been seen by thousands of people since it was opened to visitors following excavation by Dr. Jesse Walter Fewkes. Jesse Fewkes worked at Mesa Verde between 1908 and 1922. He excavated some sixteen dwellings, including Spruce Tree House, Sun Temple, and several ruins in the Far View locality.

This Pueblo III cliff dwelling is third in size at Mesa Verde and consists of some 114 rooms and 8 kivas. Two kivas located at the north end of the ruin have been restored with cribbed roofs based upon the intact kiva roofs found at Square Tower House. These two kivas with their roofs at plaza level make that courtyard of Spruce Tree House resemble all cliff dwellings, and Anasazi pueblos as well, when they were occupied. An outdoor plaza work area would be surrounded on one, two, or three sides by living quarters. The Anasazi lived and worked outside in all seasons. The living area was protected by the great stone overhang of the cave roof. Spruce Tree House receives maximum sunshine in winter and shade in summer.

Two- and three-story rooms face the roofed kivas. Some of the doors are square, others rectangular, and others T-shaped. Second-story roof timbers extend from one of the buildings. A balcony was constructed there originally that allowed access to those rooms. Behind these rooms was a large refuse space.

Spruce Tree House is one of the best preserved of the cliff dwellings. There are many intact roofs

Spruce Tree House across from the museum at Mesa Verde National Park contains 114 rooms and 8 kivas. This Pueblo III village, occupied between A.D. 1200 and 1300, is the best preserved of all Mesa Verde's cliff dwellings, with three-story walls extending to the cave roof, many intact roofs and balconies, and painted plaster covering many wall surfaces. The visitor can

discern individual workmanship of different stone masons from wall to wall. Spruce Tree House formed the core of a community of fourteen sites holding 150 to 200 people packed into this canyon head next to a strong spring. The other Spruce Tree Canyon sites range from one to fifteen rooms each.

and doorways. Slightly to the north of the center of the ruin is a three-story building with a collapsed third-story front wall. Still in place toward the back is a horizontal roof timber and just under that, on what would have been the back wall, is an abstract wall painting. A short distance to the north in the head of Spruce Tree Canyon is the strongest known spring in the Mesa Verde. Along the sides of the canyon are a number of small masonry buildings that were used or occupied by members of the Spruce Tree House community.

Two ancient trails entered Spruce Tree House from the mesa top. One of the trails may be seen to the south of the ruin, leading to a ledge, on which two white painted sandstone slabs have been propped, and thence to the mesa top. Another trail goes up the west side of the canyon. The visitor trail makes a horseshoe turn around a set of hand and toeholds cut out of the bedrock on the cliff face.

Down the canyon to the south is Pictograph

Point, a ceremonial shrine that may have been associated with Spruce Tree House.

Pictograph (Petroglyph) Point

Pictograph Point would be more accurately labeled "Petroglyph Point." Petroglyphs are pecked, grooved, or incised figures in the rock. Pictographs are painted on the rock surface. Here all the figures are pecked into the rock surface of the canyon wall.

Displayed on the cliff are hand prints, both right and left hands, human-like figures, a mountain sheep, turkeys, animals, a wavy line that may represent a trail, zigzag lines that are probably mountains, spirals and lines, and, perhaps, a tablita. The tablita is a carved wooden tablet with a circular cutout to be worn by performers on the top of the head as a headdress in modern Indian dances (page 58).

Text continued on page 94

91

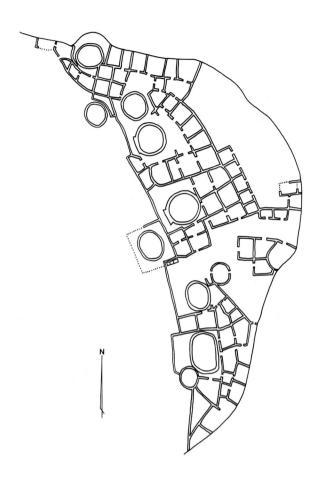

The toehold trail climbs the west side of the canyon across from Spruce Tree House. The Anasazi regularly traveled along such routes from their houses in the sandstone cliffs to their mesa-top farmlands.

Ground plan of Spruce Tree House showing the locations of rooms and kivas relative to one another. Roofs over the kivas would form open courtyards. Second- and third-story rooms and varying levels are not shown, but streets and refuse deposits are apparent. Trails entered the ruin from right and left along the base of the cliff.

The so-called main street runs from the front of Spruce Tree House to the very back of the cave. The two-story rooms on the left are seven deep and are almost perfectly preserved, with roofs still in place showing how some residents climbed through hatchways to reach the second floor. Such an open passageway also functioned as outdoor work space; remains of several stone-lined hearths probably once held fires over which meals were cooked by the people who lived in these rooms.

At left, the cliff dwellers of the Mesa Verde often plastered the inner walls of their living rooms. Lower walls were usually a reddish color while the upper walls were white. The occupants of this second-floor room in Spruce Tree House added a rectangular geometric pattern in red on the white upper wall. Smoke blackening in the left hand corner above a bright red stain marks the location of the fireplace.

North Courtyard of Spruce Tree House formed by the roofs over two underground kivas. These roofs have been restored to create an image of life in a Mesa Verde cliff dwelling during the 1200s. The second-floor rooms at the back of the courtyard were entered from the roofs of a row of one-story rooms now collapsed, while the third-floor rooms had to be reached via a balcony across the extended roof beam ends. Hearths and stone-slab storage bins in the courtyard indicate the Anasazi prepared food and cooked in the open spaces in front of their homes.

The rooms at the north end of Spruce Tree House reached to the very top of the overhang. Here the Anasazi constructed a stone masonry column support for a horizontal log upon which the topmost room wall was built. This architectural device is known from only one other Mesa Verde cliff dwelling, Spring House, and illustrates how an individual builder solved a difficult problem.

The spiral is a common rock art symbol. It is seen as part of the Sun Dagger on Fajada Butte at Chaco Canyon and at Holly at Hovenweep. One is displayed at Pictograph (Petroglyph) Point. It may represent the sun or a water source. The site itself was probably an Anasazi shrine, a sacred place. Similar panels of Anasazi rock art are associated with most ancient communities in the Southwest.

Hopi tribesmen from Arizona suggested the following possible interpretations of the petroglyphs: The spiral immediately below the large hand print represents the sipapu from whence the Anasazi emerged from the earth. The two figures to the left are symbols of the Eagle Clan and the Mountain Sheep Clan. Farther to the left are representations of the Parrot Clan. Below the Parrot Clan bird figures and to the left are two figures that may be horned toads or lizards, representing either the Horned Toad Clan or the "Lizard Spirit." The figures to the left may be "whipping kachinas." These figures are associated with a line pecked into the cliff that may have represented the Anasazi migration route. Still farther to the left is the figure of an animal that may represent an animal spirit or possibly the Mountain Lion Clan. To the right and below the mountain sheep are five humanoid figures that may be "whipping kachinas" in the act of influencing and directing the people.

Cliff-Fewkes Canyons

The magnificent Anasazi Sun Temple sits on the point where Fewkes Canyon joins Cliff Canyon in Mesa Verde. It is the focal point of a cluster of dwellings located in the cliffs of the two canyons. Jesse Walter Fewkes considered it to be a ceremonial structure, which it probably was, but it was not a temple dedicated to a sun god.

Beginning early in Pueblo III times, probably about 1150, the Anasazi began to move off the mesas and into the cliffs and by 1200 began the construction of the great cliff dwellings. The Cliff-Fewkes Canyon Settlement consisted of thirty-three cliff dwellings, with over five hundred living and storage rooms and sixty kivas. Included in this settlement are Cliff Palace and Sunset House on the east side of Cliff Canyon across from Sun Temple and Mummy House, Oak Tree House, and New Fire House on the north side of Fewkes Canyon. The Fewkes Canyon sites were also served by Fire Temple, another ceremonial structure. All of these sites are visible from Ruins Road.

Sun Temple was constructed with two concentric D-shaped, rubble-cored walls divided into compartments which enclosed a pair of kivas. On the west side of the D-shaped structure is an extension with a third kiva, other compartments, and a circular building that probably was the base of a tower. Sun Temple was constructed almost entirely of pecked stones forming the interior and exterior linings of the temple. The kivas were probably roofed and built aboveground, since it would have been impossible to build subterranean kivas into the bedrock below Sun Temple. Courtyard space surrounded the kivas within the D-shaped structure. Another tower was constructed outside.

Sun Temple was contemporaneous with other structures in the settlement and was built on this point probably because it is located directly above the largest spring in the Cliff-Fewkes Canyon system. Across from Sun Temple on the east wall of Cliff Canyon are Cliff Palace, Sunset House, and numerous smaller buildings.

Sunset House includes thirty rooms and four kivas constructed on two levels. The lower level contains three groups of rooms—two rooms and a kiva at the north end, three two-story rooms in the front center, and seven rooms and one kiva at the south end. There are three dry-wall masonry turkey pens at the rear. The ledge is irregular and the cave floor damp, so it was not very desirable for living. The upper ledge, however, was dry and would have been a reasonably pleasant place for habitation, although its west-facing location means that the sun did not reach the site until fairly late in the day. Water came from the spring below Sun Temple, and access was by several trails from the mesa top, two near Cliff Palace and one near Swallows Nest to the south. Several trails led to the narrow canyon floor.

Cliff Palace is the largest of the Mesa Verde cliff dwellings. It contains some 220 rooms and 23 kivas and during the thirteenth century housed probably 250 to 350 people. Toward the center of the ruin is a round tower that tapers inward as it rises, and to the south are two square towers. The six kivas that front Cliff Palace are supported by retaining walls.

Text continued on page 98

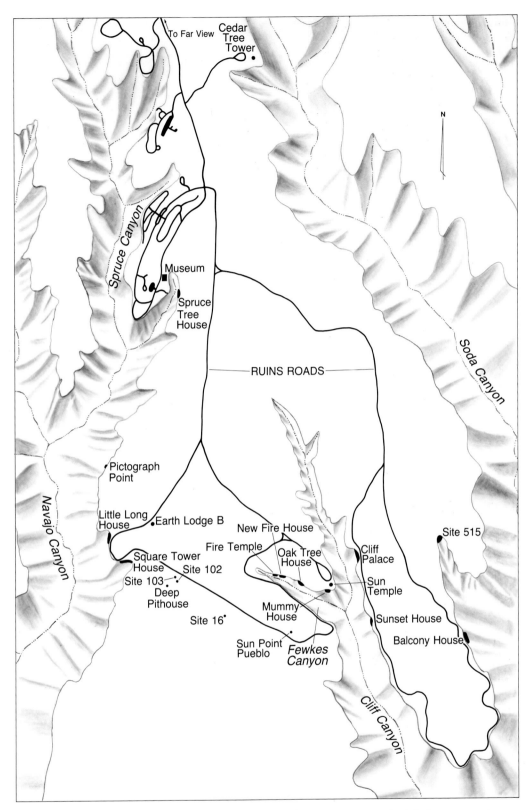

To Far View Cedar Tree Tower

N

Spruce Canyon

Museum

Spruce Tree House

Soda Canyon

RUINS ROADS

Pictograph Point

Navajo Canyon

Little Long House • Earth Lodge B

New Fire House

Site 515

Fire Temple

Oak Tree House

Cliff Palace

Square Tower House Site 102

Site 103

Deep Pithouse

Sun Temple

Mummy House

Site 16

Sunset House

Sun Point Pueblo Fewkes Canyon

Balcony House

Cliff Canyon

Many of the Anasazi ruins on Chapin Mesa may be reached or viewed from the Ruins Road. Stabilized sites chronicle the history of Anasazi development from about A.D. 600 to 1200. The many cliff dwellings visible from overlooks in Cliff and Fewkes canyons make up the Mesa Verde's largest settlement of some 600 to 800 people residing in 33 cliff dwellings, including Cliff Palace, Sunset House, and Oak Tree House. All of Mesa Verde at that time housed about 2,500 Anasazi.

Sun Temple basic structure consists of two circular kivas built above ground within a D-shaped courtyard surrounded by two concentric walls. The space between these two walls has been segmented into small compartments connected to one another by doorways. An extension of another kiva and several more compartments on the west end maintained the overall D-shape. A circular tower stands outside to the east. Sun Temple occupies the point between Cliff Canyon (behind) and Fewkes Canyon (lower right) directly above Mummy House (in shadow, lower right).

Cliff Palace from the round tower to the "speaker chief tower." Small storerooms are located on the narrow ledge just below the cave roof. The circular tower to the right provided added ceremonial space for two adjacent kivas. Restored terrace walls across the front of the ruin illustrate how the cliff dwellers leveled the sloping cave floors to build their houses and kivas.

Ground plan of Cliff Palace from the excavations of J. W. Fewkes in 1909. Access to this cliff dwelling was gained along the zones labeled "walk" at both ends of the cave, the same way modern visitors enter and leave this largest Mesa Verde cliff ruin.

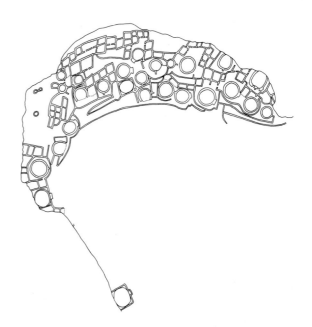

Cliff Palace, the largest individual cliff dwelling on the Mesa Verde with some 220 rooms and 23 kivas.

North end of Cliff Palace shows the best-preserved buildings in this large cliff dwelling. Excavator J. W. Fewkes labeled the tallest building "speaker chief tower," suggesting that the village sun watcher announced his findings from there. Most likely, however, these rooms were ordinary residences.

red paint was powdered hematite mixed with water and fine clay. The white is a nearly pure form of clay, called kaolin. Most of the residence rooms were plastered, and many were painted a reddish color for the bottom section and a whitish color for the top. The plaster was made of a fine clay or mud.

Along the north side of Fewkes Canyon running northwest from Sun Temple are Mummy House, Oak Tree House, New Fire House, and Fire Temple. All were a part of the Cliff-Fewkes Canyon Settlement. Mummy House consists of twelve rooms and two kivas and is located directly below Sun Temple. Jesse Walter Fewkes named the ruin after a well-preserved mummy found in the two-story building located in the small ledge above the main block of rooms.

Oak Tree House contained fifty-two to fifty-five residential rooms and six kivas located on two separate ledges. At Oak Tree House as well as the other dwellings in the cliffs, the people disposed of trash down the talus slope in front of the cliff dwelling. These talus slopes of trash have been invaluable to the archaeologists in determining the age and relationship of the habitation sites by an analysis and comparison of the pottery sherds found in the debris.

Next to Oak Tree House and to the northwest along the cliff wall in Fewkes Canyon is New Fire

The four-storied building contains interior wall paintings, each with three major segments. The lower portion of the room wall was painted solid red; above this the wall is painted white. Where the red joins the white there are several red triangles grouped as if to represent mountains and a row of red dots. The third element consists of two figures, depicted in red on the white wall, displaying abstract textile designs. All the paintings were located in the third story. Originally there were floors for each of the stories. Access to the upper stories was by hatchways from the lower stories through the floors. The T-shaped doorway at the top of the tower indicates that there may have been a balcony outside that doorway.

Decorated rooms were not uncommon during Pueblo III times. The paintings at Cliff Palace are more elaborate and better preserved than most. The

Even though no two of Cliff Palace's twenty-three kivas are exactly alike, they all follow a generalized pattern: circular in plan, generally dug beneath courtyard level so their roofs would form part of the courtyard, central fireplace, ventilator tunnel on the south side, a raised air deflector, and usually six masonry pilasters rising above an encircling banquette to support a cribbed log roof. The variation among kivas probably reflects the different ritual needs and ideas of the kin groups (lineages) who built and used these distinctive Anasazi buildings.

Painted interior walls on the third floor of a four-story building in Cliff Palace. The upper portion of the wall has been painted white, the lower portion red, with red triangles extending upward as if representing mountains on the horizon. Rows of red dots run between the triangles. Both rectangular patterns painted in red on the white upper walls resemble textile patterns. While the interiors of many cliff-dwelling living rooms were decorated, few were as elaborate as this one.

House. It was constructed on two levels with the residential houses on the top level and the kivas and additional residential units below, making a total of twenty residential rooms and three kivas. The overhang is very low, restricting the buildings in the back to one low story.

Fire Temple is a ceremonial structure analogous to the great kivas found at many large Anasazi towns in the Southwest. It differs by being rectangular rather than round like the great kivas at Aztec Ruin and Chaco Canyon. Another rectangular great kiva may be seen at Long House on Wetherill Mesa.

In the center of the major space is a masonry-lined elevated fire box and masonry-outlined floor vaults. The open space may have served as a dance platform and probably was never roofed. There are rooms at either end of the platform, with an altar in the rooms to the northwest. Fire Temple stands nearest to the spring at the head of Fewkes Canyon and as a ceremonial center served the inhabitants of Fewkes and Cliff canyons.

The Fewkes Canyon ruins are all situated on the northeast wall of the canyon. The canyon itself is very difficult to get into with no access trail into it along the northeast wall. The only access is along the southwest wall across from the space between Oak Tree House and New Fire House. There is an access route to the northeast of Sun Temple where a toehold trail goes down the cliff. It is then possible to follow the base of the cliff in Cliff Canyon to Fewkes Canyon and then up to Mummy House. The access to the cliff dwellings was difficult from the bottom of both canyons because of the steep and slippery slopes covered with dense brush.

The Cliff-Fewkes Canyon group with the Sun Temple and Fire Temple may have been the nuclear settlement for all of the Chapin Mesa cliff dwellings including Balcony House and Site 515, Square Tower House and Little Long House, Spruce Tree House, and a cluster at the head of Pool Canyon on the Ute Reservation to the south.

Square Tower House

Square Tower House, Little Long House, and several small structures—one- and two-room storage rooms—constituted a mid-size cliff dwelling settlement. Neither of these ruins is now open to the public.

Water could have been obtained from three sources. A weak spring runs immediately below Square Tower House. At one time there was a spring in the draw near Little Long House, and the Anasazi had constructed a dam above the spring which allowed the water to percolate through the bedrock sandstone into the spring. In addition, a natural depression in the sandstone above the pour-off next to Little Long House holds water much of the year. Toeholds leading to the depression indicate the Anasazi obtained water from it.

Text continued on page 104

Fewkes Canyon on Chapin Mesa. Several cliff dwellings in the north canyon wall belong to the Cliff-Fewkes Canyon community. Two communal ceremonial buildings served the entire community—Sun Temple on the north canyon rim directly above Mummy House, and Fire Temple in the north cliff near the head of Fewkes Canyon. The Anasazi built a dam across the bare rock area above the canyon head to feed water into the spring below. The wooded mesa top had been cleared for farmlands, firewood, and construction timbers. The Cliff-Fewkes Canyon community with Sun Temple and Fire Temple may have been a ceremonial center for other Mesa Verde settlements such as the Spruce Tree Canyon and Square Tower–Little Long House groups.

Mummy House (above) near the mouth of Fewkes Canyon in the Cliff-Fewkes Canyon community. Only the wall stubs of ten rooms and two kivas remain on the lower ledge of this cliff dwelling, but several rooms must once have stood two and three stories high in order to permit the Anasazi to climb up to the perfectly preserved two-story building tucked beneath the upper shallow overhang. A well-preserved mummy found in this building prompted the name. Sun Temple stands on top of the cliff at the upper left.

Oak Tree House (below) in Fewkes Canyon is the second largest cliff dwelling in the Cliff-Fewkes Canyon community with six kivas and fifty-two to fifty-four rooms. Most of the rooms squeezed onto the narrow upper ledge were for storage, only a few were living rooms. They were entered by ladders from the roofs of multistory rooms—now fallen—in the lower cave. The retaining walls supporting terraces on which the rooms and kivas were built have been restored to protect the original standing walls from deteriorating.

New Fire House (above) in Fewkes Canyon contains the remnants of twenty rooms and three kivas on two separate ledges. A set of small steps or toeholds leads onto the upper ledge between two sets of buildings. A ladder resting on the wall between the two left kivas led to those steps. The Anasazi employed similar steps or toehold trails to traverse cliffs throughout the Mesa Verde and all Anasaziland.

Fire Temple (below) was a rectangular great kiva built beneath a cliff overhang near the spring at the head of Fewkes Canyon. The large central rectangular chamber contains an encircling bench, a red and white painted wall, a raised circular masonry fire box, and two oblong masonry floor vaults. It may never have been roofed. Rooms have been attached on both the right and left, with one of the left group containing a raised altar. Ceremonies held here and at Sun Temple were probably attended by all the residents of the Cliff-Fewkes Canyon town and perhaps by people from other cliff dwelling villages on Chapin Mesa.

Little Long House · Square Tower House

The west cliffs of Chapin Mesa (above) in the vicinity of Twin Trees show the late Pueblo III cliff dwellings Little Long House (extreme left) and Square Tower House (extreme right). Together with five other small cliff ruins, these buildings housed 120 to 150 Anasazi in more than 110 rooms and 12 kin kivas. They shared water sources in a spring below Square Tower House and a reservoir/seep complex next to Little Long House. They also shared the only two trails to the mesa top to their farmlands and wood supply, now covered by pinyon-juniper woodland. During earlier times, the Basket Maker III Earth Lodge B village stood near the center of the mesa top and the subsequent Twin Trees villages at the extreme right of the photograph. The distant La Plata Mountains loom above the Mesa Verde's north rim in the background.

Square Tower House (below) lies beneath a high shallow overhang in an alcove in the west wall of Chapin Mesa below Twin Trees. It had seven kin kivas and more than seventy rooms. Several rooms were perched high in a cliff crack above and to the right of the cliff dwelling. Excavator J. W. Fewkes called this the "crow's nest." The nearest trail to the mesa top led out of the right side of the shelter along the base of the cliff and through a narrow crack behind a large boulder leaning against the cliff. (Photograph taken with the assistance of L. A. Villarreal.)

The "square tower" for which Square Tower House was named by the Wetherill brothers actually is a four-story building that once had a three-story building in front of it and a two-story building in front of that. Immediately to the right of the "tower" is a well-preserved section of kiva roof used as a model by the Park Service for the reconstruction of kiva roofs in Spruce Tree House.

Square Tower House faces south-southwest presenting an excellent view from the overlook. It gets its name from the four-story building that appears to be a tower but actually is four domestic rooms built one above the other. Originally a three-story structure stood in front of the "tower" and a two-story building in front of that. These latter two buildings are gone, leaving only the four-story structure standing.

Square Tower House, located in Navajo Canyon, was a relatively large cliff dwelling containing some seventy or more domestic rooms and seven kivas. There is a splendid view of Square Tower House from a visitors' overlook off Ruins Road.

Two of the kivas have portions of their roofs intact. These kivas provided the model for the cribbed roof construction that capped the roofs of other Pueblo III kivas, including the restored kivas at Spruce Tree House. The roofed kiva is nestled between the "tower" and the building immediately to the right.

Two trails led into Square Tower House, one a toehold trail to the south of the visitor overlook. It dropped down the sandstone cliff and then continued along the base of the cliff, going behind a large sandstone block that had fallen from the cliff and tilted back against it, and thence into the southeast corner of the ruin. The second trail came down some distance to the northwest, down a sandstone projection and around a small tributary canyon, through the lower portions of Little Long House to the cliff point immediately to the west of Square Tower House and into the ruin from the west.

Little Long House, around the cliff to the northwest of Square Tower House, faces west and is constructed on two ledges with a total of some twenty-four rooms. Four kivas were built on the lower ledge.

Balcony House is tucked beneath the cliff on the east side of Chapin Mesa overlooking Soda Canyon. Of all the cliff dwellings on the Mesa Verde, this one displays the most defensive setting. After climbing up a steep toehold trail and traversing a narrow ledge, visitors would have to crawl through two low tunnels behind the leaning boulder at the extreme left, then enter the ruin at the left end of the cave. Residents of Balcony House could get water from one spring in the cave behind the two-story building toward the left or from a second spring under the base of the cliff at the extreme right. Turkeys were penned at the base of the cliff just left of the National Park Service ladder. A disproportionate ratio of forty-five rooms to two kin kivas is balanced by the other eleven cliff sites in the Balcony House village along the adjacent cliffs.

Balcony House

From the point of view of the visitor, Balcony House at Mesa Verde is one of the most exciting and spectacular ancient ruins in North America. It sits under an overhang on the west wall of Soda Canyon and is accessible from the Balcony House–Cliff Palace road by a series of ladders.

Balcony House is one of several cliff dwellings that formed a small settlement consisting of some twelve separate sites scattered along the west cliffs of Soda Canyon, with a total of eighty-one rooms and six kivas. The population of the community is estimated to have been over a hundred people. At the head of a small tributary canyon just north of Balcony House is Site 515. It contained eleven rooms and three kivas. Pueblo III settlements in the Mesa Verde generally had a ratio of eleven rooms to one kiva, but in order to come up with the appropriate ratio it is necessary to take the entire settlement into account.

With forty-four rooms to two kivas, Balcony House is out of proportion. However, if Site 515 and the other sites along the canyon wall are taken into consideration as a whole, the kiva-to-room ratio is proportional to other cliff dwellings. Site 515 may have been the most important site in the settlement because there the Anasazi constructed a reservoir to collect water coming out of a seep at the base of the cliff and a dam in the ravine above the cliff to cause the runoff water to soak into the sandstone. This is the same water conservation system that is found at Long House, Spruce Tree House, and Little Long House.

The trail into Balcony House came into the site along the ledge from the south behind a huge sandstone boulder that had slipped from the cliff face eons ago and left a narrow crevice between the boulder and the cliff face. The Anasazi sealed off the narrow passageway with a stone masonry wall, leaving only two doorways separated by a small crawl space, thus making the entryway to the cliff dwelling easily defensible.

In ancient times the access trail led south from the boulder along the ledge until it narrowed to

One or two persons could adequately defend this entrance by positioning themselves above the two tunnels to strike any intruder trying to crawl in. Burdens, of course, could be raised or lowered into the cave by ropes.

The perfectly preserved balcony for which Balcony House was named. Its construction of poles covered with twigs or split juniper shakes set at right angles, then bark, and finally mud typifies roof construction employed by all the Anasazi. Inhabitants of the two second-floor rooms would emerge onto the balcony through the rectangular doorways, then climb down ladders to the courtyard below. These four rooms are excellent examples of the Mesa Verdean house-building skills.

nothing. At that point they built a small circular tower and a toehold trail leading down to the top of the talus slope. The trail then led north along the top of the talus slope, past the turkey pens and the spring beneath Balcony House, and onward to the north several hundred yards to a toehold trail leading to the mesa top. There was also a very steep toehold route down just below the south block of rooms. Access to Balcony House was so difficult that supplies probably were lowered into the living area by ropes. Water was provided by a spring in the back of the cave. Another water source was located under an overhang below the north end of the ruin. The Anasazi built dry-wall masonry turkey pens at the south end of the same overhang.

The north half of Balcony House is interesting for two reasons: one is the well-preserved balcony along the two-story building, and the other is the retaining wall built up to form a parapet protecting

the outer edge of the courtyard. The balcony was constructed on the extensions of the first-floor rooms' ceiling support beams that extended out from the walls. Small poles were laid on the beams, and several inches of juniper bark and mud were added to these to form the walkway. This balcony provided access to the second-story rooms. The square openings were doors, not windows.

Balcony House was divided into two halves by a dividing wall. The north half had the parapet retaining wall, the south half did not. Both kivas were built in the south section. The physical division of Balcony House by the central wall probably came about because of a duality in the community orga-

North Court in Balcony House on the east side of Chapin Mesa. Besides the remarkably preserved balcony on the two-story building, this courtyard is unusual for the low guard wall across its front. The obvious protection afforded small children against falling over the edge was not copied by other cliff dwellings. A series of poles stretched across the middle of the room at the far end of the guard wall formed a drying rack for foodstuffs.

nization—something akin to the duality that exists in modern pueblos between the Winter People and the Summer People. Responsibility for the ceremonial and governmental activities may have been passed back and forth between two segments of the community that included not only Balcony House but Site 515 and the other habitations as well. The same concept of duality might have been present in the Cliff-Fewkes canyons, with Fewkes Canyon people gathering at Fire Temple and the Cliff Canyon people at Sun Temple.

Communication between the halves is evidenced by the opening in the wall. It may also be inferred that relations between north and south changed from time to time as there is a walled-up doorway in the wall. At the time the cliff dwelling was abandoned, communication between the north and south sections was limited to a narrow passageway against the cave's back wall.

At the north end of the cliff dwelling is a small room with an intact roof. Inside this room is a series of poles that stretch across the room and were used for hanging objects for drying or for storage. These objects included strings of corn ears or strips of squash, clothing, tools, and utensils.

In the south half of Balcony House a long pole extends out at second-story level. It was part of the roof support for a room that was built between the two kivas. In the back of the cave there is smoke blackening from the ancient cooking and heating fires. The long pole extends from a building with an intact T-shaped doorway. The small openings on either side of the doorway are smoke holes for the back room. The two kivas filled most of the south

An Anasazi's view of the south courtyard in Balcony House through an opening or "window" in the wall that separates the two courtyards. We are looking at a room whose walls collapsed into the adjacent kivas, leaving only the one roof beam projecting from the room next door. Rectangular openings of this size, like the two flanking the T-doorway in the visible wall, were the only windows in Anasazi architecture. This solid wall across Balcony House, with only one narrow opening at the back of the cave through which people could pass, separated social groupings within the site.

court. The floors, fire pits, and sipapus were pecked out of the bedrock.

On the mesa tops, kiva ventilators faced south. This alignment was often impossible in the cliff dwellings as the ventilators needed to face the cave entrance for an adequate draft. At Balcony House the ventilator tunnels were angled partially to the south. This required the underground ventilator tunnels to go much farther than if the ventilators had been constructed directly facing the cave entrance on the east. The kivas were masonry lined with stone pilasters upon which the cribbed roofs were constructed.

The southern courtyard would have been an open work area in ancient times when the kivas were roofed at plaza level. The result would have been similar to the area at Spruce Tree House, where the kiva roofs have been reconstructed.

Wetherill Mesa

Wetherill Mesa, a long finger of land that lies between Long Canyon and Rock Canyon, is located west of Mesa Verde park headquarters about two miles as the raven flies, but about twenty miles by road by way of Far View.

Just as with the canyons that surround Chapin Mesa, the cliffs around Wetherill Mesa are laced with Anasazi masonry habitation and storage rooms. There are, however, four major sites: Long House, Step House, Mug House, and Kodak House. These sites may have been a part of an interrelated community with Long House at the center because of its great kiva and its central location with respect to the other three sites.

Long House lies under a great overhang at the head of a small canyon tributary to Rock Canyon. It faces south. In the center of Long House is the rectangular great kiva of the Fire Temple (Fewkes Canyon) variety. It has a raised masonry fire box in the center, two masonry-lined floor vaults to the right and left of the fire-box, and a masonry-lined sipapu. On the west end of the great kiva is a small block of rooms that may have included an altar-like structure that is characteristic of great kivas.

Text continued on page 112

Wetherill Mesa, Mesa Verde National Park, from above Long House. The tableland slopes from about 8,500 feet elevation along the north rim of the mesa past 7,000 feet near Long House to less than 6,500 feet to the south where the mesa is cut by the Mancos River canyon. Steep canyons, such as Rock Canyon that houses the Long House cliff dwelling, cut the Mesa Verde into many long and narrow finger mesas. Wetherill and Chapin Mesas are but two. (Photograph taken with the assistance of L. A. Villarreal.)

Long House on Wetherill Mesa, the second largest cliff dwelling on the Mesa Verde. Some 150–200 people occupied its more than 150 rooms and 21 kin group kivas. The name derives from the long extent of this ruin around the full arc of this magnificent overhang. In the front center of the cave, National Park Service excavators in 1960 uncovered the remains of another rectangular great kiva in the style of Fire Temple on Chapin Mesa. Upper ledge rooms on the left were primarily for storage and were reached by ladder from the roofs of rooms below. A single long crude wall riddled with peek holes encloses space on the high ledge above the center of the ruin.

Long House, Wetherill Mesa. One of the best preserved Pueblo III cliff dwellings.

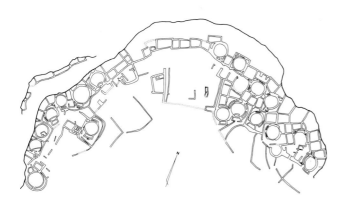

Ground plan of Long House on Wetherill Mesa at Mesa Verde National Park. The rectangular great kiva lies in the center between two clusters of houses and kivas that appear to represent a two-part (dual) division, each with its own trash slope (after Cattanach 1980).

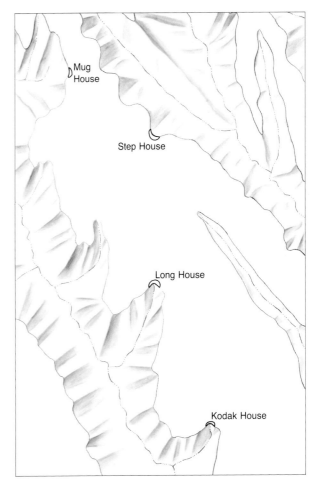

Mug House

Step House

Long House

Kodak House

Wetherill Mesa, Mesa Verde National Park.

Rectangular great kiva in Long House with typical features such as raised masonry fire box in the center of the large chamber, flanking masonry-lined floor vaults, low benches at both ends, and the altar room extension on its west side. A stone-lined sipapu may be seen between the fire box and the bedrock

sandstone back wall. A shale lens (dark band) just above floor level forces water out of the bedrock at this level, although the main spring used by Long House residents occupies the east end of the main cave. Ceremonies held in this structure probably attracted people from all of Wetherill Mesa's cliff dwellings.

At the left end of the east wall of the great kiva an opening to a small passageway with a set of steps leads up and into the room block. Immediately to the left and above this passageway are the bases of the walls of what once was a five-story building that extended upward to a height just above the highest wall section remaining on the lower ledge of Long House. The roof of that five-story building provided the base from which a ladder could extend upward to the upper ledge. The upper ledge has no rooms; it has a front wall only that suggests it may have been a defensive refuge.

To the northeast of the great kiva on the ledge is a block of residential rooms and a kiva. The kiva's original roof was not cribbed like most Pueblo III kivas. The roof cross members were laid directly on the kiva walls with smaller timbers laid crosswise to fill the roof.

Under the Pueblo III construction at the east end of Long House was a Basket Maker III pithouse.

Both here and at Step House, Basket Maker people lived in the cliffs, while most of their contemporaries on Wetherill and Chapin mesas resided on the mesa top. To the left of center in the ruin stands a rectangular kiva. The kiva has a circular hearth, ventilator, and a masonry deflector.

Near the west end of the ruin, construction occurs on two levels. The upper-level rooms were reached from the tops of the multistory buildings below. Ladder grooves are visible just to the left of the jacal wall. The visible upper-level doors demonstrate that originally the Anasazi built room upon room to a height sufficient to reach the upper ledges with the aid of ladders. Access to these ledges allowed construction under the upper overhangs. On the central level at the west end of Long House is a row of kivas. One contains a kiva wall painting, in pottery-decoration style, and a series of loom-anchors are pecked into the bedrock floor.

In the western portion of the ruin is a split

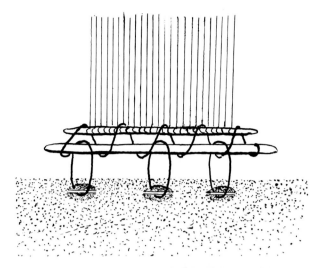

The upright looms on which the Anasazi wove cotton robes and textiles were often set up in the small kin kivas where they were tied both to roof beams and to loom anchors in the floor. This set of three loom anchors was carved out of the bedrock sandstone floor of Kiva E on the west side of Long House on Wetherill Mesa (sketch by Joan Foth).

boulder beneath which is a masonry supporting wall constructed for stabilization by the National Park Service. The boulder had slipped previously and damaged buildings that had been constructed on top of it. In many of the cliff dwellings the Anasazi built on, around, and under large boulders that had fallen from the overhang. Just to the west of the split boulder is a three-story building with a preserved roof. On the level of the second story of the building on the extreme west side of the ruin are three kivas in a row from west to east. Below the building (near the steps constructed by the National Park Service) is a kiva with multicoursed masonry walls built upon the bedrock.

The water supply for Long House came from a strong spring that flowed out on the intermediate ledge in the center of the cave. The Anasazi developed the spring by cleaning out the debris and pecking little grooves into the sandstone bedrock to lead the water over to a series of pecked depressions in the floor of the cave, where it could be scooped into jugs. Above the cave on the mesa top they built a dam to stop the runoff and allow the water to soak into the sandstone and percolate out at the spring in the back of Long House. Another possible water source is a second seep just behind the great kiva.

The Step House Cave cliff dwelling is located almost directly north of Long House. It is on the west side of a small canyon off Long Canyon and faces east. The Pueblo III ruin is located in the north end of the cave, and the stabilized remains of four Basket Maker III pithouses are found at the south end. Actually, six pithouses were found, all of which dated from the early 600s. Two of them were beneath the Pueblo III ruin. These circular pithouses belonged to a pithouse community on top of which the Pueblo III peoples built some 600 years later—a hundred years longer than the span of time from the discovery of America until today.

A staircase made of sandstone talus blocks leading out of the south end of the cave in ancient times inspired the name "Step House." The modern trail has been constructed below the original entryway. The Pueblo III buildings are built on several levels around large fallen blocks of sandstone. One of the three kivas is squeezed down in between several of these chunks of sandstone. Numerous stone-axe sharpening grooves have been worn into the top of one of these boulders. Axes and awls were sharpened by rubbing the edges back and forth on the face of a stone boulder. As time passed grooves were worn in the stone the size of the tool head. Arrows and darts were sharpened in the same way. Most cliff dwellings have a particular boulder that the Anasazi utilized as a tool-sharpening center. The three kivas manifest a variation in style. One has a large number

A partially preserved roof resting directly on the walls covers this kiva near the center of Long House.

113

Square kivas, although fewer in number than the round kivas, were not uncommon. At Long House this square kiva was constructed adjacent to an oval kiva.

of niches in the side wall. The northernmost kiva has a row of rectangular-bodied mountain sheep painted on the plaster.

Kodak House (not now open to the public) is a large Pueblo III site constructed in the next canyon head south of Long House. This cliff dwelling had nearly seventy rooms. It was badly damaged by nineteenth-century pot hunters, who ruthlessly demolished many of the standing structures in an effort to find artifacts of value.

Kodak House is an example of the continuing problem of the destruction of our American heritage by looters of ancient sites. Looting not only destroys the ancient sites, but it renders them useless for study by archaeologists. The insatiable demand by art collectors continues to spur looters to dig, blast, and bulldoze to find graves containing salable pots.

Text continued on page 119

Step House Cave (above) in the east cliffs of Wetherill Mesa overlooks Long Canyon. Late Pueblo III Mesa Verde cliff dwellers built a small hamlet of three kin kivas with associated living and storage rooms on the pile of boulders in the right side of the cave. These masonry houses and the rubbish discarded by their occupants covered a village of six Basket Maker III pithouses, four of which have been stabilized in the center of the cave. The Basket Maker III people lived here during the early 600s and buried several of their dead in the back of the cave. A series of stone steps leading down the talus slope into the left end of the cave were built by the prehistoric Anasazi, inspiring the name Step House.

Four Basket Maker III pithouses (below) dating from around A.D. 600 from Step House Cave on Wetherill Mesa. One house has been partially reconstructed to illustrate what the finished buildings probably looked like. Parts of two other contemporary houses now covered by the later cliff dwelling completed this village.

115

Close-up of stabilized Basket Maker III pithouse in Step House Cave. Visible preserved construction features include the upright sandstone slabs lining the lower wall, an encircling banquette on which the side walls rested, four charred roof-supporting posts (this house had burned), and a circular hearth.

The ancient inhabitants of Step House reached their mesa-top farm land by climbing a set of stone steps along the large talus slope at the south side of the overhang.

Kodak House, located in an alcove of Rock Canyon on the west cliffs of Wetherill Mesa, was named by Gustav Nordenskiold because he stored his camera there during his pioneer archaeological investigations on the Mesa Verde in 1891. Rooms were built along two separate ledges with kivas on the lower ledge. Like the other inhabitants of Wetherill Mesa, these people probably attended important ceremonies at the great kiva in Long House, about a mile to the north.

In the foreground is the small Pueblo III cliff dwelling at Step House constructed during the 1200s. To the rear are the much earlier Basket Maker pithouses dating from the 600s.

Tree House at Ute Mountain Tribal Park, a picturesque Pueblo III Anasazi ruin near the head of Lion Canyon. The ruins of Lion Canyon may be visited with a Ute guide.

Lion House was a part of an Anasazi community of cliff dwellings built along the north side of Lion Canyon including Tree House, Morris No. 5, and Eagle Nest House that housed some 250 people in the middle 1200s.

Ute Mountain Tribal Park

The Tribal Park (part of the Ute Mountain Ute Indian Reservation) is a 125,000-acre tract along the Mancos River set aside by the tribe to preserve Precolumbian ruins. The first professional work was done in Lion Canyon by Earl H. Morris in 1913 and 1915. He named Eagle Nest House and Morris No. 5. David A. Breternitz directed additional excavation work here for the University of Colorado Mesa Verde Research Center in the mid 1970s. The ruins were then stabilized by the National Park Service.

Along the road into the park are several ruins and some interesting rock art at Kiva Point. The ruins herein discussed have been stabilized for visitation, but they retain the charm of ruins recently discovered. Pottery sherds are scattered about, and the trails are not surfaced. Of all the Anasazi ruins open to visitors, with the exception of Keet Seel,

the Johnson–Lion Canyon ruins are the most exciting to see because they project the feeling of Anasazi ruins when first discovered by the Wetherills.

The ruins are situated only a few miles southeast of the Mesa Verde National Park but can be reached only by road from the junction of U.S. 160 and Ute Reservation Road that goes east along the Mancos River. The road leaves the Mancos Canyon about fifteen miles east of U.S. 160 and snakes its way southward to the top of the mesa where it swings around the east end of Johnson Canyon, back about three miles to the west to the head of Lion Canyon.

Lion Canyon contains several spectacular Pueblo III cliff dwellings: Fortified House, Tree House, Lion House, Morris No. 5, and Eagle Nest House. These and other small ruins may be visited with an approved Ute Mountain Tribal Park guide by making reservations at the Tribal Park Headquarters at To-

119

Lion House and other Lion Canyon cliff dwellings were constructed in two phases: the first 1130–60 and the second 1195–1230. The upper-story room shows a difference in masonry wall construction from the ones below.

waoc, Colorado. Johnson–Lion Canyon ruins are a part of the Pueblo III Anasazi settlements of the Mesa Verde.

The Johnson Canyon Anasazi lived on the mesa tops in times prior to the construction of the cliff dwellings. They began to move from the mesas into the cliffs beginning about 1130 and continued to build in the overhangs until 1160, after which there was no further significant building until 1195. Then a second phase of construction continued until about 1230.

The cliff dwellings may have been at least partially abandoned during the thirty years prior to 1195, because the second building sequence involved dismantling the early construction in the cliff alcoves and using the material to build the buildings occupied during the second phase. The tree-ring dates show the last construction to have been in 1240 and 1241. How long was the canyon occupied after that? Possibly ten or twenty years, which would indicate abandonment around 1250 or 1260—some thirty or forty years before Mesa Verde was abandoned.

The Johnson Canyon Anasazi were probably closely associated with the Mesa Verde people. These sites in total constituted only one village of some 200 to 250 people and, like Balcony House, Square Tower—Little Long House, and Spruce Tree House, may have been an outlying village of the Cliff–Fewkes Canyon Settlement. Tree House, Lion House, Morris No. 5, and Eagle Nest House nestle from east to west in the cliff overhangs on the north side of Lion Canyon. They can be visited in sequence by following the trail that connects them.

Tree House is a jewel set in the verdant head of a small canyon off Lion Canyon. It has a tower-like cliff dwelling with a T-shaped door and is built like a wasp nest against the canyon wall. The cylinder-like room block reaches up to additional dwellings on the ledge above.

Lion House is the next cliff dwelling down the canyon. It has a stub wall still standing, showing that originally there were multistoried rooms. At the time it was abandoned, Lion House had seven kivas and more than forty-five rooms.

Morris No. 5, the next cliff dwelling, has only the ruins of a few standing walls on two levels. There is an excavated kiva with a cribbed roof on stone pilasters, a fire pit, and a floor-level ventilating system with a curved deflector wall. Also numerous axe- and awl-sharpening grooves are incised into the rock.

The ruins were discovered by the Wetherill brothers (Richard, John, Al, Clayton, and Win), who did some collecting shortly after the discovery and found several well-preserved mummies, one of which had been cut in two and sewn back together. They left their mark by carving "Wetherill" into one of the boulders.

The most interesting and spectacular ruin in the Ute Mountain Tribal Park is Eagle Nest House. The long masonry building on the second level is substantially intact. A series of poles extending out from the building walls originally supported a balcony similar to that of Balcony House at Mesa Verde.

Fortified House is located on the south side of Lion Canyon and is particularly interesting because of the water impoundment in the sandstone built to furnish domestic water and to enhance the spring below.

Text continued on page 123

The most spectacular cliff dwelling in Lion Canyon, Ute Tribal Park, is Eagle Nest House. The very well preserved buildings on the upper ledge had to be reached by climbing up toeholds at the extreme right of the picture. All the cliff dwellings in Lion Canyon constituted a village housing about the same number of people as did Cliff Palace located only about six miles northwest. (Photograph taken with the assistance of L. A. Villarreal.)

The path along the cliff running through Morris No. 5 from Tree House and Lion House gives the visitor the sensation of seeing these ruins as they were when first discovered by the Wetherill brothers in the late nineteenth century.

121

Eagle Nest House. The extended beams visible along the front of the building supported a narrow balcony used for access to the top rooms. This Pueblo III cliff dwelling, built as it was next to a sheer cliff, is stark evidence of man's adaptability to his living conditions. With no banisters, guard rails, or protective walls, the children must have learned to move about safely at an early age.

The Montezuma Valley

This lovely canyon-incised valley stretches northwest from the Mesa Verde in Colorado to the Abajo Mountains and Comb Ridge in southeastern Utah. Now, as in Anasazi times, it is rich, well-watered, dry-land farming country. The valley covers 2,500 square miles. It is drained by intermittent stream systems of the Yellow Jacket–McElmo, Montezuma Creek, Recapture and Cottonwood washes, all of which enter the San Juan River from the north.

The Montezuma Valley Anasazi are not well known because the ruins here have not been excavated, but they were here, some 30,000 of them in the 1100s and 1200s. The Mesa Verdeans, scratching a living from the thin soil of the mesa tops, must have been poor relations by comparison with the Montezuma Valley folk.

A series of eight Classic Pueblo towns, verging on crossing the threshold into the smallest of urban settlements, marks the Montezuma Valley as an important population center of the Anasazi. Beyond 2,500 to 3,000 residents, such settlements would need to restructure their society in order to meet the conflicts of the larger communities. Here, as elsewhere in Anasaziland, the Anasazi seemed determined to hold the population of their towns below 3,000 people.

As viewed from the Mesa Verde's north cliffs these towns (from left to right) are: Yucca House at the base of Ute Mountain, Mud Springs in the McElmo Canyon, Sand Canyon and Goodman Point ruins on the elevated Goodman Point, and Wilson, Lowry, Lancaster, and Yellow Jacket ruins just to the right of Abajo Mountain. With their associated rural populations and broad cultivated lands, these Pueblo communities would have made an imposing sight and all together probably housed more than 30,000 people.

Traces of pre-Anasazi Archaic and Basket Maker II occupation of the valley are scarce, but there are a few. By the seventh century late Basket Maker III people were living throughout most of the valley in villages such as the Gilliland and Payne sites enclosed within palisades of wooden posts.

Joe Ben Wheat from the Colorado State Museum has excavated a large pithouse near Yellow Jacket, similar to the proto–great kivas from Shabik'eschee and the Mesa Verde. Pueblo I villages, varying considerably in size, have been excavated across the Montezuma Valley from the Dolores River on the northeastern frontier to Alkali Ridge and White Mesa near the western edge. The Dolores Archaeological Project has uncovered great kivas in the Dolores River valley at Grass Mesa and Singing Shelter, while additional unexcavated ones associated with Pueblo I sites are known from Nancy Patterson Site in Montezuma Canyon and from Comb Ridge where the San Juan River crosses it. The Duckfoot Site west of Cortez represents the typical modular layout found in Pueblo I settlements.

By Pueblo II, in the tenth century, newly developing patterns of social and political organization began to exert themselves in the layout of towns and villages. These patterns can best be seen in the classic Pueblo III settlements, most of which grew out of and overlie their earlier beginnings in Pueblo I and II.

Dominating Pueblo III life in the Montezuma Valley were eight towns along its eastern side, where the best farming conditions exist today. The largest, Yellow Jacket Ruin, housed as many people as inhabited all of the cliff dwellings of the Mesa Verde. Each town had plazas and either a great kiva, as at Lowry, or a concentric wall structure, as at Sand Canyon Ruin on west Goodman Point.

Concentric wall structures were a sort of tower-kiva with one or two walls in either a circular or D-shaped plan surrounding a central kiva. Examples include the excavated tri-wall structures at Aztec Ruin and Pueblo del Arroyo and the D-shaped Sun Temple at Mesa Verde. Important religious ceremonies were probably performed by inhabitants of both the town and nearby villages and hamlets.

Text continued on page 126

123

An Anasazi looking northwestward from Mesa Verde's north rim about 800 years ago would see the Montezuma Valley teeming with some 30,000 inhabitants. About half lived in the eight towns marked by clusters of smoke from cooking fires (left to right): Yucca House at the base of Ute Mountain at the left, Mud Springs near the head of McElmo Canyon in the center, Sand Canyon and Goodman Point Ruins on the high north side of McElmo Canyon, and Wilson Ruin, Lowry, Lancaster, and Yellow Jacket ruins in front of Abajo Mountains that dominate the horizon in Utah. (Watercolor painting by Joan Foth.)

In addition to the rituals, the occupants of each town shared a managed water supply—usually including an artifical reservoir—and surrounding farmlands. Internal streets provided communication between segments of the community and probably continued as roads beyond the town limits to surrounding villages and perhaps shrines.

The Lowry Ruin complex provides a good example of one of these towns. The excavated pueblo represents about 5 percent of the total domestic building units that are scattered over roughly one square mile. A spring, enhanced by a reservoir, and several natural pools in a small central canyon provided water. The great kiva and a plaza in the north section provided the community's ceremonial focus, while at least three roads interconnected various building segments. Additional features include shrines, terraced farming areas, and outlying field houses and religious sites.

Yellow Jacket Ruin, the largest town, probably housed around 2,700 people in some forty-one separate buildings. Its layout included at least two, and possibly four, plazas, a central north-south avenue, crossing streets, about 165 kin-group kivas, a great kiva, an apparent bi-walled tower, six shrines, and an artificial reservoir to impound water above a spring. Natural farmland surrounds the town site. The surrounding countryside contains some eight villages of 200–250 inhabitants each, numerous small hamlets, dozens of pottery kilns located away from the villages, and several apparently purely religious structures. At least one roadway segment passes between two of the villages.

Although towns do not occur in the central and western portion of the Montezuma Valley, the villages found there tend to cluster. The Hovenweep sites are a good example, all within easy walking distance of one another and the central Square Tower Group. Great kivas do not occur here, but smaller D-shaped concentric wall structures, called horseshoe houses, may have served similar funtions.

Toward the northwestern edge of the valley, Edge-of-the-Cedars Ruin and the villages on Alkali Ridge probably belong to one or more such settlement clusters. Additional villages and other small settlements east and north of Cortez, Colorado, such as Wallace, Ida Jean, and Escalante-Dominguez, may represent rural villages associated with nearby towns or a separate cluster in themselves. Undoubtedly more will be identified as investigations progress throughout the valley.

Lowry

The excavated portion of Lowry—a room block and great kiva—lies at the end of a dirt road about nine miles west of Pleasant View, Colorado. The ruin is an oasis of pinyon-juniper woods surrounded by cultivated bean fields, but it tells us that these Anasazi settled in fertile country good for farming.

Lowry Pueblo Ruin is one of forty separate structures that make up the second largest Pueblo III town in the Montezuma Valley of southwestern Colorado. This town sprawled over nearly one square mile. Its twenty-four habitation sites contained some 108 standardized pueblo units, each marked by a small kin-group kiva, totaling close to 1,200 rooms and housing perhaps 1,500 to 1,800 persons. The house blocks were arranged in two distinct sectors on opposite sides of their common water supply in a manner similar to Taos and Zuni pueblos.

A number of features served the entire Lowry community. A spring in East Cow Canyon, between the two housing sectors, maintained a continual flow in the canyon. An artificial reservoir on the canyon rim above this spring supplemented its flow. A short distance downstream, three naturally formed permanent pools supplied water to about one-third of the town's residents. Land suitable for farming surrounds the town on its west, north, and east sides. A shallow draw running south from Lowry Pueblo contains fertile soil within the confines of the town, and many stone-walled terraces allowed farming in the canyons to the south. Each residential sector had a plaza in which public portions of ceremonies could be performed. The Lowry great kiva occupied part of the northern plaza, and two of five known shrines stood in the southern plaza.

A series of roadways connected various parts of the Lowry town and led outside to surrounding villages, hamlets, and farmland. One of these roadway segments is visible as a thirty-foot-wide shallow ditch leading southwestward from the north plaza between Lowry Pueblo and the great kiva. A vehicle track runs along part of its length.

Of all the features in the Lowry town, only Lowry Pueblo and the great kiva have been excavated. This was done by Dr. Paul S. Martin of the Field Museum of Natural History in Chicago from 1930 through 1934. He recognized at least thirty-seven ground-floor rooms but guessed as many as fifty may once have been present. Probably second- and third-story rooms would bring the total to between sixty-five and eighty rooms plus eight kivas.

However, various episodes of remodeling indicate not all rooms and kivas were in use at one time.

The earliest rooms and a then-detached kiva were built in 1089–90 according to tree-ring dates. The large room size and masonry style resemble construction details found in Chaco Canyon sites, but the kivas contained typical local features. The most extensive building occurred between 1103 and 1120, all in the local Montezuma Valley style. Three smaller subsequent additions brought the building to its final form. The excavated rooms and kivas of Lowry Pueblo have been repeatedly stabilized to protect them against visitor and weather wear.

Features worthy of note at Lowry include the contrast between Chaco-style and local-style rooms. The Chaco-style rooms are two to three times larger and built with tabular pieces of sandstone fitted very closely together. The local Mesa Verde–style rooms are smaller, the building blocks tend to be larger and less evenly laid, and the thicker mud mortar spaces have been chinked with small sandstone spalls. The large kiva built within the room block near the south end retains a remarkably preserved mural painted on the plaster of its lower wall. The design closely resembles a typical pottery decoration. The triple sets of horizontal poles between pilasters are unusual.

Stabilizers have roofed this kiva with a skylight and opened a passage into the kiva's southern recess to allow visitors to view this kiva. Unfortunately, stabilization efforts on the plastered mural have been unsuccessful and it is presently (1985) boarded up to protect it.

The Lowry great kiva was the first such structure to be excavated in Colorado. It is a circular, masonry-lined, partially subterranean building apparently designed for communal ritual activities. Its inside diameter measures forty-five feet, and it exhibits features typical of other great kivas from Chaco Canyon and Mesa Verde: masonry fire box, masonry floor vaults, four square seats for roof-supporting columns, encircling bench, north and south stairways, and north altar room. A single tree-ring date suggests building after 1106.

Lowry Pueblo forms the west wing of a broad U-shaped arrangement of houses in the north sector of the town. The U opens toward the south forming the north plaza where the great kiva stands. To the south is rich farmland up to the rim of East Cow Canyon. The visible features of the Lowry town mostly belong to the Pueblo III stage (1100–1300) with some Pueblo I (750–900) and Pueblo II (900–1100) construction beneath. The excavated portion of Lowry does not exceed 5 percent of the total ruin; it does, however, evidence at least four hundred years of occupancy (pages 130–131).

Escalante and Dominguez

On the banks of the Dolores River, north of Cortez, are two small Pueblo III ruins thought to be the pueblos mentioned in the journals of the Franciscan priests Francisco Atanasio Dominguez and Silvestre Velez de Escalante, who rode across the Montezuma Valley in 1776 in search of a passage from New Mexico to California. The ruin at the foot of the hill next to the parking area is Dominguez and the one atop the hill is Escalante.

Their setting on the south rim of the Dolores River valley looking downstream, over the Dolores Reservoir to the north, fits the journal description. Fray Escalante wrote, "On the 13th we made camp, both to allow the Padre to improve, and to take a bearing on the polar elevation of this site and meadow of El Rio de los Dolores where we found ourselves. . . . Upon an elevation of the river's south side, there was in ancient times a small settlement of the same type as those of the Indians of New Mexico. . . ."

Text continued on page 131

Aerial view of the Yellow Jacket Ruin, the largest Pueblo III (1100–1300) Anasazi town in the Montezuma Valley, housing some 2,500–2,700 persons. The settlement extends for nearly half a mile from the edge of the plowed field (lower left) on the north to the junction of the two branches of Yellow Jacket Canyon (upper right) on the south. A central avenue passes from the great kiva near the north house to a south plaza bisecting many east-west rows of houses marked by mounds and kiva depressions. The yellow green vegetation next to the blue green sagebrush at center left represents an artificial water supply.

Edge-of-the-Cedars Ruin near Blanding, Utah, is a Pueblo III village that may have housed around 250 people. Anasazi villages in the western Montezuma Valley, such as this one, were much smaller than the towns found along the valley's eastern side, but they partook of the same cultural pattern. Only a portion of Edge-of-the-Cedars village has been excavated and stabilized.

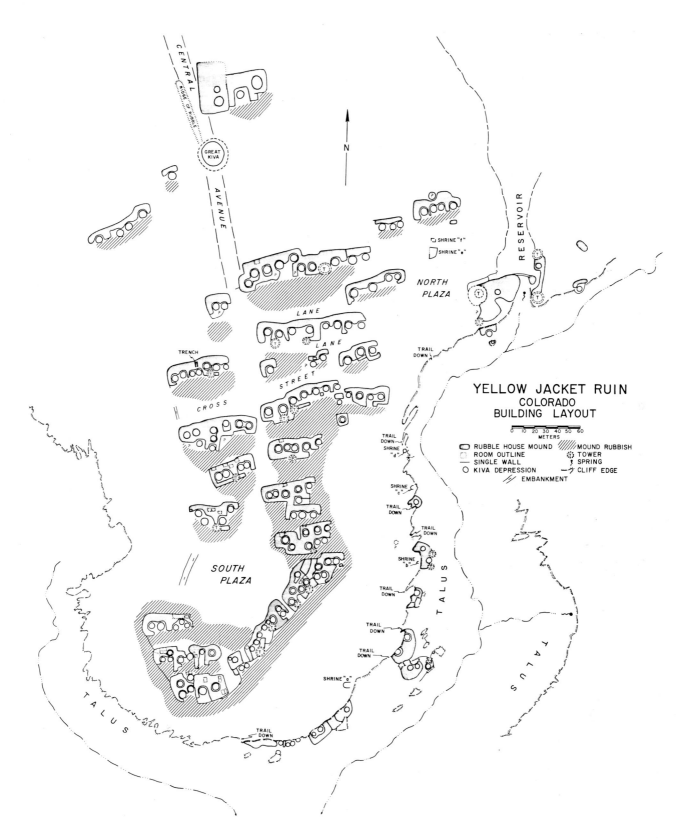

A ground plan of the Yellow Jacket town in the Montezuma Valley. In addition to the many residences, there are at least two plazas and possibly four, six shrines, a great kiva, and several streets and lanes.

Although the buildings have not been excavated, except for vandalism, the outlines of building rubble piles and kiva depressions are clearly visible on the ground.

129

Lowry's great kiva measures forty-five feet in diameter below bench level. It contains typical features—four masonry boxes from which roof-support columns rose, masonry floor vaults between the columns on the east and west sides, an encircling bench, an altar room attached to the north side, and an entry staircase. This building and the two plazas in the Lowry town probably held religious ceremonies attended by not only the town inhabitants but also by the residents of villages and hamlets from several miles away.

The excavated Lowry Pueblo and great kiva. More than fifty rooms and eight kin kivas, only five of which may have been in use at any one time, were recognized during the excavations by Paul S. Martin in the early 1930s. The earliest building took place about 1090 and continued well into the 1100s. The oldest rooms display Chacoan architecture, but all later building is typical of Montezuma Valley ruins. A large kin kiva beneath the protective roof retains a well-preserved mural decorated in a style typically found on painted pottery vessels. This structure forms the west wing of the northwest house block that surrounds an open plaza in which the great kiva stood. A roadway leads to the right from between the pueblo and the great kiva. (Photograph taken with the assistance of John Q. Royce.)

Interior of large kin-group kiva in the south end of Lowry Pueblo. Three sets of poles stretched between each pair of pilasters provided shelves on which to store objects. This demonstrates that kin kiva banquettes were not used for seating. Below the banquette can be seen the pottery-style design painted in white on the gray plaster lining the lower kiva walls.

Escalante is the larger of the two ruins. It is essentially a unit pueblo of rooms arranged around one kiva. Double rows of rooms are located on the west, north, and east sides. There is a single row to the south. The kiva displays Chacoan features: low banquettes with a floor-level shallow southern recess, eight low masonry pilasters, subfloor ventilator, and one crude floor vault. Seven of an estimated twenty to twenty-five rooms have been excavated and stabilized. Several of these are in the large Chacoan style. The masonry of both the rooms and kiva and the pottery, however, are more at home in the Northern San Juan than in Chaco.

The Dominguez Ruin, at the foot of the hill, is one of several small sites around the hill's base. It consisted of only four rooms and a kiva. A burial in one of the rooms contained the remains of a woman interred with a substantial quantity of turquoise jewelry and other artifacts. The burial is unusual because the artifacts in the grave indicate the possibility of an elite status of the deceased, which does not fit with the Pueblo III social makeup of the Montezuma Valley.

Duckfoot Site

The Crow Canyon School of Cortez, Colorado, conducted excavations at Duckfoot starting in 1983. The site is located in the Montezuma Valley about five miles west of Cortez and consists of a block of seventeen rooms, three pithouses, and a refuse pile in the Pueblo I stage, dated stylistically to the late 800s.

The rooms were arranged in a double row running approximately east-west, with nine storage rooms forming the north row and six living rooms making up the south row. Two additional small rooms were squeezed between the living spaces in the south row. The three pithouses occupy space about fifteen feet south of the room blocks.

The Duckfoot Anasazi employed considerable variety in constructing their houses. Most room walls consisted of mud plastered over a framework of branches woven horizontally among upright wooden posts with large upright stone slabs built into the bases of the walls. On the other hand, inhabitants of the central third of the rooms laid up sandstone blocks in profuse mud mortar as crude masonry walls. Some walls seemed to combine masonry and posts with mud.

Most likely such variation reflected the preferences of individual builders. The central block of two living rooms and five smaller storerooms belonged to the central pithouse, while the east and west blocks, each including two living rooms and three storerooms, were linked respectively to the east and west pithouses. Presumably, the people occupying each such unit were related to one another and made up a small lineage or clan. Each of the living rooms contained a hearth and traces of food-preparation activities, such as corn-grinding stones, and probably marked the presence of a distinct household. Thus, Duckfoot would have housed six households each divided into three lineages or clans of two households.

Besides this clear picture of Pueblo I society, the excavations of Duckfoot uncovered traces of a prehistoric drama. Many of the rooms had burned. The only pithouse completely excavated by fall 1984—the west pithouse—had also burned. A large quantity of household equipment including over twenty pottery vessels and a complete corn-grinding outfit—a metate propped up on river cobbles with two pottery platters to catch the meal and a mano or handstone—were buried by the collapsing roof. Clearly this structure had been inhabited up to the moment fire consumed it (page 133).

Text continued on page 135

Escalante Ruin sits atop a hill overlooking the Dolores River valley. Two Franciscan priests, Francisco Dominguez and Silvestre Velez de Escalante passed this way in 1776 and mentioned two ruins in such a setting. The ruin is probably Pueblo III. It features double rows of rooms built around one kiva. Escalante Ruin has some Chacoan features that have led some archaeologists to argue that it was a Chacoan outlier. The site is easily reached by road from Cortez, Colorado. In the background may be seen the preparations for the reservoir behind McPhee Dam that precipitated the Dolores Archaeological Project, the most expensive antiquities study to date in North America—more than 200 archaeologists excavated and surveyed the region between 1978 and 1983. Most of the finds were Pueblo I Anasazi.

The kiva at Escalante Ruin displays Chacoan features including eight low masonry pilasters and a floor-level recess. The masonry, however, is more the Mesa Verde style.

Dominguez Ruin, at the foot of the hill below Escalante Ruin, is one of several small sites around the base of the hill. A woman was interred in a vacant room with an unusually large amount of jewelry. Some archaeologists cite such burials as evidence for the existence of an elite class, but quantity of personal jewelry or pottery vessels does not by itself evoke the symbolism associated with elite-class burials elsewhere in the ancient world.

The Pueblo I Duckfoot Site occupied in the late 800s, being excavated by the Crow Canyon School of Cortez in 1984.

Pottery vessels found at the bottom of an excavated Pueblo I pithouse at the Duckfoot Site, Montezuma Valley, Colorado. These pots are used by archaeologists as evidence for the reconstruction of pueblo life in the 700–800s. This pottery is plain gray and neckbanded utility ware, probably used for cooking and storage of water, food, or valuables.

Duckfoot Site rooms were arranged in east-west rows with storage rooms on the north and living rooms on the south. In the plaza to the south were three pithouses (forerunners of kivas).

The collapsed and burned roof debris also surrounded two human skeletons, one sprawled across the hearth, the other along the north wall. Neither had been accorded a proper Anasazi burial; both had died violently. The burning roof material had charred very small portions of their bones, indicating their flesh was still present when the burning occurred. Yet both bodies lay atop some charred poles and the knee of one was elevated by the debris below.

How did these two people die? Were they trapped in the pithouse as it burned, unable to escape? Were they killed outside and thrown into the burning pit? Was this a prehistoric murder or the devastation of an enemy raiding party? The answers will probably never be known, but it is certain that these bodies are evidence of violence that occurred 1,200 years ago (page 83).

Hovenweep

Introduction

Hovenweep, a paradise for photographers, has light like no other place. The orange of the sandstone ruins glistens against a cloud-flecked sky—a sky so blue it looks unreal. Ruins, clinging to the canyon rims, offer themselves for close-ups or cross-canyon shots that sparkle when printed and will reward even the most amateur picture-taker.

Hovenweep includes clusters of masonry-walled buildings concentrated at the heads of shallow arid canyons along the Colorado-Utah border about forty-five miles west of Cortez, Colorado. They were a part of the Northern San Juan–Montezuma Valley settlement pattern of 1100 to 1300. Prior to 1100 the Indians of the Hovenweep district were living in clusters of unit pueblos on the mesa tops; then for reasons that are not clear, these people moved to the heads of the canyons during Pueblo III. It was

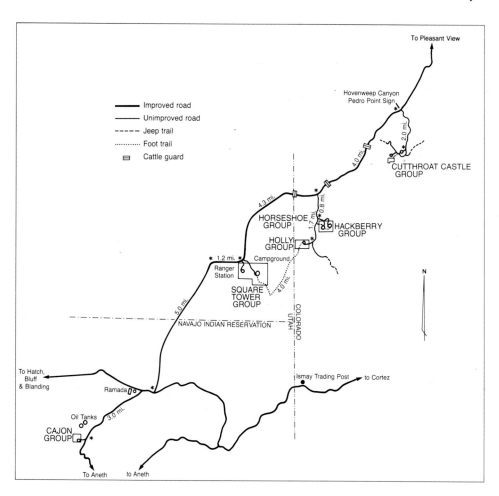

Locations of the various ruin groups in Hovenweep National Monument in Utah and Colorado. From west to east are Cajon, Square Tower (monument headquarters), Holly, Horseshoe, Hackberry, and Cutthroat. A seventh group on Goodman Point lies far to the east.

135

The setting for ruins of the Square Tower Group at Hovenweep National Monument. The greatest cluster of ruined buildings occupies the lower left quadrant of the photograph from Tower Point (between the two canyon forks) past Rimrock House, Eroded Boulder House, and Twin Towers on the left and Unit Type and Stronghold houses on the right. Nearly thirty kin kivas were once scattered along the slopes on both sides of this canyon among the many stone masonry housing units. At the head of the longer left-hand fork stand the Square Tower (for which the group is named), Hovenweep House, and Hovenweep Castle along with another eleven kivas. A number of granaries tucked beneath the cliffs and rainwater check dams are scattered about among the main residences.

the same phenomenon that occurred about the same time at Kayenta, Canyon de Chelly, and Mesa Verde.

Jesse Walter Fewkes partially excavated several of the Hovenweep sites in the 1920s. His excavations, however, were confined to the larger more visible structures, and he did not excavate or restore habitation sites, only the community buildings such as Hovenweep Castle and Hovenweep House. Names such as "Hovenweep Castle," "Stronghold House," and "Square Tower" were given years ago by what each ruined building resembled, not what they were. Hovenweep Castle was part of a pueblo, not a castle. Around the buildings visible in the canyons are sagebrush-covered rubble piles that outline the pueblos that were flourishing in Pueblo III times before abandonment.

The ruins in Square Tower and Ruin canyons

near the Hovenweep National Monument ranger station are the center of the Hovenweep villages. To the east are Cutthroat Castle ruins, Hackberry ruins, Horseshoe ruins, and Holly ruins. To the southwest are the Cajon ruins. All are open to visitors. In addition to these are Cannonball to the southeast and the Pedro Point Group to the north and northeast. Because of the very limited excavation and the lack of kiva counts, it is difficult to estimate population accurately, but based upon the number of ceremonial structures and the size of the pueblos, the Hovenweep group of sites probably housed a population of 2,500 or more.

Each village was built in a canyon watered by a spring. They all utilized similar site layouts and construction techniques, and all were located within easy walking distance of each other. There were no

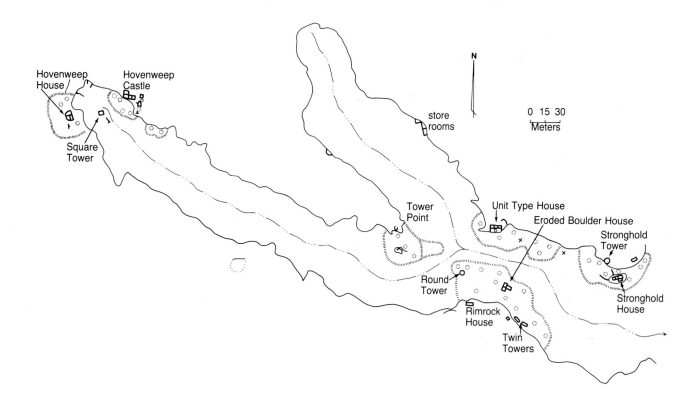

Ground plan of the Square Tower/Ruin Canyon Group of ruins. Standing buildings and walls are represented by solid heavy lines, the extent of collapsed building rubble is indicated by dashed lines, and visible kiva depressions by small circles. This was the largest of the Hovenweep villages housing some 400 to 450 people. Water was available from the spring at the head of Square Tower Canyon and the confluence of the two tributary canyons.

great kivas, but each village had a ceremonial tower or a horseshoe house–type building—a **D**-shaped structure constructed with two concentric walls with a kiva in the center in the same style as the Sun Temple at Mesa Verde.

The ceremonial center for the Hovenweep settlements was probably the Ruin Canyon complex made up of Square Tower, Tower Point, and Twin Towers ruin groups. Both sides of the canyon were heavily populated. The complex included several prominent structures: Hovenweep Castle, Hovenweep House, Square Tower, Rim Rock House, Twin Towers, Stronghold House, and Unit-type House.

Mesa Verde masonry and architecture and the predominance of Mesa Verde pottery at all of the villages indicate that these people were a part of the Montezuma Valley–Mesa Verde culture. They were descendants of Anasazi who had lived in the valley from Basket Maker II times, perhaps from the begin-ning of the Christian era or before. But these people, like the other Anasazi of the Northern San Juan, Kayenta, and Chaco Canyon regions, abandoned their homes, their villages, and their farms during the late 1200s and moved to the south. Some went to the Rio Grande region and some to the Tusayán region of the Little Colorado River, which in historic times became Hopi country.

Square Tower Group

Square Tower, more or less the center of the Square Tower Group, sits on a large sandstone boulder in the bottom of Square Tower Canyon, near its head. On the canyon rim to the east of Square Tower, the Anasazi built Hovenweep Castle. It is the still-standing portion of a much larger building, the ruins of which lie on the slope just under the rim between the castle and the tower. To the west beneath the overhang at the head of the canyon is a small cliff dwelling. On the west rim of the canyon is Hovenweep House, a D-shaped ceremonial structure similar to the Horseshoe House. The brush around Hovenweep House covers the rubble of attached unexcavated buildings including two kiva depressions.

On the canyon rim to the north are the remnants of a dam that captured rainwater runoff, allowing it to soak into the sandstone and enhance the flow of the spring immediately below it. It was a common practice for the Anasazi to build water impoundments above a spring in order to hold the water and allow it to slowly percolate down through the sandstone until it reached an impervious layer of shale, from whence it flowed into the canyon as a spring.

A second cluster of ruins is located a short distance down the canyon from Square Tower between Twin Towers and Stronghold House. These two ruin clusters to the west and south of the ranger station make up the Square Tower Group of Hovenweep ruins. The National Park Service has laid out two visitor trails in addition to the Square Tower loop: Tower Point loop and Twin Towers trail. The ruins along these trails include the tower at Tower Point, Round Tower, Eroded Boulder House, and Twin Towers on the southwest side of the canyon; and Stronghold House and tower, and Unit-Type House on the northeast side. In the canyon are numerous rubble piles representing collapsed buildings.

SQUARE TOWER. Square Tower was built on a large sandstone boulder. Originally it was three stories high, constructed of masonry dressed and laid in typical Pueblo III Mesa Verde–Montezuma Valley style. It has a keyhole doorway facing down canyon. The small openings may have been for roof support beams or for lookout.

Anasazi towers were probably not defensive structures, but rather part of ceremonial enclaves. The location of this one in the bottom of the canyon makes it useless as a lookout tower or as a defensive stronghold. In other Anasazi sites towers are usually associated with kivas. However, its location near the spring gives rise to the speculation that it is a ceremonial structure that was in some way associated with the spring. In addition, it is located between two other possible ceremonial structures: Hovenweep Castle to the east and the D-shaped horseshoe building to the west.

The Pueblo III Anasazi were intrigued with towers. They were difficult to build and not very

The Square Tower near the headquarters of Hovenweep National Monument. This structure built of sandstone masonry rises two stories high from its foundation on a sandstone boulder near the bottom of the canyon. Such a location would not support a protective purpose, but it does lie just below the canyon's most productive spring.

suitable to live in, yet they are found throughout the Northern San Juan region. They most probably had ceremonial significance in Anasazi culture akin to totem poles for the Indians of the Northwest, obelisks for the Egyptians, or stone heads for the Olmecs and Easter Islanders.

HOVENWEEP CASTLE. Hovenweep Castle was not intended by the original builders to be a freestanding tower, since they constructed residential rooms one or two stories high against these buildings. The buildings collapsed and the towers remain. The northernmost tower is a D-shaped structure facing the canyon. The doorway and other openings may have been placed to mark the summer and winter solstices and the vernal and autumnal equinoxes. These towers could have been either ceremonial or only a part of the domestic construction.

Hovenweep Castle (above) at the head of Square Tower Canyon (below). The standing walls on the cliff edge represent only the best-preserved portion of the main living quarters for this ruin group.

Square Tower Canyon with the square tower in the foreground and the ruins of Hovenweep Castle on the cliff rim. Traces of six kin kivas and additional residential rooms may be found on the talus slope immediately below the standing ruin.

Artist's reconstruction of the pueblo of which Hovenweep Castle formed only a part. Most of the buildings actually stood on the talus slope below the sandstone cliff. (Drawing by Lisa Ferguson after Don Ripley.)

There is at least one kiva depression on the top of the rim rock and six more in the ruins of an unexcavated residential pueblo on the talus slope below. At least three small pueblos sat at the head of Square Tower Canyon, one in the canyon just below the Hovenweep Castle, another across the canyon built around Hovenweep House, and a small cliff dwelling under the overhang at the head of the canyon. The population at this end of the canyon was probably well over one hundred people.

HOVENWEEP HOUSE. The aerial view of Hovenweep House shows it to be in the center of a sizeable pueblo. The outline of the building is clearly shown on the canyon rim by the rectangular rubble pile now covered with sagebrush. Just to the northeast of the rubble pile is a round green spot with a tree in the center. This was a reservoir that furnished water for the people and also served to enhance the spring under the overhang just below.

Hovenweep House was a horseshoe-type religious building similar to the one at the Horseshoe House Ruin.

TOWER POINT. The tower at Tower Point, sitting as it does on the point of junction of two canyons, does lend itself to the interpretation that it was a watchtower. It commands a view up the canyon toward Square Tower House and down the canyon to the southeast toward Ute Mountain and the Twin Towers Trail ruins. It stands alone on the mesa top; but, it is likely that buildings ran right up to it as at Hovenweep Castle. We must remember that the entire interior of the canyon below the tower was occupied and that this tower may have been as much a part of ceremonial functions for the people living in the canyon as Square Tower or Hovenweep House.

From the Tower Point it is possible to visualize how the canyon looked during the 1200s. Within the canyon directly below Tower Point is Round Tower. It is surrounded with rubble, including at least three kiva depressions, indicating it was associated with residential rooms, although Round Tower itself was probably a ceremonial structure. Slightly beyond Round Tower is Eroded Boulder

140

Hovenweep House, a slightly distorted horseshoe house, at the head of Square Tower Canyon. The scattered stones on either side of the standing building mark fallen walls from once-standing adjacent structures.

The Tower Point tower, Rimrock House, and Twin Towers in the Square Tower Group. Most of the former buildings in this sector have collapsed into piles of rubble on the slope below the standing structures.

House and beyond it are the Twin Towers. The sagebrush on the slope that surrounds these three buildings and extends down into the canyon from just below the rim delineates the rubble remains of Anasazi houses. The villagers incised some rock art at Eroded Boulder House—a spiral and geometric figures. Rim Rock House, probably residential, on the southwest rim of the canyon would have overlooked the buildings below. The eleven or more kiva depressions indicate that this was a large residential area. Twin Towers were two-story apartment-type buildings containing sixteen rooms. Each of the ovoid-shaped buildings was constructed on a separate boulder (page 142).

Across the canyon from Twin Towers stood another large pueblo built against the huge boulder that is topped by Stronghold House. Although Stronghold House buildings now appear to be isolated, they were merely the top story of the pueblo rooms built up from the canyon below. On the rim of the canyon next to Stronghold House is Stronghold Tower. Only a portion remains because the

canyon side of the tower was constructed on a log that bridged the crevice in the canyon. When the log rotted away, more than half of the tower fell into the canyon. Below the tower is the telltale rubble pile indicating residential rooms.

The rubble and kiva depressions extend up the canyon on its northeast slope from Stronghold House to Unit-Type House located on the rim of the canyon across from Twin Towers, indicating that both sides of the canyon were filled with pueblo rooms from Tower Point to Stronghold House housing perhaps 400–500 people.

UNIT-TYPE HOUSE. Unit-Type House follows the same design as the unit pueblos of Mesa Verde—a block of rooms with a kiva on the south and a trash dump south of the kiva. The kiva has a banquette and stone pilaster configuration with a floor ventilating system. It has also been suggested that the openings on the east side are arranged to allow a determination of the solstices, equinoxes, and perhaps the nineteen-year cycle of the moon.

Holly

The Holly Ruin group, a Pueblo III village, was a part of the Hovenweep cluster of settlements. It is located at the head of Keeley Canyon about two miles northeast of the Square Tower Group.

At the site are the remains of five named buildings: Tilted Tower, Holly Tower, Curved Wall House, Great House, and Isolated Boulder House. The Tilted Tower was originally a multiroom structure on the canyon rim, part of which may still be seen there. Sometime after abandonment the boulder on which it was constructed shifted and much of the masonry fell into the canyon. To the west and north of Tilted Tower are room-block ruins on the canyon rim and directly below is a talus slope with three kiva depressions indicating these all formed parts of a sizeable residential building on the canyon side.

The Twin Towers in the Square Tower Group. The separation between these two buildings was necessitated by the separation of the two sandstone boulders upon which they were built. These were probably two-story dwellings built with curved walls to conform to the shapes of the rocks on which they stood. Such solid foundations have preserved them from the ravages of normal deterioration.

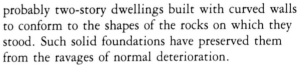

Stronghold House, the southeasternmost unit in the Square Tower Group. Construction of this building on the separated portion of bedrock sandstone ledge is responsible for its remarkable preservation. Whether the Anasazi intended this setting to be defensive is not known. They could have reached it via ladders from the tops of buildings built along the slopes adjacent to it.

Rimrock House (on the canyon rim) and Eroded Boulder House (beneath the boulder overhang) stand among the rubble of many fallen buildings as testimony to the sizeable masonry village that existed at the canyon junction below Tower Point about 800 years ago. The rubble atop Eroded Boulder House indicates that the ruins below the overhang were only a portion of the building.

Unit Type House (above) near the junction of the two heads of Square Tower Canyon. Some eight to twelve rooms surround a kin kiva on three sides. Because of the bedrock, the kiva had to be built on the rock surface instead of below the ground surface and hence stands at the same level as the residential rooms around it. This building exemplifies the typical unit pueblo concept used by the Anasazi in the arrangement of their living rooms, storerooms, and small kin kivas.

Holly Group at Hovenweep (below). To the left is Holly House with Holly Tower in the center and Tilted Tower to the right. Additional ruins cover the talus slopes between the standing buildings including some twelve kiva depressions. A stone and earth dam at the edge of the cliff behind Holly Tower fed the spring in the canyon head.

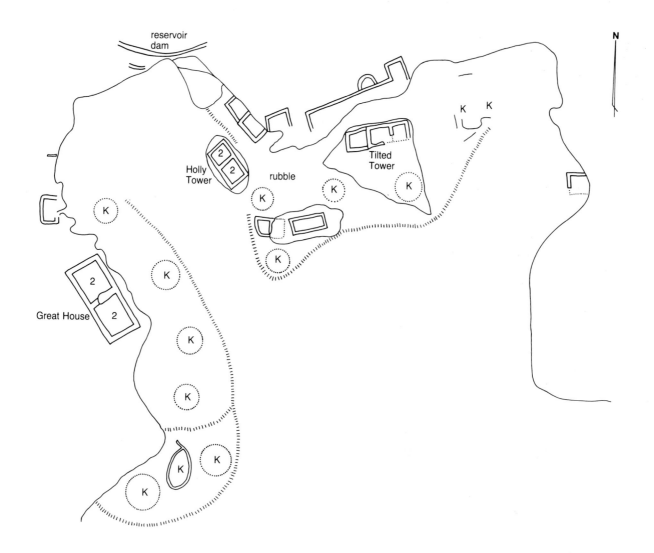

Ground plan of the Holly Group, showing standing and discernible buildings, the boundary (dashed line) of collapsed building rubble, and visible kiva depressions ("K"). The Holly people probably got water from a seep just below the man-made dam and reservoir to the north of Holly Tower. A collapse of the cliff edge at this point has probably buried the spring. Numbers indicate number of stories standing.

On the other (west) side of the canyon, below the Curved Wall House were similar room blocks, now fallen into rubble piles. Thus it appears that the head of the canyon was a pueblo with two standing structures to the east—Holly Tower and Tilted Tower House—and two structures to the west—Great House and Curved Wall House. On the canyon rim to the north the Anasazi constructed a dam for domestic water and to enhance the spring below. Alone on a turtleback rock south of Tilted Tower House stands Isolated Boulder House. Its function is not clear, but it was not likely residential.

Located as it is at the head of a canyon with room blocks in the canyon and on the rim and with ceremonial towers and structures built in prominent places in or near the Pueblo, Holly Ruins are very similar in site location and design to other sites in the Hovenweep cluster: Horseshoe, Hackberry, and Cajon. Holly Tower is a graceful little building fitted on a boulder with an entrance on the north. Some hand and toeholds of its entrance trail are still visible.

On the west rim are Great House and Curved Wall House. These buildings were constructed in Mesa Verde Pueblo III style with pecked stone masonry two to three stones thick. In Curved Wall

145

The rectangular tower at Holly Group. This two-story building was built on a sandstone boulder in the center of the small canyon head where it could be reached by a set of toeholds cut into the rock itself. The building fits very closely the limits fixed by its foundation and rises gracefully amid the structures of the group around it. This represents one of the finest examples of Montezuma Valley architecture.

House the stones were faced to fit the curve of the external wall that encircled the rectangular interior. This structure was not a residence; it did have a tunnel leading out of the bottom through a crack in the rimrock to the room blocks and seven kivas below. The Holly Group once housed 120–150 people.

Like other ancient ruins—Egyptian, Greek, Roman, Maya, and many others—these Anasazi houses have eroded away, leaving only the ruins of the public buildings. If twentieth-century towns were abandoned, soon all that would be left would be the ruins of the post offices, court houses, schools and churches, the football stadiums, and a few store buildings, and only then if they were built of stone or brick. So when we look at the Anasazi ruins we must mentally fill in the habitations to visualize how things looked in the 1200s.

Holly, too, had a device for determining the sun's position at solstice and equinox time, very similar to the Sun Dagger on Fajada Butte at Chaco Canyon. The solstice marker consists of one complete three-ring concentric circle on the west, a second circle, or spiral, that has either partially eroded away, or was deliberately only half completed, in the center, and a spiral on the east. They are tucked under the rock ledge south of Great House and are so placed to mark the summer solstice and the fall and spring equinoxes, but not the winter solstice.

Horseshoe

Horseshoe Ruin, located about one mile northeast of Holly, was a small village housing only fifty to sixty people contemporaneous with and similar in style to Holly. There was a dam on the canyon rim creating a reservoir, house blocks in the canyon, and ceremonial structures to the east and west of the pueblo. The most significant building is Horseshoe House itself, a D-shaped structure with a curved wall on the north side, subdivided into compartments in the general pattern of the Sun Temple at Mesa Verde, although slightly smaller. Its masonry is among the finest in Hovenweep. There may have been a kiva in the open portion of the D. The outer circle of rooms is walled off from the center room.

Beneath the canyon rim on the north side is a small cliff dwelling with a kiva. In the cave are ancient hand prints. In the rubble along the talus to the southeast are three or four kiva depressions plus the remains of fallen houses.

Hackberry

Hackberry was a medium-sized Pueblo III village, probably as large as Cliff Palace at Mesa Verde, having between 250 and 350 inhabitants. It had a settlement pattern similar to that of Holly and Horseshoe: a cluster of room blocks around springs at the head of the canyon. Between rubble mounds at the canyon head and the canyon rim were dams designed to enhance the springs below. There are ruins both on the rim and in the canyon. This settlement was built on the east branch of Hackberry Canyon less than a mile east of Horseshoe.

Beneath the overhang at the head of the canyon is a grotto with existing springs and the ruins of a cliff dwelling. On the walls are a series of Anasazi hand prints. Very little excavation has been done at Hackberry. Visible remains of one building rise above the rubble mound on the east rim of the canyon.

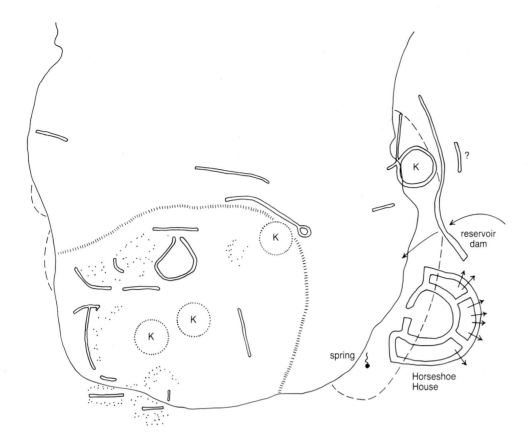

Ground plan of the Horseshoe Group (above). The standing Horseshoe House, a kiva beneath the west end of the overhang, and numerous terrace walls are marked by stone wall symbols, while a small rubble mound with three visible kiva depressions ("K") is outlined by a dashed line. The Horseshoe House stands directly above a good spring whose flow had been enhanced by the man-made dam and reservoir immediately west of the building. Arrows indicate "peep" holes through the wall.

The Horseshoe House (below) for which the Horseshoe Group is named. It consists of a central kin kiva surrounded on three sides by compartments formed by partitioning the space between the circular kiva wall and a partially enclosing curved concentric outer wall. These compartments could not be entered at floor level from either the kiva or from the outside. A low stone dam runs along the cliff edge from in front of the building to the lower left of the picture. A kin kiva and several rooms occupy the overhang below Horseshoe House.

147

This isolated tower standing on the sandstone point to the west of Horseshoe House has an excellent view of the canyons to the south. Despite this overlook, the tower probably served a primarily ceremonial function rather than a defensive one. It probably stood two stories tall.

Ground plan of the Hackberry Group. Standing buildings and walls are indicated by stonewall symbols, the limits of collapsed building rubble by dashed lines, and visible kiva depressions by K's. Several two-story rooms stood beneath the overhang west of the springs. Numbers indicate number of stories standing.

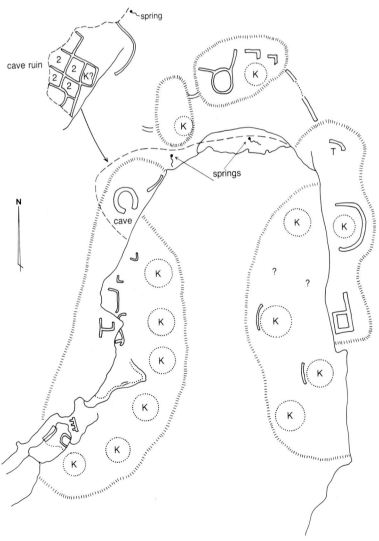

148

The overhang and spring beneath the canyon head at the Hackberry Group. About twelve rooms and a possible kiva once stood here. The spring at the extreme right is one of two that provided drinking water for the residents of the Hackberry Group.

Cutthroat

The Cutthroat Castle Ruin, the most interesting and spectacular of the outlying ruins of the Hovenweep cluster, is situated on an offshoot of the Hovenweep Canyon about eight miles northeast of the Hovenweep ranger station. Cutthroat was a Pueblo III village of substantial size, perhaps having a population of 150 to 200, built straddling an S-shaped stream that was probably dammed in ancient times to provide a reservoir between the two sections of the village. Several terraces were built along the stream. Even today subsurface moisture probably exists since cottonwood trees grow along the stream bed.

Cutthroat Castle sits on the north side of the stream. It was a three-storied horseshoe house built on a sandstone slab. The central kiva was partially surrounded by a wall. This complex was further connected to a rectangular tower. A passageway from beneath led from a small room block into the main building through a split in the ledge. Oval towers were built to the north and west. These ceremonial structures are surrounded by the rubble remains of the pueblo's room blocks.

Across the stream bed to the south is another sagebrush-covered rubble pile, from which another round tower arises adjacent to a kiva depression and some standing walls of other buildings (pages 150–151).

Cajon

At Cajon (about eight and one-half miles southwest of the Square Tower Group) are the ruins of a Pueblo III village constructed in the same configuration, around a spring at the head of a canyon, as Hackberry, Horseshoe, and Holly. A dam up the wash created a reservoir for domestic use and enhanced the spring under the overhang. The spring is strong today and used by the Navajo Indians to water their horses (pages 152–153).

Text continued on page 153

149

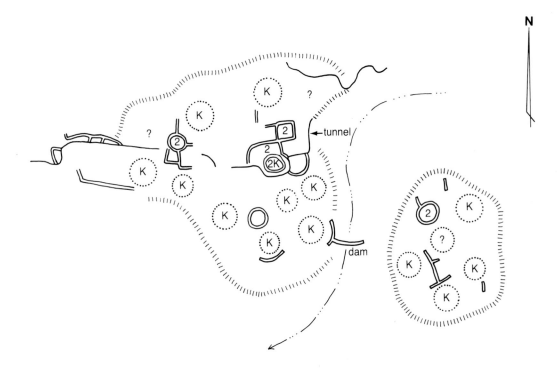

N

Ground plan of the Cutthroat Group (above). Solid heavy lines mark visible walls and standing buildings, the fringed lines outline collapsed building rubble, and the K's mark visible kiva depressions. Numbers indicate number of stories standing.

The Cutthroat Group (below). Virtually all of the ground in the photograph is covered with building rubble from collapsed houses and kin kivas. The standing walls represent only a fraction of the structures that once stood here. The green trees in the center of the group mark the probable location of a spring that once supplied water to this community.

One of the well-preserved round towers at the Cutthroat Group. The carefully pecked sandstone blocks have been laid in mud mortar without the benefit of small chinking spalls between them.

The main preserved building at Cutthroat consists of a horseshoe house with several attached rooms on the right. A tunnel leads through a crevice in the bedrock floor behind the kiva in the center of the photograph to a two-story rounded room below the ledge.

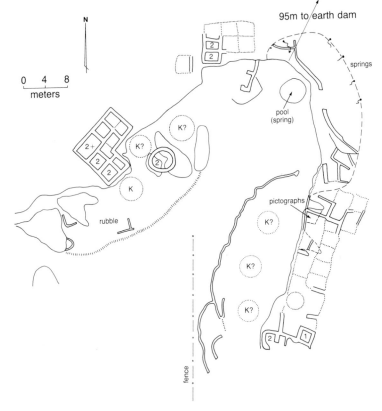

General view of the Cajon Group. A strong
spring flows out of the back of a cave in the
head of the canyon and the buildings flank
this spring on both sides. Piles of building
rubble marking the remains of at least seven
kin kivas and associated houses cover both
talus slopes and the rim of the canyon. An
earthen dam about 100 yards upstream behind
the cave trapped rainwater runoff that
percolated through the rock to feed the
spring. (Photograph taken with the assistance
of John Q. Royce.)

Ground plan of the Cajon Group. Several standing
buildings and recognizable room outlines are indicated
by stonewall symbols and dotted lines, seven visible
kiva depressions are marked by dotted circles, and
rubble mounds surround the visible ruins on both
sides of the canyon. The deep cave in the canyon head
contains a very strong spring still used by the Navajo
Indians to water stock. Numbers indicate number of
stories standing.

152

A rubble pile with some standing walls and four kiva depressions extends down the canyon slope on the east side, indicating that room blocks of the pueblo once stood there. Under the ledge are some small cliff dwellings. On the cliff wall is a pictograph painted in Mesa Verde pottery style with interlocking key-shaped frets connected to a rectangular scroll. On the same wall the Anasazi painted a four-legged creature with a bird-like body and a zigzag line.

To the west of the spring cave are several buildings on the rim of the canyon below which a talus slope with three kiva depressions indicates there once were additional buildings on the west side of the canyon. Also on this western slope of the canyon stands an exotic round tower with its walls following the undulations of three boulders. Cajon was once the home of eighty to a hundred Anasazi.

A circular tower built on and around several large sandstone boulders on the slope of the west ruin at the Cajon Group. The builders carefully fitted their masonry blocks to the boulders to produce the desired circular building plan on a remarkably uneven surface. The space between the large boulders served as a lower-story room with one or more stories on top.

The western cluster of buildings at the Cajon Group. All three of these buildings stood at least two stories tall. Additional buildings including three kin kivas once stood among these visible structures but have since fallen to rubble.

Aztec Ruins. The stabilized Aztec West Ruins are in the foreground and the unexcavated east portion of the town extends to the Animas River. The restored great kiva occupies the center of the plaza. In the rear of the pueblo, next to the road, is the tri-wall Hubbard Site. The pueblo contained some 405 rooms and 28 kivas. Aztec Ruin was located in the fertile Animas River valley that had been inhabited since very early times. (Photograph taken with the assistance of John Q. Royce.)

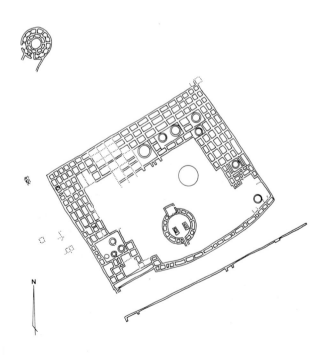

Plan of Aztec West Ruin (after Morris 1928).

Aztec Ruins

The Aztec Ruins lie on the north bank of the Animas River near Aztec, New Mexico. There was a popular belief in the late 1800s that the ruins scattered across the Southwest were the remains of cities built by the Aztecs or Toltecs of Mexico, and this precipitated the name *Aztec*, but there is no actual connection between these Anasazi ruins and the Precolumbian Mesoamericans.

The excavated and restored pueblo, known as the Aztec West Ruin, is the largest of twelve structures on the twenty-seven-acre Aztec Ruins National Monument. The Hubbard tri-wall structure to the north of the West Ruin has also been excavated. The unexcavated portion of the tract includes the East Ruin, another tri-wall structure, and several house mounds. Some archaeologists suggest the site was occupied only in late Pueblo III times; others suggest it was inhabited for a much longer period, at least from Pueblo II.

The fertile Animas River valley was occupied from very early times. In a few places beneath the

154

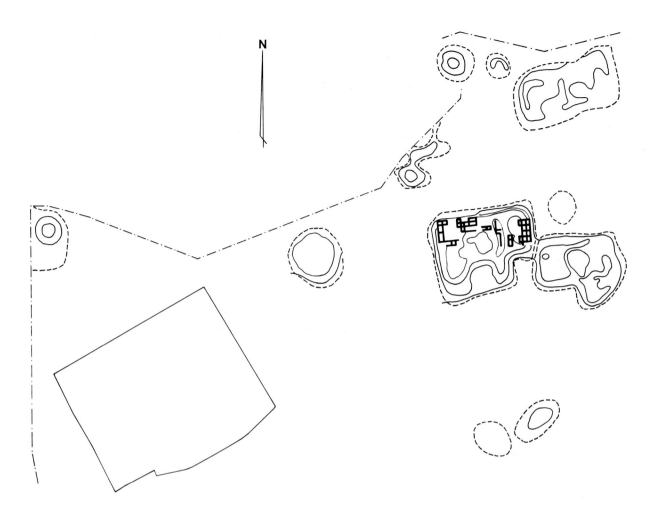

Plan of Aztec community (after Vivian 1959).

excavated portions of the Aztec Ruins were traces of earlier kivas and some aboveground dwellings. A substantial population may have lived in scattered settlements along the river, but evidence of these settlements has been destroyed by modern farming.

Some archaeologists suggest that the West Ruin of Aztec (like the Salmon Ruin, located twelve miles to the south on the San Juan River) was built by the Chacoans, arguing that the site plan, masonry, core and veneer walls, room sizes, kivas, and great kivas are strikingly similar to Salmon, and Chacoan in style. They also suggest that Aztec and Salmon were constructed and then abandoned by the Chacoans almost contemporaneously. Both were built around 1100, abandoned by 1150, and reoccupied by Northern San Juan peoples (Mesa Verdeans) during the 1200s. Other archaeologists suggest that the West Ruin is actually more characteristically Northern San Juan in style than Chacoan. True, there is a kin kiva in the room block on the north side of the plaza that is Chacoan; however, this doesn't nec-

essarily mean that the entire site was Chacoan. It is more likely, they argue, that at most a Chacoan colony lived at Aztec during the early 1100s.

The Aztec West Ruin contained an estimated 405 rooms and 28 kivas, including the Chacoan style and Northern San Juan–type kivas, in addition to the restored great kiva. Some of the rooms are spacious, high-ceiling Chacoan rooms. Portions of the pueblo were three stories high. Later the large rooms were reduced in size, older doorways were blocked up, and new floors were laid upon the debris which partially filled some of the rooms. Mesa Verdean kin-group kivas were built, and the great kiva was remodeled and restored.

The Hubbard Site tri-wall structure (located in the northwest corner of the Aztec Ruins) with a centralized kiva was a late construction. This ruin is sixty-four feet across and was built with three concentric circular walls. The space between the walls was partitioned into a series of small rooms, twenty-two in all. Most of the rooms and the center kiva

Banded west wall of Aztec West Ruin. The green sandstone blocks used to produce the two bands had to be imported to the site. The fine tablet band is suggestive of Chacoan masonry, but the remainder of the stone work and the green bands are more characteristic of Montezuma Valley construction.

Doorways through rooms on the east side of the Aztec West Ruin.

were accessible only by hatchways in the roof. The tri-wall was built over earlier kivas. Tri-wall buildings are a Northern San Juan architectural development similar in style and function with the Sun Temple of Mesa Verde and the horseshoe houses of Hovenweep. Pueblo del Arroyo in Chaco Canyon has a similar tri-wall structure.

In the 1880s residents of Aztec broke through the walls on the first floor of the West Ruin to explore and collect relics. Seven of these rooms have intact ceilings. The breaks in the wall have been repaired and used by the National Park Sevice as a passageway for visitors through this series of rooms. Along this passage the visitor may see a mat covering for a door.

The great kiva was rebuilt by Earl Morris. At times during visiting hours recorded Indian ceremonial music softly plays, producing a solemn atmosphere that fits the restored interior of the kiva. No other Anasazi building has been as completely restored; it is worth a trip to Aztec to enjoy this experience. The inner portion of the great kiva has a circular floor about forty-one feet in diameter and eight feet below ground level with stairs leading into it from an altar room on the north side. The roof is supported by four columns made of alternating masonry and wood. Under each of the pilasters were three circular sandstone disks. A bench

encircles the room at floor level. In the center is a fire pit flanked by two rectangular vaults. Originally there was a stairway on the south side, but later it was eliminated. The existing wooden stairway has been installed by the National Park Service.

Fourteen arc-shaped chambers surround the great kiva at ground level. At one time each of these rooms had a door that opened onto the plaza and another opening into the kiva. Later the outside doors were sealed, and the only means of access was the narrow ladders extending up from the bench level on the inside of the kiva (pages 157–158).

The remains of a ditch that carried water from the river to the flat lands around the pueblo indicate that the fields were irrigated. The Anasazi of Aztec Ruins seem to have had everything needed for survival, even in dry times: fertile soil and plenty of water. Morris felt there was almost constant armed harassment by outsiders who were not so fortunately situated. He found only circumstantial evidence for his conclusion. In comparing burials, for example, he noted that earlier burials were done with great care and contained numerous grave offerings, including imported luxury items, whereas the later

156

The restored great kiva in the plaza of the Aztec West Ruin.

burials were hastily made and did not include grave offerings. Morris observed also that the great kiva and the entire east wing were destroyed by fire. He further noted the south row of rooms built of cobbles by the second occupants closed the pueblo except for a narrow entrance to a hallway at the southwest corner of the pueblo. The result was to make Aztec into a fortified town.

Whatever the reasons, Aztec was abandoned sometime after 1252. The residents may have retreated to the cliff dwellings of Mesa Verde or they may have gone to the Rio Grande valley as a part of the Great Migration that emptied the Northern San Juan region by 1300.

Salmon

Salmon Ruin was constructed by the Chacoans on the San Juan River, some thirty miles north of Chaco Canyon, at or near the end of the ancient Chacoan Great North Road. The site and an accompanying museum are located on the Bloomfield-Farmington highway.

Tree-ring dates indicate it was built in the short span of seven years between 1088 and 1095. Some archaeologists feel Salmon is the companion town to Aztec located on the Animas River about twelve miles to the north. They suggest that both pueblos were built by the Chacoans about the same time (Salmon just before 1100 and Aztec just after), with essentially the same plan and style, and both were abandoned by the Chacoans at about the same time: Aztec by 1130 and Salmon by 1150. Both sites were later reoccupied by the Northern San Juan peoples (Mesa Verdeans). It is as if a colony of workmen and their families were dispatched from Chaco Canyon with instructions to build a pueblo according to a definitive plan. They came, chose a spot along the river with excellent nearby farmland, and then brought in sandstone and roof timbers (from as far away as thirty miles) to begin construction.

The walls were constructed of thin, carefully matched sandstone slabs with typical Chacoan precision. When completed, 250 large rooms were arranged in suites as family dwelling units. The pueblo was built in the shape of a great E with an east-west back wall 450 feet in length with two sections extending southward from each end, creating a large central plaza. In the center of the main building was a tower-kiva, and toward the south end of the plaza they built a great kiva. Three kin-group kivas were built in the room blocks around the plaza.

Text continued on page 161

157

View from the south.

Two photographs show the great kiva restored by Earl H. Morris in 1934. An altar in the north room had a painted white circle on its top. Stairs lead down to the circular floor of the kiva, in the center of which was a masonry fire box, flanked by two rectangular vaults that may have been foot drums. The roof was supported by masonry and pole columns; large stone disks served as footings for the columns. Fourteen small rooms encircled the inner sanctuary.

View from the north.

158

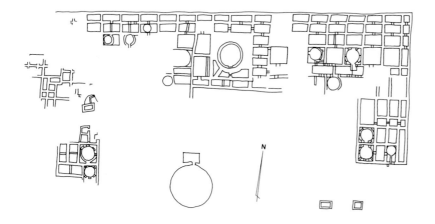

Salmon Ruin plan (after Irwin-Williams 1976, revised 1977).

Salmon Ruin lies on the San Juan River near the end of the ancient Great North Road from Chaco Canyon thirty miles to the south. This northeast view shows the tower-kiva in the center, the great kiva to the left across the plaza, and the E-shaped design of the pueblo. Salmon Ruin tree-ring dates indicate construction between 1088 and 1095, and it was occupied by the Chacoans until about 1150. Northern San Juan peoples (Mesa Verdeans) reoccupied Salmon Ruin around 1200. They subdivided some of the large Chacoan rooms, built kivas around the plaza, and reworked the great kiva. (Photograph taken with the assistance of John Q. Royce.)

Built by migrants from Chaco Canyon around 1075, Chimney Rock Pueblo sits on a high mesa 1,000 feet above the canyon floor. It consists of thirty-six ground-floor rooms and two Chaco-style kivas. This pueblo was a part of a much larger settlement—not Chacoan—containing as many as 2,000 people that Frank W. Eddy, who excavated the site, calls the Chimney Rock Tribe. The entire district was abandoned by 1125. (Photograph taken with the assistance of L. A. Villarreal.)

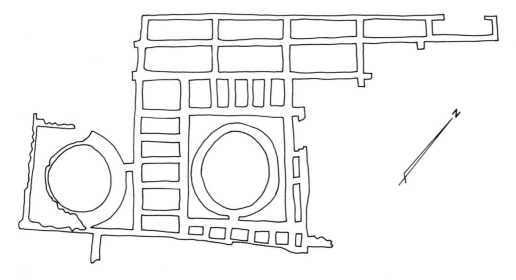

Plan of Chimney Rock Pueblo (after Eddy 1977).

Chimney Rock Ruins are located on a ridge high above the Piedra River valley near Pagosa Springs, Colorado. From west to east are: the great kiva, Parking Lot Site, Chimney Rock Pueblo, and the huge Chimney Rocks. In the background is the Continental Divide in the San Juan Mountains.

The great kiva was similar to the restored great kiva at Aztec Ruin. It was forty-six feet in diameter and entered by way of an antechamber room on the north side. The roof was supported by four stone and wood columns. In the center of the circular room were two rectangular vaults or foot drums. The tower kiva resembles the one at Chetro Ketl in Chaco Canyon. It was constructed inside a room block with special footings to support its extra thick walls, and it probably extended somewhat above the roofs of the adjoining buildings.

Salmon was abandoned by the Chacoans about the middle of the twelfth century after only about sixty years of occupation, but after perhaps fifty years it was reoccupied and partially rebuilt by peoples from the Northern San Juan. These Northern San Juan people subdivided the larger Chacoan rooms, built kivas around the perimeter of the plaza, and reworked the great kiva. The masonry work of the Chacoans is easy to distinguish from the less-refined construction of the walls of the second occupation.

A fire occurred at the pueblo in 1250 (during the Mesa Verdean occupation), and some fifty children and one woman were killed when the kiva roof, onto which they had climbed for safety, collapsed, causing them to fall inside the burning kiva. Another great fire broke out in 1270 destroying the great kiva and much of the pueblo. It is impossible to say, but this destruction may have caused the final abandonment that took place in that year. All of the Northern San Juan was being abandoned during the last half of the 1200s, and Salmon may have been abandoned only a few years earlier than the rest of the region. The Mesa Verde Salmonians joined the migration south and east to the Rio Grande valley as their Chacoan predecessors had done one hundred years before.

Chimney Rock High Mesa Sites

Sometime around 1075 migrants from Chaco Canyon (eighty miles to the south) climbed to the high narrow ridge at the foot of the twin spires of Chimney Rock. From here they could see the wind-

161

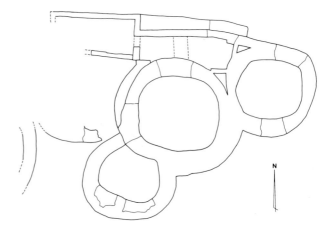

Chimney Rock Parking Lot Site plan (after Eddy 1977).

Parking Lot Site 400 yards west of the Chimney Rock Pueblo. These three circular thick-walled rooms resemble kivas but were probably residential units—Pueblo II aboveground pithouses—occupied between 950 and 1125. Next to the access road where it branches is another site called the Access Road Site consisting of circular living rooms similar to those of the Parking Lot Site. (Photograph taken with the assistance of L. A. Villarreal.)

ing green valley of the Piedra River to the west, the wild mountains of the Continental Divide to the north, and the towering chimneys of rock to the east. To this tiny, barren, waterless high mesa, a thousand feet above the canyon floor, they carried tons of dirt, rubble, and rock to build Chimney Rock Pueblo on the most spectacular building site in all Anasaziland.

The Chacoans were not the first people to occupy the high country around Chimney Rock; other Anasazi had been living there for a thousand years. The Chimney Rock archaeological area consists of the ruins of the High Mesa site group and six other communities surrounding it. Frank W. Eddy estimates that some 1,200 to 2,000 people lived in these villages during the 1000s and that these people were a social unit that Eddy calls the Chimney Rock Tribe. He also suggests there must have been a religious impetus to inspire building on this high mesa where the nearest good farmland and an abundance of water lay in the valley a thousand feet below. The Indians of the modern Taos Pueblo, whose legends indicate they came from the Chimney Rock area, consider the twin spires to be a shrine dedicated to the twin war gods of Taos mythology.

An access road winds northwest up the mountain from Highway 151 to the parking lot on the Chimney Rock High Mesa. Here are five restored ruin clusters: the Parking Lot Site, Great Kiva Site, Access Road Site, the Guard House, and the Chimney Rock Pueblo. Visitation arrangements can be made at the Pagosa Springs ranger station.

Three circular thick-walled aboveground rooms are linked together at the Parking Lot Site. They resemble kivas but, as Eddy points out, they lack the bench, pilasters, keyhole recess, loom holes, and sipapu features of Chacoan or Mesa Verdean kivas. He concludes they were domestic living rooms, designed in the same way as pithouses but built above ground. Pithouses were common in the Northern San Juan from 400 to at least 1050. To dig one on this rocky ridge would have been virtually impossible; thus the Anasazi compromised an ancient tradition by building a masonry pithouse on top of the ground.

Immediately to the north and attached to two of the circular rooms were two long rectangular rooms. One had been used for grinding and perhaps food preparation, while the other provided storage. All the rooms were entered through doorways, the pithouses through hatchways in the roofs.

The Parking Lot Site was a Pueblo II village occupied between 950 and 1125, consisting of the excavated rooms plus five circular crater-shaped mounds probably marking additional pithouses. These people were living side by side with the inhabitants of the Chacoan pueblo a few hundred yards up the ridge. This phenomenon of the Anasazi concurrently exhibiting different life-styles, here pithouse people and pueblo people, was not uncommon. At Chaco

162

Canyon at about this same time people lived in large pueblos on the north side of the wash and in small pueblos on the south side.

About 200 yards to the southwest of the parking lot are the ruins of the great kiva that served as the ceremonial center for the Chimney Rock Tribe. It was a circular stone-masonry building, with an inside diameter of about forty feet. Around the inside walls were fourteen subfloor rectangular cists probably used to store ritual paraphernalia. In the center of the single large room was an altar flanked by subfloor vaults. The great kiva had been roofed, but the exact kind of roof is unknown.

Next to the great kiva on the north side is the stabilized ruin of Building 16, an aboveground pithouse with a fire pit and ventilator designed as in the Parking Lot Site houses. On the north side stood two masonry rooms, one for storage and the other containing five mealing bins holding metates for grinding corn. Building 16 was part of a Pueblo II village with sixteen unexcavated mounds. It may be that Parking Lot Site, Building 16, and Access Road Site all belonged to the same village.

The Access Road Site was partially destroyed by an early dirt road. The surviving portion of the ruin is very similar to the Parking Lot Site and Building 16 with circular masonry living rooms and attached work and storage rooms. It, too, was part of a village with some thirteen crater-shaped mounds.

About 400 yards to the northeast of the parking lot across the high narrow ridge called the Causeway is the Guard House, an excavated circular masonry room enclosed by a rectangular retaining wall. Beyond that on a small rock platform, at an elevation of 7,600 feet with a sheer drop-off on two sides, are the ruins of the Chimney Rock Pueblo.

Frank Eddy suggests Chimney Rock Pueblo was constructed by migrant priests from Chaco Canyon who arrived at the high mesa about 1076. He believes that they were men because they brought all the building skills—men's work—but no pottery—women's work. He further suggests that as men they could be accepted into a matrilineal society without disrupting the local customs. They built an L-shaped complex with two Chaco style kivas and thirty-six ground-floor rooms. With a combination of precisely laid wide and narrow courses of tablet-size stones, the masonry is certainly Chacoan, as are the big rooms and the kiva appointments.

Why they came can never be known, but they didn't stay long, only fifty years. By 1125 the site was abandoned along with the entire Chimney Rock district. The reasons for the abandonment of Chimney Rock are more obscure than in other Anasazi regions. Chaco was abandoned because of adverse environmental conditions and a breakdown in the social organization. Chimney Rock and Chaco Canyon were abandoned at about the same time, but there is no evidence of drought or social breakdown at Chimney Rock. Perhaps the Chacoans were recalled by the people of Chaco Canyon, but why did the other Anasazi leave?

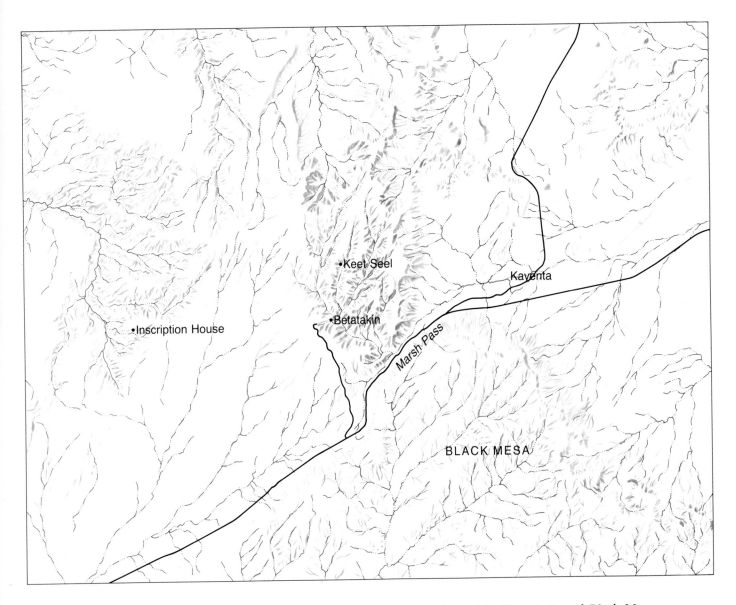

The Kayenta region showing locations of Inscription House, Betatakin, Keet Seel, and Black Mesa.

Kayenta Region

Introduction

The Kayenta ruins, Keet Seel and Betatakin, are chefs d'oeuvre for lovers of cliff dwellings. Both require some hiking, Keet Seel far more than Betatakin, but getting to the ruins, from the mesa to the canyons, gives the visitor the feeling of being in a time warp, of being part of the Anasazi culture of the 1200s.

Keel Seel and Betatakin are part of the Navajo National Monument located between Kayenta, Arizona, and the sacred Navajo Mountain that overlooks Lake Powell. Here are high (nearly 8,000 feet) forest-covered mesas cut by deep, wide canyons. To the northeast is Monument Valley, with some of the most breathtakingly beautiful scenery in the world, and to the south the huge Black Mesa that was home of the earliest dated Anasazi. Tsegi Canyon in Pueblo III was the hub of northern Arizona Anasaziland extending from Canyon de Chelly to the Grand Canyon.

From Basket Maker times through Pueblo III the Kayenta Anasazi made up the northwest branch of the Anasazi tree; the other three branches are the Anasazi of the Northern San Juan (Mesa Verde and the Montezuma Valley), Chaco Basin, and the Little Colorado River regions. The Kayenta cultural development focused on the Tsegi Canyon–Marsh Pass region. The most active zones were the northern end of Black Mesa; Long House, Klethla, and Monument Valleys, and Tsegi Canyon. Canyon de Chelly was an eastern and the Grand Canyon a western offshoot of the Kayenta culture.

Kayenta Anasazi remains have been found beginning in early Basket Maker II (radiocarbon dates from the northern end of Black Mesa reveal houses and small villages in use as early as 750 B.C.) to the end of Pueblo III in A.D. 1300—over two thousand years of continuous occupation and cultural development. Basket Maker III, Pueblo I, and Pueblo II stages are all well represented throughout the central Kayenta region. This region was the source of population movements during Pueblo II, both to the north across the Colorado River and to the west as far as the Grand Canyon and the Virgin River drainage of southern Nevada and southwestern Utah. Populations begin to move out into those areas between 900 and 950 and peaked between 1050 and 1150. They moved up the Colorado and Green rivers into southeastern Utah as far north as Moab. The population movement was never large, involving only a few hundred people.

These areas to the west and north were abandoned by about 1150. The Anasazi left the Grand Canyon and the Green and Colorado River settlements and returned to the Kayenta region. By 1270 the Kayenta people in the Tsegi, Navajo Mountain, and Hopi districts were concentrated in large villages: Awatovi on Hopi Antelope Mesa; Long House, on the northwest rim of Long House Canyon that runs southwest from Marsh Pass; Betatakin and Keet Seel in Tsegi Canyon; and Inscription House, a cliff dwelling located about fifteen miles west of the monument headquarters.

During the last half of the 1200s perhaps half of the population of the great valleys near Tsegi Canyon moved out of the valleys into the canyons and built cliff dwellings such as Betatakin and Keet Seel. Jeffrey S. Dean suggests the migrations were brought about as a result of arroyo cutting that lowered the water table, making farmlands unusable. The occupation of the canyons lasted only until around 1300 when all of the Kayenta–Marsh Pass Region was abandoned, possibly triggered by continued destruction of farmlands, and the people moved

Inscription House Ruin is the third largest Pueblo III cliff dwelling in the Navajo National Monument. It is located in a steep canyon west of the Shonto Plateau and Tsegi Canyon. Like the similar Kayenta sites of Keet Seel and Betatakin, it represents one of the latest Anasazi villages to be built prior to abandonment of the San Juan River drainage.

south to the Hopi Mesas where they, with others, became the ancestral Hopi.

Betatakin and Keet Seel are late Pueblo III (Tsegi Phase) cliff dwellings, constructed in canyon offshoots of Tsegi Canyon. The masonry was crude in comparison with the masonry at Chaco Canyon or Mesa Verde. The walls were generally only one row of stones thick, the stones were trimmed but not dressed, and mud mortar predominated over stone. The Kayentans continued the use of jacal walls (vertical posts and stays tied and filled with a coating of mud plaster) to the end of Pueblo III. Generally the front wall containing the door would be of jacal and the other three of masonry. The use of mud plaster in construction enabled them to stick the rooms on steeply pitched surfaces.

The room clusters of the Tsegi Phase Kayenta architecture were similar to Mesa Verde Pueblo III cliff dwellings, particularly Mug House, with the exception of the ratio of rooms to kivas. The Tsegi Canyon people built a living room and several storage rooms that opened onto a courtyard, but they did not regularly build kin-group kivas. At Betatakin only one square kiva has been identified; at Keet Seel there are only four kivas. Additional kivas may be in the lower caves or nearby as is the case of the Turkey Ruin near Keet Seel. Also there are no great kivas in the Kayenta region. We can only assume that the few kivas constructed by the Kayentans served both as kinship (household) kivas and ceremonial centers. If the Kayentans performed community ceremonies, they may have used open plazas.

The central element of the Tsegi Canyon sites was the courtyard as the focal point of the room cluster. The room cluster housed a family or a small extended family constituting the basic unit of the cliff dwelling. The site organization was akin to a modern apartment house (except that it was economically self-sufficient), with each family occupying a series of rooms. The cliff dwelling was not simply an assemblage of individual rooms.

Entry to Tsegi Phase living rooms was either by door or roof hatchway; there are some T-shaped

Betatakin Canyon opening into Tsegi Canyon at the Navajo National Monument, Arizona. The Anasazi began building cliff dwellings in these canyons in the late 1200s. Betatakin is located here and Keet Seel about eight miles to the north. By around 1280 some 700 Anasazi were living in the Tsegi Canyon district. By 1300 all the Indians had abandoned the canyons and moved to the south.

doors. The floors were leveled and the inside walls plastered. Living rooms were heated by a slab-lined fire pit located under the hatchway or smoke hole. Drafts were controlled by deflectors or more complex entry boxes if the room was designed for a doorway at ground level.

Granaries, storerooms, kivas, and grinding rooms were additional forms of construction. The granaries were finished on the outside and crude on the inside since they were designed to protect food from insects and rodents. The storerooms often had jacal walls built for storage of things other than food. The grinding or mealing rooms contained a series of stone bins that housed metates for grinding corn with stone manos; sometimes the bins were set up in the courtyards. It is generally believed that the bins were

Betatakin cliff dwelling constructed beneath a cave overhang in the north canyon wall.

set up in tandem in this way to allow the women to visit while performing this daily task. Some archaeologists have suggested this tandem arrangement provided for course, medium, and fine corn grinding, but this theory has not been clearly demonstrated.

The Kayenta Anasazi were farmers living on corn, beans, squash, domestic turkeys, and wild game. They cultivated cotton. Their pottery falls into two major kinds: utility pottery for cooking and storage, and decorative pottery used for eating bowls, for water-carrying ollas, and for storage of personal belongings such as charms and jewelry. The Kayenta pottery displayed greater variation in color, shape, and design than their Chaco or Mesa Verdean counterparts. The Kayentans made a negative decorated black-on-white by using large quantities of black painted on the white slip, producing a pottery that looked more like white-on-black. In addition red, black-on-orange, black-on-red, and polychrome pottery of three and four colors made the Kayenta Anasazi outstanding in the production of ceramics.

Jeffrey Dean postulates that the Tsegi Phase Anasazi chose to abandon the Kayenta region because the large villages could no longer be supported. It was a choice of splitting into smaller self-sustaining groups or leaving Kayenta. They chose to leave. They moved to the Hopi Mesas where they could maintain their village culture.

Betatakin

For reasons that are not clear—dry weather, erosion, lowering of the water table, or changes in the social structure—many of the Kayenta Anasazi began to move into the canyons from the valleys (Klethla, Laguna Creek, Long House, and Monument Valley) during the last half of the thirteenth century. The leisurely and deliberate migration into Betatakin Canyon from another village somewhere in the Kayenta region is one classic example of the population shift during late Pueblo III, or Tsegi Phase, of ancient Anasazi life in northern Arizona.

The Betatakin Cave, nestled in the cliff side of a lush, well-watered canyon filled with oak, Douglas fir, aspen, and box elder trees is now and was then

Betatakin Ruin. The tree-ring dates tell us that construction began about 1267 and that the population peaked in the mid 1280s with about 125 Anasazi. They farmed the canyon floor. Portions of the cliff dwelling have collapsed, but in its heyday more than 100 rooms, some multistoried, filled the cave. The only identified kiva is the rectangular room just to the right of the stone steps.

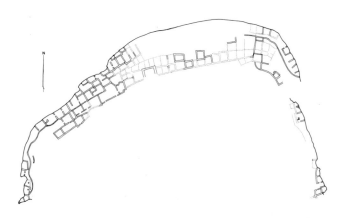

Jeffrey S. Dean's plan of the Betatakin Ruin showing the foundations of the rooms. Construction filled the entire arc of the cave. South orientation under the overhang made the cliff dwelling cooler in summer and warmer in winter.

an attractive and hospitable site. It is shady in summer—an important feature in these canyons where the temperature climbs to 100 degrees—and sunny in winter when this high country often is below freezing for weeks at a time. The cliff dwellings were protected from the north winds, and even on the coldest of days, if there was sunshine, they were reasonably comfortable. A mile to the east where the Betatakin, Keet Seel, and Tsegi canyons join, there was land for farming in the alluvial soil of the canyon floor. It probably required extensive clearing of thick stands of oak and aspen and substantial preparation for irrigation, but it was better than the land nearer the home village.

Jeffrey Dean's research at Betatakin—his analysis of tree cutting and construction dates—enabled him to reconstruct the forty-year life of this Tsegi Phase Anasazi village. Betatakin Cave served as a seasonal camp for a few years around 1260, and then in 1267 and 1268 four households (about twenty

169

people) founded the village. These people seem to have been an advance party assigned to prepare the site for a move by the residents of the main village. They cleaned the site, and then they cut trees into standard lengths and stockpiled these construction beams. Later in 1272 more beams were cut, sized, and stockpiled. It may be that things improved at the home village delaying the move to Betatakin, for the major move didn't come about until the period between 1275 and 1277.

By the mid-1280s the population peaked at about 125 people. Some 700 people may have resided in the Tsegi Canyon by this time. Dean suggests arroyo cutting in the big valleys around Kayenta lowered the water table, destroyed farmlands, and forced the cultivation to shift upstream into the canyons. Sometime after 1286 the Betatakins began to leave the cave, and by 1300 the entire region was abandoned, possibly because arroyo cutting continued upstream and destroyed the canyon fields and irrigation systems in the same manner as the fields in the big valleys had been destroyed. These people probably moved southward to the Little Colorado River region where, during Pueblo IV, they became the ancestral Hopi.

The planning and preparation of the new site and the deliberate and unhurried movement from the earlier village to Betatakin indicate a community decision-making process, yet there is no evidence of an elite class. The architecture of the village conforms to the Tsegi Phase general plan of construction involving room clusters or suites composed of a living room, storage rooms, and a courtyard. Some of the buildings were two stories high, and the courtyard was located on the roof of adjoining structures, but no room clusters were bigger or better in any

way than any other. Nothing in the architecture indicates an elite person or group. In fact no evidence at any of the prehistoric Anasazi sites indicates the existence of an elite class. Nevertheless the record at Betatakin indicates some sort of community decision-making.

The Betatakins built five kinds of buildings: living rooms, storerooms, granaries, grinding rooms, and kivas. All are easy to identify except the kivas. Dean concludes that there was only one kiva in the cliff dwelling (K55). K55 is a large rectangular room with rubble-cored walls, a bench along the north wall, a triangular bench at the northwest corner, and four loom-anchor holes. The men did the weaving, mostly in kivas all over Anasaziland; their vertical looms were fastened to the roof and to the floor by making a set of small holes with cross sticks inside, to which a rope looped around the lower loom frame pole could be fixed: two or more such holes anchored the loom's lower frame for weaving. Since the front wall is missing, any evidence of a recess, ventilator, or fire pit has been lost. Dean based his conclusion on the large size of the room, the extra height of the ceiling, and the fact that the room is not associated with any room cluster. There is a second rectangular kiva located in a small cave upstream from Betatakin.

About thirty feet above the rooms in the center of the cave is a low masonry wall built along the edge of the ledge. It was probably reached by a ladder extending from Room 33 and was used for rodent-free storage.

The principal access to the ruin begins at the

Square kiva located in the center of Betatakin Ruin.

A Betatakin cliff-dwelling living room. This masonry room had a fire pit in the center with a deflector between the pit and the entrance. One of the roof timbers is still in place. The blackened walls attest to the amount of smoke that was a part of Anasazi life.

170

top of the talus slope on the west side of Kiva 55. From here a pecked stairway leads upward to the left where it joins the ledge at Room 105. The main passageway runs eastward along the ledge to the east end of the ruin and westward to Courtyard 36. Although a collapse of a portion of the overhang destroyed a large section of the ruin (sometime after the cliff dwelling was abandoned by the Anasazi), the remains display well-preserved rooms and buildings, looking much as they did 700 years ago.

Keet Seel

Keet Seel can be seen only after about eight miles of a hot and thirsty hike. The trail begins at the horse barn to the north of the monument headquarters and runs along the top of the mesa about 1.5 miles to Tsegi Point; this is the easy part. The trail then drops down about 1,000 feet along a switchback, sandy, manure-filled trail to the canyon below. This part is a lark because it is downhill with magnificent vistas at every turn; it's the struggle from the canyon floor back to the mesa top over the same sandy, manure-strewn trail on the return that tests the hiker's mettle. Once in the canyon the trail leads six miles up Keet Seel Canyon past four waterfalls, crossing and recrossing the ankle-deep water in the wash, past Navajo hogans and spectacular rock formations with names like "Battleship Rock" and "Kachina Mother," until it slips through a narrow part of the canyon and reaches Keet Seel. The hike may be a thirsty one without a pack full of water bottles because the dreaded giardiasis (caused by an intestinal parasite) has rendered it inadvisable to drink the river water. Overnight hikers can camp in a delightful grove across from the ruins and near a spring.

Anasazi rock art depicting what may be a Hopi Fire Clan symbol. The Hopi Indians believe they are the descendants of the Anasazi, and it is likely that after the Tsegi Canyon cliff dwellings were abandoned, the Kayenta Anasazi migrated south to the valley of the Little Colorado River and the Hopi Mesas.

Around 1250 the Anasazi began constructing the presently visible village of Keet Seel (sometimes spelled "Kiet Siel") in a cliff overhang on the west side of Keet Seel Canyon some five miles from where it branches off from Tsegi Canyon. The large rock shelter had been occupied in earlier times and then abandoned by the Anasazi before the Tsegi Phase people arrived.

The tree-ring dates indicate a surge of timber cutting and construction activity between 1272 and 1275, which tapered off and ceased entirely by 1286. By examining the room clusters and dating the construction, Jeffrey Dean estimates the population of Keet Seel was about sixty people in 1272, and by 1286 the total population may have been between 125 and 150. After 1286, construction ceased; at least there are no tree-ring dates after that time. Within twenty-five years Keet Seel was abandoned. During the later years before abandonment there must have been migration in and out of the village: room blocks were vacated and then rebuilt, unoccupied rooms were turned into granaries, and beams from vacant rooms were used in building new ones.

Keet Seel, the best preserved of the larger ruins in the Southwest, retains the charm of a recently rediscovered ruin. Corncobs and pottery sherds are scattered throughout the ruin. A large log some twenty feet long laid across the pueblo entrance may have been placed there symbolically by the Anasazi, some archaeologists suggest, to bar entrance to the cliff dwelling. The extremely dry climate in this part of Arizona, coupled with the protection of the cliff overhang, resulted in the preservation of the

Rooms with original intact roofs at Betatakin.

Keet Seel is the best-preserved large cliff dwelling in the Southwest. Built in the last half of the 1200s, it may have housed as many as 150 Indians. The masonry retaining wall stretching some 180 feet along the front of the cliff dwelling, enclosing a rubble-fill foundation for buildings behind, attests to the engineering skill and cooperative effort of the builders. This village, along with the other Anasazi habitations in the Tsegi Canyon system, was abandoned by 1300.

The plan of Keet Seel shows the outline of some 150 rooms. In addition to these are the remains of several rooms and a round tower at the base of the cliff.

ruin and a number of otherwise perishable objects such as baskets and corncobs. There is little evidence of restoration or stabilization, except for the visitors' ladder to replace the original hand and toehold trail.

Although we assume that the majority of construction at Keet Seel was the work of individuals and families, the Anasazi mounted a community effort, perhaps as early as 1272, to build a 180-foot-long retaining wall extending from the central cross log to the east end of the cliff dwelling. They filled the area behind the wall—over ten feet high in places—by carrying, probably with baskets and tump lines, tons of dirt and rubble to create a foundation for the east end of the village. They also cooperated in the layout of the cliff dwelling by providing for three streets to allow easy access to all the room clusters.

At about the center of the village on the lower level facing the "Rampart Street," the Anasazi built a rubble-core walled, keyhole-shaped kiva (K 46) with a fire pit, a ventilator, and a rectangular storage area or perhaps a foot drum. The walls were plastered

Keet Seel Canyon, a tributary of Tsegi Canyon, winds through Skeleton Mesa. Here the stream has cut a deep arroyo in front of the Keet Seel Ruin destroying portions of the farm lands originally cultivated by the ancient Anasazi.

"Rampart Street" at Keet Seel runs along the top of the fill behind the retaining wall. At the end of the street is the barrier log and beyond that the west section of the ruin. In the right foreground is a keyhole-shaped kiva. The vertical poles were set by the Anasazi, their function unknown.

and painted with two four-inch white bands. Next to this kiva they constructed a D-shaped ceremonial annex (Room 74) with a jacal front wall. Room 74 was not a residence or a storage room, yet it does not have kiva features. There are four kivas in the ruin and two, possibly three, additional kivas at nearby Turkey Cave Ruin, and possibly others at the base of the cliff below the ruin.

Jacal walls continued in Keet Seel during Pueblo III, although they had virtually disappeared elsewhere in the Four Corners area. The builders set small posts along the wall line and filled the space between them with twigs or reeds set vertically, tied with split yucca leaves, and filled with mud plaster.

More than 150 rooms were built on the bedrock floor of the overhang, several perched like wasp nests on the bedrock of the lower west side. Erosion has destroyed most of the buildings at the base of the cliff; there may have been a fairly large group of structures that were a part of Tsegi Phase Keet Seel including additional kivas. Visible remains include

several rooms and a two-story round tower. Dean has identified twenty-five room clusters consisting of one living room and one to four storage rooms arranged around a courtyard; the cluster around Courtyard 12 at the east end of the ruin is an example. These room clusters or suites at Keet Seel correspond to the suites found in Pueblo III cliff dwellings at Mesa Verde.

Keet Seel's rock art includes several painted figures on the cliff face: a human figure with one arm flailing downward and the other upward, a flute player, and two anthropomorphic figures with large semicircular heads with a hooded extension coming off one corner. These may represent masked figures, for there are historic references to kachina masks with that general shape. The bird figure with the white body and blue neck is probably a turkey. At the east end of the cave are some pecked geometric figures. Nearby Turkey Cave displays numerous positive and negative hand prints and a row of birds—turkeys or ducks.

A Keet Seel plaza. The Anasazi cliff dwellers for the most part worked and cooked out of doors. In the foreground is a fire pit. The plaza is surrounded by small living rooms. The fire-blackened ceiling of the cave indicates there were multistoried living rooms built to the roof of the cave. In the center of the plaza are the stub remains of a burned jacal-walled room.

A group of potsherds (vessel fragments) from Keet Seel in Navajo National Monument, Arizona, representing several styles of pottery used by the Anasazi. In the top center is a rim fragment of a gray corrugated cooking vessel. It is surrounded by several polychrome painted pieces—red, black, and white on an orange background. Five black-on-white potsherds in the two bottom rows reflect slightly different ages; the two in the lower right corner were made during the 1000s and 1100s while the other three date from the late 1200s. Three-color polychrome pottery was a popular trade item to eastern Anasazi regions.

Canyon de Chelly

Introduction

Canyon de Chelly National Monument's unique natural setting makes it an exceptional and exciting place to visit. Two huge, narrow canyons, de Chelly and del Muerto, with 1,000-foot-high walls, come together just east of the monument headquarters at Chinle, Arizona. Unless you bring your own Jeep and arrange for a Navajo guide, the only way to see ruins in the canyons is to take the rubber-neck tour in multiwheel-drive, open top, military personnel movers. There is one exception: White House Ruin in Canyon de Chelly may be visited by way of a hiking trail from the south canyon rim. The reason is that the canyon bottoms are filled with deep dry sand, quicksand, and running washes, making them impossible for standard cars, and this is restricted Navajo country in which hiking is prohibited. The tours are great fun. They deliver the visitor to the ruins and the rock art sites, furnish lunch, and provide an opportunity to marvel at the almost unbelievable grandeur of these wind-carved and desert-varnished canyons. In addition, self-guided motor tours to both the north rim of Canyon del Muerto and the south rim of Canyon de Chelly afford excellent views of the canyon ruins, Navajo hogans, and cultivated fields.

The Canyon de Chelly (pronounced "d'Shay" and derived from the Navajo word *tseqi* meaning "rock canyon") district made up the settlement area for the eastern branch of the Kayenta Anasazi from Basket Maker II (as early as A.D. 1) through the abandonment at the end of Pueblo III, around 1300. The Kayenta region included northeastern Arizona south of the San Juan and Colorado rivers and west of the Lukachukai-Chuska Mountains.

The Canyon de Chelly and Canyon del Muerto (a Spanish word meaning "death") complex is located at the upper reaches of the Chinle Wash where the headwaters come out of the Chuska Mountains to the east. The streams from the Chuskas that join to form Chinle Wash have cut through the de Chelly sandstone producing very deep, vertical-walled, flat-floored, and well-watered canyons, which provided an almost unique habitat for the Anasazi and their Archaic predecessors as far back as 1000 B.C.

The Kayenta Anasazi occupying the canyons were farmers who lived on the standard prehistoric Pueblo Indian fare—corn, beans, squash, game, wild fruits, seeds, nuts, and, during Pueblo III, domes-ticated turkeys. Tests at Antelope House show that cotton seed, beeweed, prickly pear cactus, and mule deer were a regular part of the diet. The subirrigated (water flowing beneath but close to the ground surface) canyon bottoms were farmed then much as they are farmed today by the Navajo Indians. In addition to corn, beans, and squash, these Anasazi grew cotton, wove it into textiles, and likely traded it to other peoples. In order to conserve the flat lands for farming, the pueblos were built either in or against the cliffs. From 700 to 1150 the plateaus around the canyons were also occupied. Population increased sharply in the entire district during the hundred years before 1150, and then it declined steadily for the next 150 years until the abandonment.

Canyon de Chelly runs east-west. Canyon del Muerto branches off the main canyon about three miles east of the monument headquarters and extends generally northeastward. Most of the occupation at all times occurred in this canyon at three major sites: Antelope House, Big Cave, and Mummy Cave. Visitors may enter Antelope House and view Mummy Cave from the canyon floor or from the North Rim overlook. Big Cave, however, is not accessible to visitors.

The other large ruin, White House, is located in Canyon de Chelly. It, too, is open to visitors. All three of these ruins, Antelope House, Mummy Cave, and White House, are Pueblo III ruins retaining the general form, except for the partial destruction by time and the elements, they exhibited when they were abandoned by the Anasazi during the late 1200s.

These Canyon de Chelly Anasazi, like their cousins in the Kayenta region, did not build many kin kivas, and no great kivas have been found. At Mummy Cave, however, a rectangular, roofless structure may have functioned as a great kiva similar to the Fire Temple at Mesa Verde. It is questionable whether this structure can be attributed to the Kayenta Anasazi because it is so similar to Mesa Verdean construction that it may have been built and utilized by people from the Montezuma Valley, or at least the construction was strongly influenced by them. The Canyon de Chelly people did construct a ceremonial center at the Standing Rock Site composed of three large kivas.

Although the region had been occupied continuously from the beginning of the Christian era by Kayenta people, during the 1200s a small number of people from the Northern San Juan or Mesa Verde region arrived, bringing with them or making after their arrival Mesa Verde–like pottery and architecture. They built the central tower at Mummy

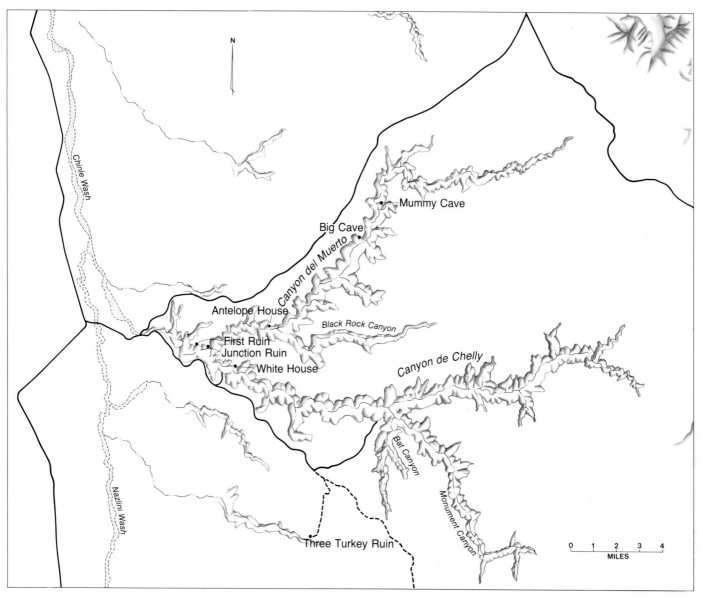

Canyon de Chelly National Monument consists of two major canyons that join a short distance east of Chinle, Arizona. Canyon de Chelly gave its name to the monument and contains White House and a number of smaller Anasazi ruins, while Canyon del Muerto extends to the northeast and contains most of the prehistoric ruins including Antelope House, Mummy Cave, and Big Cave.

Cave. At White House the large rooms and Chacoan masonry indicate the influence or presence of Chaco Canyon Anasazi. But at no time—even at the peak of occupation—were there many more than 600 to 800 people living in the canyons. Then by 1300 all were gone. Probably they migrated southwestward to the Tusayán region of the Little Colorado River in what is now Hopi country.

Some evidence indicates the canyons were temporarily occupied later by the Pueblo IV Hopi ancestors. It was never a significant occupation—probably just a few short-time visitors. So the canyons were empty of human habitation until the coming of the Navajo, probably in the 1600s.

White House Ruin

From the White House overlook on the south rim of Canyon de Chelly an easy trail (about 1¼ miles) drops some 500 feet to the canyon bottom and then goes across the ankle-deep wash to the White House Ruin. The lower portion of the ruin may be visited, but the cliff dwelling is closed.

The tree-ring dates taken from the beams used in the construction of this Pueblo III cliff dwelling

Canyon de Chelly and Canyon del Muerto were occupied by the Anasazi and their progenitors from as early as 1000 B.C. They farmed both the canyon floors and the mesa tops. The population of Pueblo III Anasazi peaked in the canyons about A.D. 1150, when there may have been as many as 800 people, and declined thereafter until abandonment by 1300. The Canyon de Chelly–Canyon del Muerto Indians are a part of the Kayenta Anasazi culture.

indicate that construction continued from about 1060, on the lower level, to as late as 1275. The big rooms and distinctive close-set, accurately coursed masonry are suggestive of Chacoan influence in its construction. Originally the two levels of buildings were connected by four-story buildings on the lower level. Unfortunately, many of the canyon-level rooms have been damaged or destroyed by high water in the wash. At its peak, White House included some eighty rooms and kivas and probably housed 100 or more people.

First Ruin

First Ruin may be seen both from the canyon floor and the south rim at Junction overlook. It was constructed on a ledge on the north side of Canyon de Chelly just west of the junction between the main canyon and Canyon del Muerto. This Pueblo III ruin

Navajo farms in Canyon del Muerto. The Anasazi farmed these canyon floors for hundreds of years prior to 1300. The Navajo arrived in the 1600s.

was named by Cosmos Mindeleff as the first ruin he examined in 1882. This small cliff dwelling had ten rooms and two kivas.

Junction Ruin

Similarly situated and located on the north side of the main canyon a few hundred yards to the east of First Ruin is a companion cliff dwelling, Junction Ruin, so named because of its location at the confluence of the Canyon de Chelly and Canyon del Muerto. This Pueblo III structure contained fifteen rooms and one kiva.

Antelope House

Antelope House was built on the canyon floor on the north side of Canyon del Muerto about four miles northeastward from the junction with the main canyon. The downstream room block was con-

structed before 1140 and contained large, plastered and decorated rooms with some multistoried construction. The later room blocks, to the north, were much less refined. The rooms were smaller and seem to have been built as needed. After 1200 a circular plaza was built between the two room blocks.

Visitors are allowed to enter this Pueblo III ruin that contained ninety-one rooms, two and possibly three large kivas, and several smaller kivas in the room blocks. Much of the pueblo has been eroded away by floodwaters. The masonry is Kayenta style—not nearly as sophisticated as Chacoan or even Mesa Verdean. The rough masonry was plastered both inside and out. In some of the rooms in the south room block are white painted designs of parallel lines, and in one there is a gesticulating stick-figure representation of a human-like being.

Text continued on page 184

White House Ruin (below). The canyon wall is streaked with desert varnish (a crust of manganese or iron oxide) that overlays 200-million-year-old sand dunes cut by the Chinle Wash. White House Ruin is accessible to visitors from a trail beginning on the south rim of Canyon de Chelly.

First Ruin (above), a Pueblo III ruin with ten rooms and two kivas, located on the north side of Canyon de Chelly west of the Canyon del Muerto junction.

White House cliff dwelling housed some 100 Anasazi. The ruin represents occupation for some 250 years beginning about A.D. 1060. The wash has destroyed many of the canyon-level rooms. The accurately set masonry walls indicate an influence by the Chacoan Anasazi.

Junction Ruin (fifteen rooms and one kiva) is a companion ruin to the First Ruin.

Antelope House on the Canyon del Muerto floor. The
visible ruins are all late Pueblo III occupied during the
1200s. This pueblo was abandoned about 1270, earlier
than the other canyon habitations, possibly because of
flooding.

Still standing, Antelope House tower is a portion of the multistoried pueblo that contained ninety-one rooms, several plaza kivas, and other kivas in the room blocks.

Antelope House Ruin is open to visitors. Beneath these Pueblo III buildings, Basket Maker III ruins dating back to A.D. 693 have been found.

Painted plaster on the interior of Antelope House. These inside walls were plastered with mud and painted with humanoid and geometric figures.

The visible ruins are all late Pueblo III, (the 1200s), but beneath this construction archaeologists have found a late Basket Maker III pithouse that can be dated at 693. For reasons that are not clear, perhaps because of flooding, Antelope House was abandoned about 1270—twenty or thirty years earlier than the rest of the habitations in the canyons.

The ruins are named for the paintings of antelope on the nearby cliff walls, done by the Navajo in the early 1800s.

Mummy Cave

Mummy Cave lies under a great overhang in the northern portion of Canyon del Muerto about twelve miles above its junction with Canyon de Chelly. Visitors are not allowed in the cliff dwelling, but it is visible from the canyon floor and from the Mummy Cave overlook on North Rim Drive.

The most spectacular portion of this ruin was constructed in late Pueblo III times on the ledge between the two alcoves that make up the cliff dwelling, by people from the Northern San Juan. Tree-ring dates indicate that these seven rooms, including a three-story tower, were built about 1284. The tower, with its second- and third-story roof beams protruding from the walls, was built on the south side of the visible complex with straight-coursed masonry and knife-sharp corners. Rooms to the north were connected to the tower and may have served as a method of transit between the north and south alcoves. At the time of abandonment, probably by 1300, seventy to eighty rooms and at least three kivas were in use in all of Mummy Cave: fifty to sixty in the south cave and twenty in the north.

Portions of the Pueblo III cliff dwelling were built over much earlier Basket Maker II habitations in the south cave and were supported by two retaining walls. The most intriguing aspect of the construction in this cave is a large enclosed space measuring some thirty by twenty feet with many of the attributes of a roofless great kiva similar to the Fire Temple in Fewkes Canyon at Mesa Verde. The lower four feet of the existing walls were finished with a reddish brown plaster and the upper portions with a wide band of white. Inside were niches, benches, and a paved platform. The north end of the area connected with a circular kiva with interior abstract decorations in red and white. This Mesa Verde–style cliff dwelling, constructed here at the time the Northern San Juan was being abandoned, indicates that some of the Montezuma Valley people moved southwest.

Farther to the southeast in the cave are the remains of several Basket Maker II rooms and storage cists dating from A.D. 300 to 400. There are seven exposed houses built with vertical sandstone slabs fastened together and to the bedrock by straw-tempered mud. The inward sloping walls and the use of horizontal poles indicate a domed or cribbed roof. Inside one of the houses was a hearth. Some had benches pecked into the bedrock and smoothed; other benches were constructed with sandstone slabs or adobe platforms; and some used horizontal timbers

The lower east end of Mummy Cave was originally occupied about 2,000 years ago by Basket Maker II Anasazi. These people constructed ten small houses and numerous storage cists by mudding sandstone slabs upright to the sloping bedrock cave floor and covering them with logs, branches, and mud. Later Kayenta Anasazi constructed the more visible structures in the east cave, covering the older houses with their rubbish.

Mummy Cave Ruin on the east wall of Canyon del Muerto. The prominent buildings on the ledge between the two caves were probably built by people from the Mesa Verde region. At the time of abandonment, there were some eighty to ninety rooms and at least three kivas in the cliff dwelling.

around the base of the walls. Numerous cists were used for storage. In all, some twenty-two Basket Maker II structures have been found, and probably many more are covered by the Pueblo III construction. Another engaging aspect of Mummy Cave is that after the Basket Maker II Anasazi left, the cave was not reoccupied for some 750 years, the same span of time as that from Richard 1st of England's Third Crusade to the present.

Grand Canyon

The modern Hopi Indians claim the Grand Canyon as the place ("sipap") where their ancestors emerged from the underworld a very long time ago. The Kayenta Anasazi ancestors of the Hopi first expanded westward into the Grand Canyon during the 900s when a few people camped there while hunting away from home. By 1050, several hundred Anasazi had moved onto the canyon rims and into the canyon itself, where they constructed hundreds of small sites over a broad territory. Whatever attracted them to the Grand Canyon, they all left by 1200, returning eastward to the Kayenta heartland.

Three of the small houses built by the pioneering Anasazi of 900 years ago may be visited. The Tusayán Ruin lies a short distance from the south canyon rim about three miles west of Desert View at the east end of the south rim road. It consists of a single room block with masonry living rooms—some two stories tall—forming the center of a broad U-shaped plan. Smaller one-story storerooms formed wings on both the east and west sides. A kiva, with its roof supported by four wooden posts, occupies the northwest corner. A second kiva, built in the ancient refuse pile south of the east wing, replaced the original one after it burned.

Text continued on page 191

185

Mummy Cave three-story cliff dwelling built, probably by people from the Mesa Verde region, in about 1284, not long before the abandonment of the entire region. The masonry is more refined than typical Kayenta–Canyon de Chelly masonry.

Three Turkey Ruin at the Three Turkey Ruin Tribal Park is not open to visitors, but it may be seen from the Three Turkey Ruin overlook located on a west branch of the Fort Defiance road about seven miles from the end of the paved Canyon de Chelly south rim road. Three Turkey cliff dwelling is a small, well-preserved Pueblo III Anasazi ruin occupied contemporaneously with the habitations of Canyon de Chelly and Canyon del Muerto.

Tusayán Ruin on the south rim of the Grand Canyon was built by the Kayenta Anasazi around 1185. Seven or eight living rooms in the two-story portion housed some thirty people. The single-story rooms were for storage. The pueblo was occupied for about twenty years and was abandoned shortly after 1200, when the people moved back to the Kayenta region.

Artist's reconstruction of Tusayán Ruin when it was occupied during the late 1100s (U.S. Department of the Interior, National Park Service, Grand Canyon National Park, index number 4681. Artist: Gene Foster.)

The masonry foundation of Tusayán Ruin shows the size of the ground-floor living rooms.

The large, squarish, mostly aboveground pithouse-type kiva had a central fire pit and roof supported by four corner posts. Entrance was by way of a ladder through the smoke hole.

Reconstruction of Bright Angel Pueblo. (Drawing by Joan Foth.)

Bright Angel Pueblo, on the Colorado River near the Kaibab Trail in the bottom of the Grand Canyon, was built by the Anasazi around 1100 and abandoned about 1140. Three or four families lived in this small pueblo and farmed the small delta by the river. There was an underground kin kiva in the courtyard in front of the room blocks. (Robert Euler, U.S. National Park Service.)

190

Bright Angel Pueblo was built in the bottom of Grand Canyon where Bright Angel Creek enters the Colorado River. It is one of several structures built on alluvial fans where trails provide access to the canyon rims. None were large, and the absence of kivas suggests that these units were inhabited only during selected seasons of the year. Five masonry rooms built above ground were probably in use during the early 1100s. A small pithouse on the same location had been occupied about fifty years earlier.

Most of the Anasazi ruins in the Grand Canyon are small isolated granaries or seasonal camps. Another example of such seasonal camps is the Walhalla Glades Ruin on the north rim with four masonry rooms and no kivas occupied in the late 1000s. The total Grand Canyon population could not have exceeded five hundred at any one time.

Besides this short span of occupation, the Anasazi regularly traveled to the Grand Canyon to hunt and to celebrate their origin tale. Traces of such expeditions date from Basket Maker II (700 B.C.– A.D. 450) to historic times. Evidence of considerable occupation of Grand Canyon by pre-Anasazi Desert Culture people lends support to the Hopi origin legend.

Chaco Canyon
Region

Introduction to Chacoan Culture

The hub of Chacoan Anasazi culture was Chaco Canyon—now a part of the Chaco Culture National Historical Park—situated nearly in the center of the high (6,000 to 7,000 feet), treeless, arid Chaco Basin of northwest New Mexico. The historical park includes the magnificent world-famous ruins of Pueblo Bonito, Casa Rinconada, Chetro Ketl, and others, as well as Fajada Butte, on top of which is the well-publicized Sun Dagger site.

The canyon in midsummer today is often very hot and dry and has the look and feel of the desert. Recent studies suggest that at the time of the occupancy by the Anasazi the climate was similar to that of the present except that prior to the middle 1100s more rain fell during the summer months. The arroyo that now runs down the middle of the canyon may have been there in ancient times, which would argue against floodwater irrigation by the Chacoans. This is a matter of dispute; some climatologists believe the canyon was more verdant in the tenth and eleventh centuries than now, and without the arroyo it would have served as a fertile area for fields and gardens.

From the hub of Chaco Canyon ancient roads ran like spokes of a wheel to settlements occupied contemporaneously with Chaco that are now referred to as "outliers." Some of the outliers are well known, like Pueblo Pintado to the east, Salmon Ruin to the north, and Kin Ya'a and Casamero to the south; the exact locations of many others have not been revealed to protect the sites from looters. The burgeoning of the Chaco culture was so spectacular that it is referred to as the "Chaco Phenomenon." Unfortunately, this flash of cultural genius was short-lived, as we shall see.

The Bonito Phase of Chacoan culture covers the period during which the Chaco Phenomenon begins, flourishes, and wanes, in exactly two hundred years between 920 and 1120. It was a time when the Chaco Anasazi developed a culture different from and more spectacular than the Northern San Juan (Mesa Verde), Kayenta, or Canyon de Chelly Anasazi. The Bonito Phase encompassed both Pueblo II and Pueblo III characteristics. The Chacoans reached the Pueblo III stage fifty years earlier than other Anasazi. In turn, after an amazing florescence, the Pueblo III phase of Chaco culture waned nearly a century earlier than its counterparts at Mesa Verde and Kayenta.

During the hundred years prior to 1020, the Chacoans began the construction and occupation of the sites that became the towns of Pueblo Bonito, Chetro Ketl, Una Vida, Peñasco Blanco, and Hungo Pavi. Both Pueblo Bonito and Chetro Ketl underwent major construction in the early 1000s. These pueblos were built along a seven-mile stretch of Chaco Canyon from Una Vida, near Fajada Butte at the east end, to Peñasco Blanco on West Mesa to the west.

The buildings in these early times were constructed of unfaced slab-type masonry—sandstone slabs laid in a double row and sealed with sand and clay mortar. They began as small Pueblo II–type structures that were added onto in later times to create the large structures.

The control of runoff water from the cliffs to irrigate fields in the canyon, as a supplement to the Chaco Wash floodwater irrigation, was begun during this formative time, and was accomplished by the construction of ditches, dams, and canals to divert runoff water to the fields and gardens.

By the end of the Early Bonito Phase—during the early eleventh century—we can infer that Chaco

Canyon had become a population center and the center of an integrated group of communities covering the entire Chaco Basin. Together with Chaco, these surrounding communities began to function as an integrated economic system.

By 1020 the Chacoans were well on their way to the creation of a scintillating Precolumbian culture. The architecture, ceramics, jewelry making, astronomy, road building, agriculture, communication systems, complex of outliers, commerce, and system of administration that developed during the Bonito Phase made them precursors of the classic Pueblo III culture of the Anasazi Southwest. All of these aspects of the Chaco culture were set in place during the Early Classic Bonito Phase.

Exact dates are unknown, but several additional pueblos were likely begun in Early Classic Bonito times: Pueblo Alto, which became the terminus of the north Chaco roads and a possible market center; Kin Ya'a, a Chaco outpost to the south with a signal tower kiva and connected with the canyon towns by a roadway; Tsin Kletsin, located southwest of the canyon; and in the Florescent Pueblo del Arroyo, one of the later pueblos; Wijiji, about five miles upstream; and Pueblo Pintado, located seventeen miles east of Pueblo Bonito.

The Florescent portion of the Classic Bonito Phase between 1055 and 1083 is so designated because this twenty-eight-year-period became the highwater mark of the Chacoan culture and also the period of the most intense building activity. It is particularly significant because the span of time is so short—about one generation. The Florescent Bonito Phase overlaps in time the early portions of the Hosta Butte and McElmo phases of Chacoan development.

The Hosta Butte Phase (1040–1110) defines a settlement pattern of Chacoans who were the suburban or rural neighbors of the urban dwellers. Possibly half of the Chaco Canyon population lived in clusters of small pueblos up and down the canyon. The small habitations around Casa Rinconada, for example, did not represent separate villages. More likely taken together they made up one village, in much the same way as Talus Unit No. 1 at Chetro Ketl was a detached housing unit connected with the large apartment-like complex. The Hosta Butte people were contemporaneous with the urban dwellers and shared most of their traits, but they employed a very different kind of architecture. The villagers lived in small clusters of room blocks of roughly finished masonry arranged in rows and incorporating kivas within the room blocks.

Chaco Canyon Chronology

PHASES	DATES	SITES
BONITO		
Early Bonito	920–1020	Pueblo Bonito
		Chetro Ketl
		Una Vida
		Peñasco Blanco
		Hungo Pavi
		Kin Bineola
Early Classic Bonito	1020–1055	Pueblo Alto
		Tsin Kletsin
		Kin Ya'a
Florescent Bonito	1055–1083	Pueblo del Arroyo
		Wijiji
		Pueblo Pintado
Late Classic Bonito	1083–1120	All Bonito Phase sites remodeled and enlarged
Late Bonito	1120–1220	No new Construction
HOSTA BUTTE	1040–1110	Casa Rinconada Group and other small sites
McELMO	1050–1154	Kin Kletso
		Casa Chiquita
		New Alto
		Tsin Kletso
		Tri-wall unit
REOCCUPATION	1250–1300	Some remodeling in older sites
ABANDONMENT	By 1300	

The McElmo Phase describes the sites constructed by apparent migrants from the Northern San Juan: Kin Kletso, Casa Chiquita, New Alto, Tsin Kletso, and probably the tri-wall unit at Pueblo del Arroyo. These people are thought to have come from the Mesa Verde and the Montezuma Valley region. They were part of the Chaco Canyon community just like the Hosta Butte people.

Was there a Chacoan system of social and economic organization, different from other Anasazi systems that produced the Chaco Phenomenon? The controversy on this point is heavy. W. James Judge suggests that the growing population in the 900s could not be supported by the canyon's agriculture, so the Chacoans developed an industry fashioning turquoise into ritual and other objects that were exchanged with other Chaco Basin villages for food and other goods. Judge argues that Chaco Canyon in the 1000s became a ritual center (similar to the Maya cities during the 700 and 800s). By 1050 it

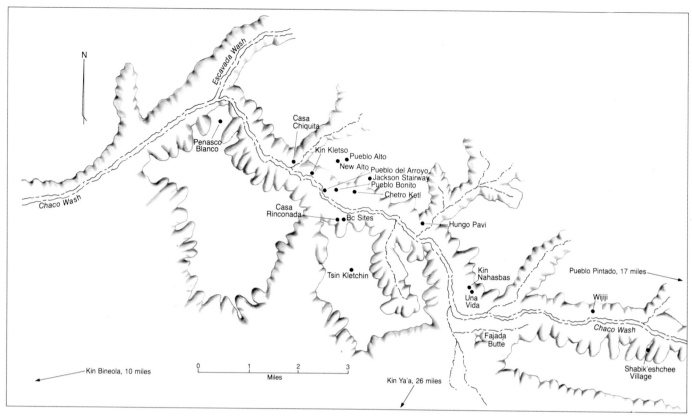

The Chaco Canyon in northwestern New Mexico, an ancient center of Anasazi population, was the scene of a remarkable development in architecture and communications by the end of the 1000s. This development was responsible for the remains of some of the most spectacular Precolumbian buildings in the United States.

Wijiji, just over two miles east of the Visitor Center by foot trail up Chaco Canyon, was a Classic Bonito Phase pueblo with ninety-two first-floor rooms and two kivas. (Photograph taken with the assistance of John Q. Royce.)

Casa Chiquita, a McElmo Phase small village of fifty rooms and three kivas, originally standing two or three stories high, contemporaneous with Kin Kletso, is located just to the right of the point where the modern road enters Chaco Canyon. (Photograph taken with the assistance of John Q. Royce.)

195

was the center of a social, ritual, and economic system. Chaco Canyon, he suggests, was a ritual rather than a residential center; the pueblos were not year-round residences but accommodations for pilgrims. The permanent population of Chaco Canyon was around 2,000, rather than some 6,000 indicated by the number of rooms in the canyon. He argues that the roads leading into Chaco Canyon were conduits for the pilgrims bringing food and goods to Chaco in exchange for turquoise and ceremonies.

Other archaeologists disagree. They point out that the source of turquoise was far from Chaco Canyon, that the Anasazi were farmers, not craftsmen, so that a mercantile center is not likely. The huge pueblos of Chaco Canyon, with the exception of Pueblo Alto, are rather typical Anasazi residence towns with residence suites, kin kivas, and great kivas; they are not hostelries. The most significant argument against Judge's hypothesis is that modern Pueblo culture, with its roots far back into Anasazi history, has no counterpart for ritual pilgrimages, or organized manufacture, trade, or exchange of goods.

Architecture

Pueblo Bonito and Chetro Ketl are partially excavated examples of four- and five-story living complexes with room-enclosed courtyards, great kivas, and kin-group or clan kivas, all built according to an organized plan. Pueblo Bonito may have housed as many as 1,000 people, with fewer persons in the others.

During Florescent Bonito times the older towns—Una Vida, Peñasco Blanco, Pueblo Bonito, and Chetro Ketl—underwent extensive remodeling. Several new pueblos were built. Pueblo Pintado is an outlier to the east with wood specimens dating between 1060 and 1061. Pueblo del Arroyo, located in the center of the canyon near Pueblo Bonito, and Wijiji, constructed on the canyon floor some five miles to the southeast, are possibly two of the latest towns to be constructed. These major building projects took place between 1055 and 1083, which is the reason for designating this period as one of florescence.

Masonry, Construction, and Ceramics

Coursed sandstone masonry is as central to Chacoan architecture as marble is to the Greek Parthenon or glass to modern skyscrapers. The Chacoans utilized several styles of stone masonry, double-rowed sandstone slabs, dressed and faced blocks chinked with bits of sandstone, and a rubble-cored wall veneered in several styles. These various types of wall construction seem to have been more a matter of style than improved efficiency.

The materials used were stone, sandy clay, and water. Two types of stone were used: the hard brown tabular sandstone from the bench above the canyon cliffs, and the bedded sandstone from the cliffs themselves.

It has been suggested that the surge of building and remodeling after 1050 was precipitated by the development of the rubble-cored masonry walls. These walls were constructed by the use of a rubble core of rocks and mud with a veneer of carefully shaped, tablet-size stones. The walls were much wider at the bottom and tapered upward to support the massive weight of the masonry rooms up to four and five stories. It can be argued, however, that these rubble-cored walls, like other types of Chacoan masonry, were really just innovations in style, and that, in fact, they are not as efficient as the walls constructed of interlocking blocks that created a solid masonry wall. Rubble-cored walls may have appeared only coincidentally at the time of the burgeoning Chaco construction. Elsewhere in Anasaziland, such walls have been recorded in Betatakin and many sites in the Mesa Verde and the Montezuma Valley.

Some archaeologists have suggested that skilled laborers shaped and set the stones while other workers did the carrying and mixing, and that the pueblos were the result of master plans conceived in the minds of the builders prior to construction, something akin to an architect's plans for a building today. They argue that in addition to laying up the wall, it was necessary to plan in advance the necessary width or thickness of the core needed for the proposed height of the building. They suggest further that the builders needed to determine the locations of the rooms, kivas, and plazas in advance and to plan for doorways, vents, and interior wall supports. Thus a division of labor is suggested as well as a system of management that other archaeologists cannot accept. These other archaeologists point out that Chaco construction is not significantly different from that found at other Anasazi sites built without managed labor, and that the pueblos at Chaco, impressive as they are, are no more than an assembly of modular pueblo units that had been well known to the Anasazi for hundreds of years. Loosely directed community efforts in rural America have constructed many a barn and farmhouse according to "plans" held jointly in the minds of the contributing laborers.

Chacoan pottery bears a number of very distinctive qualities. The utility corrugated jars display

Hungo Pavi, at the junction of Mockingbird Canyon and Chaco Canyon, just below a prehistoric stairway ascending to the mesa, was a medium-size site (seventy-three lower-story rooms and two kivas) with tree-ring dates from A.D. 943 to 1047. (Photograph taken with the assistance of L. A. Villarreal.)

a variety of decorations wrought by modifying the outside coils or by incising and pinching over the coils. Painted vessels show bold geometric figures in a kind of halftone created by hatching (close parallel lines) bounded by markedly heavier lines. A characteristic Chacoan mug can be identified by its tall cylindrical shape. The tall cylindrical shape of mugs and vases is unique to Chaco. The Chacoans also made painted pottery in a style similar to the Northern San Juan Pueblo III ware.

Population

By 1100 the number of rooms indicates that as many as 6,000 people were living in the Chaco Canyon area in some 400 sites, and it is estimated that the population was double that of fifty years earlier. In addition Chaco Canyon was closely connected with more than thirty outliers within the Chaco Basin and probably others outside the basin. The number and population of the outliers is difficult to compute. Some that have been so designated are obviously quite small sites such as Chimney Rock Pueblo near Pagosa Springs, Colorado, and Newcomb, Skunk Springs, and Dalton Pass in New Mexico. Others, such as Lowry in the Montezuma Valley, are now known to belong to large local settlements and were not outliers of Chaco Canyon. A reasonable estimate of total population during the Florescent Bonito Phase in the Chaco Basin is thought to be

between 10,000 and 12,000, with about half living in the outliers.

Ceremonial Structures

Chacoans built kin-group kivas for use by lineage or clan groups; great kivas—large, round semi-subterranean rooms likely used for community-wide ceremonies; one tri-wall structure, similarly used; and the tower-kivas, used perhaps as a combination kiva and communication tower.

The kiva is an outgrowth of the Basket Maker III pithouse and is a specialized kind of religious architecture developed by the Anasazi. At Chaco, kivas were built in two ways: they were either circular belowground rooms with the roof at ground level and located in the plaza in front of the living quarters, or they were constructed within the room blocks of the pueblos. They varied in size from ten to twenty-five feet in diameter and were covered with both flat and cribbed roofs. They were entered by a ladder through a hatch in the roof. Inside were a fire pit, banquette (not used for seating), ventilator shaft, and wall niches. Some had a subfloor ventilating system; others had floor ventilators and deflectors. Sipapus are fairly rare at Chaco. They were included in McElmo Phase kivas, but not often in Chaco-style kivas.

The Chaco-style kivas had eight log-end pilasters (short pieces of log were fitted into the kiva wall, cut end facing inward, leaving several feet of log upon which the long cribbing logs were laid) to support a cribbed roof, a subfloor ventilator, and a floor vault. The McElmo (Mesa Verde)–style kivas were constructed with six masonry pilasters, an above-floor ventilator, a deflector, and a sipapu, and they were often keyhole shaped. The kivas were probably used by lineage or clan groups as a place for social, religious, and instructional activities.

The great kivas were revived at Chaco after being out of style since Basket Maker III times. Great kivas were, however, being constructed in the Northern San Juan during the hiatus at Chaco. The proto-great kiva at Shabik'eshchee Village (Chacra Mesa, nine miles east of Pueblo Bonito), was constructed about 753, but true great kivas did not reappear until Bonito Phase times.

In the canyon are two so-called isolated great kivas, Casa Rinconada and Kin Nahasbas (located near Una Vida), both probably constructed during the middle 1000s, and several great kivas constructed within the plazas of the pueblos. The great kivas were semisubterranean with flat roofs raised several feet above ground level. Entrance was at ground level through an antechamber on the north side, which often contained an altar. Inside was a circular bench to accommodate ceremonial viewers, a sipapu, raised masonry fire box, sockets for roof-support pillars, and a pair of masonry vaults possibly serving as foot drums. The Chaco Canyon tri-wall structure, a ceremonial complex located adjacent to Pueblo del Arroyo, emulates the tri-wall structures of the Northern San Juan and so is considered to be part of the McElmo Phase. Little is known about the function of tri-walls, except that they are assumed to be ceremonial.

Tower-kivas have been found only at Chaco and Chacoan outliers and probably were used for ceremonial functions. They may also have served as part of the communications network. Tower-kivas were constructed at Chetro Ketl, Una Vida, Kin Ya'a, and Kin Kletso. Often the only spot in the pueblo from which another pueblo or signal station could be seen was the highest point in the pueblo, and frequently this was the top of the tower-kiva.

Communication System

The most unique and technically advanced aspect of the Chaco culture was the road and signal communication system. The line-of-sight communication network developed by the Chacoans may have linked communities throughout the Chaco Basin by use of fires at night. They combined shrines with signal stations. Near Peñasco Blanco, a Pueblo III shrine-signal station was uncovered that contained a cache of turquoise beads. The shrine (Site 29SJ423) was located to allow a clear view of the distant eastern and western horizons.

The roads linking the outliers ran north, south, southeast, and southwest from Chaco Canyon. The Great North Road reached Salmon Ruin and probably extended beyond. The southeast road extended to Pueblo Pintado and Guadalupe, the south road to San Mateo and Kin Nizhoni, the southwest road to Kin Ya'a, at Crown Point, and another road to Standing Rock and Peach Springs. In addition, road segments ran west toward Skunk Springs.

The roads were of varying widths; the main roads averaged about twenty feet, with some forty feet wide, and were cleared down to bedrock or to the hardpan of clay. The spur roads were about twelve feet wide. The roads were laid out to avoid obstacles in the terrain, but they were basically straight even though this required cutting through low hills. Some were bordered with low stone walls. The known network of roads fanning out from Chaco Canyon exceeds 400 miles in length. Hand-cut stairways in the rock connected the base of the canyon with roads on the top of the mesa. Roads and stairways joined Pueblo Bonito and Chetro Ketl with Pueblo Alto.

Pueblo Alto was the terminus for several roads from the north and northeast that came from nearby communities and more distant outliers. Along the roads a number of small ruins have been found that are assumed to have served as way stations. The primary purpose of this extensive roadway network, in addition to the transportation of goods, building materials, and individuals in and out of Chaco Canyon, must have been to hold Chaco Canyon and its outliers together as a social and economic network. This road system is undoubtedly the greatest single achievement of prehistoric man in the Southwest. It is the crowning achievement of the Chaco culture.

Astronomy

All ancient peoples, except some tropical dwellers, governed their lives by the changes of seasons. Like all peoples who live outdoors, the ancients were aware of the movements of the sun, moon, and stars. Modern Pueblo Indians have ritual and agricultural calendars that are meshed with the movements of the solar system, and the evidence indicates that the Anasazi, including the Chacoans, were similarly aware of solar phenomena.

The full extent of Chacoan astronomical sophistication is as yet unknown. Certainly they were

A prehistoric grand stairway descends from the mesa top to Hungo Pavi. This is one of several stairways leading into and out of the canyon.

aware of the seasonal movements of the sun and could determine the equinoxes and solstices by observing the sunrise with respect to specific points on the canyon cliffs. They also could make accurate directional alignments by observing the north star. It is unlikely, however, that the Chacoans had sufficient solar, lunar, and celestial knowledge to have created a calendar as accurate as the calendar devised by the ancient Maya.

The Chacoans did have several known artifical devices for recording the sun's movements. At Pueblo Bonito the winter solstice could be determined by the alignment of two third-story windows with the sunrise point on the cliff on that day. More impressive are the Sun Dagger spirals on Fajada Butte. These spirals were so positioned on the face of the cliff to enable the Anasazi to determine the days of the equinoxes and solstices, and perhaps the phases of the moon.

It has been suggested that the niches in the great kiva of Chetro Ketl were designed to observe the phases of the moon and even the heliacal risings

The ancient Jackson Stairs lead to the mesa top at the head of the canyon northeast of Chetro Ketl.

of Venus. Other solar and lunar alignments may be demonstrated in the future.

Water Control

Another of the singular achievements of the Chacoans was a comprehensive runoff water control and distribution system. In earlier times the Chacoans may have utilized floodwater irrigation from the Chaco Wash, although there is no direct evidence remaining of diversion from the wash. Later in Pueblo III times it became necessary to make use of the surface water that poured off the cliffs following thundershowers.

A series of water control and distribution systems along the entire canyon from Una Vida to Peñasco Blanco employed a system of dams at the mouths of side canyons to impound the runoff and direct it by canals to a headgate from whence it was directed into a grid irrigation network to water the gardens and fields. This system was so extensive and complex that, like the roads, it represented engi-

neering expertise and an extensive community effort. As a result of this system of irrigation, food production increased in conjunction with the doubling of the Chaco Canyon population just prior to Classic Bonito times.

Mexican Connection

Did the Chacoans go too far too fast during the Classic Bonito Phase for their accomplishments to have been the result of a cultural flash of insight? Could they have built the roads, the multistoried pueblos, the water control system, the Sun Dagger, the outliers, and the commercial network without the direct assistance and guidance of a more advanced culture?

We know there was contact with Mesoamerica. Macaws or parrots and copper bells from tropical regions along the Mexican coast, and other artifacts from Mexico as well as shell jewelry from the Hohokam in southern Arizona, were traded for turquoise. Specific structural features that have been attributed to the Mexican influence are rubble-cored masonry walls, square pilastered colonnades, and seating disks beneath great kiva roof support columns. Numerous ceramic objects have been found that appear Mexican in style.

The Mexican connection is demonstrable, but that the Mexican traders or others directly controlled the Chacoans is doubtful. As a result of the trade connections, an infusion of ideas may have been sufficiently great to have influenced the Chacoans to adopt such techniques as rubble-cored walls, and runoff water control, or may have given them the idea that a road network to outliers was feasible. But this hypothesis cannot take away from the Chacoans the credit for their accomplishments.

End of the Chaco Phenomenon

There was little remodeling or new construction after 1120 by the Bonito people. The McElmo people were the latecomers, and they continued to do some building during the 1100s, perhaps to the middle of the century. It is impossible to determine exactly when Chaco Canyon was abandoned. During the Late Bonito Phase (1120 to 1220) the fabric of the Chaco economic and social system began to unravel, not only in Chaco Canyon but at the small settlements and the outliers as well. But exactly when and why is unknown. The only certainty is that by the middle 1100s, the Chaco Phenomenon had died, and by 1300 all the Anasazi were gone from the Chaco Basin.

After the Chacoans had abandoned their works and moved out of the canyon, some evidence from pottery indicates that Mesa Verde people moved in, for a time at least, but they too were gone by 1300. These Mesa Verdeans came much later, perhaps as much as a century later, than the McElmo people who came from the same region. From about 1300 until sometime in the 1700s, when the Navajos arrived, Chaco Canyon's pueblos and great kivas were simply part of a ghost town.

Where did they go? These Anasazi were not a "lost civilization"; they migrated in small bands, probably lineage groups or clans, to the southeast to the Rio Grande, or to the south to the Zuni country. In these areas they mingled with and influenced the local population and developed the Pueblo IV Anasazi culture that endured until the arrival of the Spaniards.

Why did they go? The root cause may have been sixty years of drought that plagued the entire Chaco Basin south of the San Juan River between 1130 and 1190, the effect of which was a shortage of food for Chaco Canyon and the outliers. Migrations have been precipitated by climatic changes for tens of thousands of years, but for the Chacoans there may have been additional causes, all of which are speculative, but nevertheless intriguing.

The most generally espoused theory is that the leadership could not cope with the stress of food shortages over a protracted time. The Chaco road and outlier system is assumed to have been set up to provide for sharing of food. Shortages caused by temporary drought in one area could be offset by importing food (corn) from an area that was not affected. If, however, the drought continued and was widespread—as the tree-rings indicate it was in the Chaco Basin in the late 1100s—the people had no choice: move or starve. If it is assumed that the drought was not sufficiently intense to produce famine, and we really don't know, other causes may have contributed to the abandonment.

Wood was the Anasazi's single most necessary resource, next to food and water. The construction of the pueblos required thousands of logs for beams and roof supports and a huge supply of smaller branches for ceilings and floors. W. James Judge has estimated that 215,000 beams were carried into Chaco Canyon. Moreover, wood was also their only fuel for heating and cooking. The thousands of people of the Chaco Canyon required a large quantity of fuel to get them through the winters. As decades passed, the area in and around the canyon was stripped of ground cover resulting in erosion and a heavy loss of arable land and a consequent sharp reduction in food production. Irrigation of the same fields over hundreds of years increased the alkali content of the soil. This, coupled with continued use without adequate fertilizer, combined to reduce the productivity of the cropland.

As no written records exist, it is impossible to say what kind of social organization ran Chaco. Based upon the modern-day Pueblo Indian organization and what is known of the Anasazi system of government in Pueblo IV times when the Spaniards arrived, we can assume that no strong central authority took hold in Pueblo III times. Pueblo life depended on custom and voluntary cooperation between the families and the clan or lineage groups. There were no nobles or kings and no hereditary chiefs. At Chaco no evidence indicates an elite class, a priest class or a theocracy. The pueblo people left more exotic goods behind than did the rural people, but that is about the extent of the difference between them. Given these facts, the only supportable explanation for the authority that could build and maintain the irrigation works and the road and signal system, and build the huge pueblos, would be a kind of a super council of representatives from the various pueblos, outliers, and villages with both religious and secular power.

When times became troubled, the authority of such a council would at first have strained and then collapsed. Then the people, who it must be remembered were self-sufficient farmers dependent on no one for tools or know-how, packed up their meager possessions and moved out. Eventually, all were gone.

Pueblo Bonito

In Classic Pueblo times (between 1050 and 1100) Pueblo Bonito could have housed perhaps 1,000 Indians in some 600 rooms. It was the largest single Anasazi building and probably the most thoroughly excavated by the Anglos. Lt. James H. Simpson of the U.S. Army first described the ruin in 1849, and the first excavations were conducted by Richard Wetherill (who was later shot and killed by a Navajo). The Hyde Exploration Expedition began in 1896; at the end of it four years later, 190 rooms and kivas had been cleared, and some 10,000 pieces of pottery and a huge number of turquoise beads and pendants were shipped to New York. Neil M. Judd and the National Geographic Society worked here for seven years beginning in 1921. Judd also stabilized the ruin during the 1930s. Research con-

The largest and one of the most spectacular buildings constructed by the Anasazi, Pueblo Bonito in Chaco Canyon stood five stories high along the rear wall and was occupied for more than 200 years. In the last half of the 1000s it housed some 1,000 people in 600 rooms with two great kivas. During four construction periods some 800 rooms and 37 kivas were built.

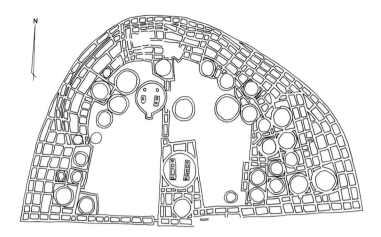

Plan of Pueblo Bonito.

tinued here and at other sites at Chaco during the 1970s by the National Park Service and the University of New Mexico under the direction of Robert H. Lister and, later, W. James Judge.

Pueblo Bonito went through four construction phases beginning with a curved multistoried block of rooms, close to the cliff. This Early Bonito Phase construction took place between 919 and 936. The second phase (during the early 1000s) added several kivas and the great curved rear wall that is now in place. The earlier smaller curved wall has been covered by the second phase wall, but it still is in there. Bonitian culture was changing rapidly at this time.

The majority of the construction took place during the Early Classic and Florescent Bonito phases of building, between 1030 and 1079, and included the two great kivas and the rooms and kivas located in the front of the complex on the east and west sides. The last phase added several kivas and the rooms on the southeast corner. The Pueblo Bonito building and remodeling process covered a period of some 200 years.

Four principal types of masonry have been identified at Pueblo Bonito. The oldest type employed sandstone slabs, double rowed, held together with a mortar of mud and sand. The second type used dressed and faced sandstone blocks chinked with thin laminate sandstone tablets. The third kind of masonry wall was rubble-cored and veneered on the outside with banded masonry made up of sandstone blocks alternating with inch-thick tablets of sandstone. The last walls were rubble-cored and faced on both sides with sandstone tablets of uniform thickness.

The significance of these masonry styles is not clear. At Pueblo Bonito they demonstrate a sequence of construction, but only at Pueblo Bonito. At other pueblos the styles as well as the sequence of construction were different. It wasn't a question of strength or durability—all of the styles beginning with the second phase were equally effective. It wasn't for beauty either because most of the masonry in the entire pueblo was plastered both inside and out. Actually the only explanation for the variations in masonry is that it was a matter of the style or preference of individual stone masons. Each Anasazi phase developed its own patterns of lithics, pottery, basketry, and architecture. The elegant, close-fitting, Chacoan masonry is an example of the development of a particular style.

Although there may have been as many as 800 rooms, the exact number is unknown because many of the upper walls collapsed after the pueblo was abandoned. In addition, many of the older rooms were filled with trash to serve as footings for the upper levels that extended to five stories along the rear wall. Probably no more than 600 rooms were ever in use at one time. Some thirty-seven kivas have been located, but, here too, not all were in use at the same time.

The site now occupied by Pueblo Bonito was originally a Pueblo I pithouse village following which, during Pueblo II times, a semicircle of rudely constructed one-story rooms were added, with storage rooms in the rear, built of wall-width stone slabs embedded in adobe mortar. This original pueblo settlement was occupied from about 828 to 935. Pueblo Bonito itself grew out of these modest beginnings.

Pueblo Bonito is a spectacular architectural achievement for a Neolithic people who had no metal tools, no wheel, and no beast of burden. Archae-

Part of the evidence for a general construction plan for Pueblo Bonito may be seen in the way the curving rear (north) wall of the pueblo was built thicker at its base and tapering toward the upper stories. This also represents a good example of the masonry-veneered, rubble-cored wall construction found in the large Chaco ruins. Although the ground plan shows this wall was not part of the original construction at Pueblo Bonito, it must have been the result of a community effort.

The living rooms at Pueblo Bonito were quite large by Anasazi standards, and they were built of unusually fine sandstone masonry. Several different styles of banded and unbanded masonry in the photograph mark the work of individual stone masons. The horizontal grooves in the walls held the ends of roof-support beams separating the different floor levels, at least three of which are clearly visible.

ologists disagree on whether this great masonry structure was conceived and constructed following a master plan throughout the four stages of construction, or whether the builders simply followed a generalized cultural concept—a putting together of smaller pueblo units using techniques known to the Anasazi since Pueblo I times. The long outer walls were probably a community effort and the interior rooms a family undertaking.

Community efforts and cooperation can be seen throughout Anasaziland, not just in the Chaco sites. The residents of Keet Seel pooled their labor to construct the large rampart wall holding up the entire east end of the site; Anasazi farmers throughout the Four Corners country combined their energies to build extensive systems of farming terraces and water collection works; town dwellers contributed to the building of the communally used great kivas and tri-wall structures.

The huge rubble-filled walls were battered—that is, tapered from bottom to top—to support the massive weight of five stories of rooms. The rooms were terraced to allow access without an interior system of stairways. In its later stages, Pueblo Bonito became like a fort. The single entrance (located in the south wall in the southeast corner of the west plaza) was originally only seven feet ten inches wide, and it was later barred by a single crosswall with only a thirty-two-inch-wide doorway in the middle. All the external doorways in the previously constructed walls were sealed. It will probably never be known whether they were building defenses against marauding tribes or against their neighbors.

Pueblo Bonito was constructed near the northeast wall of the Chaco Canyon about midway between Escavada Wash and Fajada Butte. It was, inexplicably, built in the shadow of a great balanced rock. The Navajo called the ruin *Sa-bah-ohn-nee,* "the house where the rocks are propped up" because the Pueblo Bonitians constructed a series of support timbers with tons of earth and masonry to forestall its collapse. They also placed some prayer sticks and perhaps other offerings behind the rock. There is an apocryphal story that in 1940 archaeologists removed some of the offerings from the base of Threatening Rock, but it is a fact that in January 1941, the great monolith fell, producing an avalanche of rubble that tore into the back wall of the ruins.

Kivas were constructed in the room blocks and in the plazas. The Chacoan kivas were built with a low banquette and four to ten pilasters made of juniper logs buried in the wall and extending horizontally onto the banquette. These pilasters sup-

The older kin kivas in Pueblo Bonito and other Chaco Canyon large ruins were built in the typical Chacoan style: circular with floor-level recess, encircling banquette, and an average of eight low masonry and log stub pilasters to support the cribbed log roof, a subfloor ventilator tunnel, and a centrally positioned hearth. Later immigrants from the Northern San Juan built Mesa Verde–style, keyhole-shaped kivas, sometimes within the remains of older Chacoan ones.

ported poles that encircled the kiva in ever-decreasing circles, creating a domed cribbed roof. The empty space was filled and flattened at the top to serve as the floor of an open courtyard above, or at plaza level if the kiva was not a part of the room block. Ventilation was provided by a duct in the floor connected to a shaft leading to the outside. Some kivas were constructed with four tall pilasters and a matted adobe roof.

In addition to the small kivas were two great kivas, forty or fifty feet in diameter, one on each side of the dividing row of rooms between the two plazas. A possible third great kiva may once have existed. In the dividing area rooms, many grinding stones (manos and metates) were found. The metates were arranged in a line of bins that allowed several women to work together grinding corn. The smaller kivas in the room blocks and the great kiva in the plaza suggest a way of life central to many of the Pueblo III Anasazi: the smaller kivas were used by kin groups as workshops and as places for educating children, storytelling, and family ceremonies. The great kivas, however, were probably designed and used for more formal community gatherings; perhaps they were where the people made decisions governing the conduct of the pueblo. The dividing wall suggests that a duality of social organization existed then as now in modern pueblos. In today's pueblos each entity is responsible for certain of the social and ceremonial aspects of life.

The ruins of Pueblo Bonito exhibit the arrangement characteristic of Anasazi pueblos throughout the Southwest. Masonry rooms, two or more stories high, were constructed to the rear, and generally on the north side, of the pueblo. Storage rooms were built on the back side, and the living quarters faced the plaza. Kivas were located in the room blocks and in the plaza area, but always in front of rooms. The plaza kivas were covered, making the plaza area level. At the open end of the plaza was a trash dump. At Pueblo Bonito a row of rooms constructed at the end of the plaza separated the plaza from the trash dump. Presence of the great kivas indicates the size and importance of the pueblo. They were the ceremonial centers of the complex and may have served outlying villages and habitations as well.

Pueblo Bonito was a more or less self-sufficient social entity. It was a farming community that incorporated housing, work areas, clan or lineage group kivas, and great kivas. It was not an ancient equivalent of a modern apartment complex. Pueblo Bonito was one of several associated but independent towns and villages that were built in Chaco Canyon There is, however, so much evidence of community endeavor—roadways, irrigation works, and com-munication systems—that it is probable Pueblo Bonito was a part of a much larger social entity.

Chetro Ketl

The Chetro Ketl ruin has four particularly noteworthy elements: the courtyard colonnade, the great kiva, tower-kivas, and the nearby Talus Unit No. 1. The meaning of the name *Chetro Ketl* (also spelled "Chettro Kettle") is unknown. It is probably a Navajo word that Lt. James Simpson transcribed to English spelling after his expediton in 1850. It is one of the major Anasazi pueblos of Chaco Canyon and is located about one-half mile southeast of Pueblo Bonito.

The pueblo contained over 500 rooms and more than twelve kivas, including several tower-kivas. It may have been four or possibly five stories high along the rear wall. During its excavation, over 300 tree-ring dates were obtained, producing the best building sequence for any of the Chaco Canyon pueblos. Chetro Ketl was constructed in fifteen stages from about 1010 to 1105 with abandonment some time after the last construction date of 1117. The tree-ring dates from the visible ruins belong to the Pueblo

The great plaza of Pueblo Bonito. The wall between the west and east sides of the pueblo plaza with great kivas on each side indicates a duality of social organization by the Chaco Canyon Anasazi that may have been similar to the Winter and Summer People of the modern Pueblos.

Chetro Ketl and Talus Unit No. 1 (to the left) have known construction dates from 1010 to 1117. Chetro Ketl contained over 500 rooms and 12 kivas with a great kiva. Only a small portion of the ruin has been excavated; the outline of the front wall is here clearly visible.

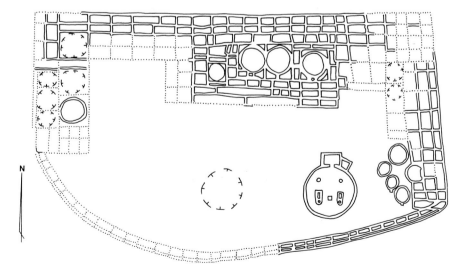

N

Chetro Ketl plan.

III, Early Classic Bonito Phase, and fall between 1036 and 1040.

The east-west rubble-filled back wall is nearly 500 feet long and supported possibly five stories of rooms, The core of the wall was made up of stones laid in adobe mortar. The wall tapered inward with increase in height and was faced with tablet-shaped stones to form a veneer. The back wall veneer utilizes Chacoan banded masonry—alternate bands of thick blocks forming a row followed by two or three thicknesses of small blocks forming another row about the total thickness of the large blocks. Another variety of Chaco banded masonry utilizes tablet-size stone layers that are two to three times as thick as the wide stone band.

Wings of rooms were built on the east and west sides of the pueblo, and a series of small rooms formed a curved wall bounding the plaza on the south. Attached to the wall of rooms on the outside were two parallel walls about seven feet tall and about two feet apart that have been called "the moat." The complex seems to follow a predetermined plan or layout in its construction and remodeling. This is particularly remarkable since the construction apparently took place over an eighty-year period involving the building and rebuilding of various of the architectural units. The general plan was adhered to over a period of three generations by an illiterate people. Only a portion of the pueblo has been excavated.

The front wall, facing the courtyard, was constructed sometime about 1087 as a row of square masonry pilasters rising from a low masonry wall that supported horizontal timbers forming the roof of a gallery. The spaces between the pilasters were later walled up to make rooms. Some archaeologists suggest that this pillar-fronted gallery is characteristic of Mesoamerican architecture of Precolumbian Mexico and consider it to be evidence of contact between Chaco Canyon and Mexico. However, pillars springing from a low wall rather than from the floor are not characteristic of Mesoamerican architecture, making it doubtful that this colonnade is solid evidence for a Mexican connection. Better evidence of the connection has been found at Pueblo Bonito, including copper bells and macaw skeletons that came from Mexico.

The round tower-kiva located on the east side of the main room block was originally three stories high with a kiva on the upper story. It was completely enclosed in the room block, and the spaces between the tower and the walls were completely

Chetro Ketl's front wall was originally constructed as square columns on the top of a low wall forming a sort of colonnade. Some archaeologists have suggested this construction is evidence of Mesoamerican influence.

A unique feature of Chacoan-style architecture is the tower-kiva, a kin kiva built in a second- or third-story block of rooms on a platform of filled-in lower rooms. This example (the tallest circular wall) from Chetro Ketl has become the model against which all others are compared. Tower-kivas are not found at all Chaco canyon ruins, but do occur at some Chacoan outliers such as Salmon Ruin and Kin Ya'a.

filled with rubble. The tower-kivas of Chaco Canyon may have been part of the signal network connecting the outliers with the pueblos of the canyon; we suppose a person standing on top of the tower could see a fire at night from another high point down the way.

The Chetro Ketl great kiva is a circular subterranean room with a diameter of more than sixty feet. The original great kiva had a diameter above the bench of fifty-four to fifty-five feet and had a maximum depth below the present plaza level of fourteen feet. This original great kiva was completely rebuilt by the construction of an outer wall and the reconstruction of bench that lies above the original bench. The niches in the original structure were sealed by the Anasazi when the kiva was remodeled. At the time of excavation, one of the original niches was found to contain a string of beads and turquoise pendants. There were more than 17,000 beads of shell and stone in strands up to seventeen feet long.

The cartwheel-size stone disks (over three feet in diameter) were found in the kiva at the bottom of four circular pits. They served as footings for four columns or large wooden posts that supported the roof. In the center of the kiva is a masonry fire box on each side of which are rectangular vaults with circular masonry seating pits for the roof-support columns. On the north side of the great kiva is an antechamber, built when the structure was remod-

The great kiva at Chetro Ketl was roofed and had a diameter of sixty feet and a depth of fourteen feet. The cartwheel-like stones were footings for the roof-support columns.

eled, which contains a masonry "altar." The exact function of the great kivas is an enigma. In Pueblo III times and earlier the kin groups used the smaller kivas and the community used the great kivas; then beginning in Pueblo IV typical great kivas were no longer constructed, and the smaller kivas were sharply reduced in number. This set the stage for the modern Pueblo use of kivas: kiva societies that combine the function of the kin kivas and the big kivas. The two large kivas in many Rio Grande pueblos serve the two halves of the community's ceremonial organization. We can speculate that the ancient great kivas were used for important gatherings where rituals or dances were performed by costumed priests with beating drums who asked the gods for rain, good crops, many children, or relief from the scourge of disease.

A much smaller site located northwest of Chetro Ketl has been designated Talus Unit No. 1. It contains some thirty rooms and five kivas. The tree-ring dates indicate that it was built and probably occupied at the same time as the larger complex. The Talus Unit was constructed on a terrace platform, which some believe demonstrates a Mesoamerican influence. However, similar terraced platforms have been found at Mesa Verde sites, such as Pipe Shrine House and Far View House that were not the result of any Mexican influence. In fact, terracing was a common method used by the Anasazi to level ground. The platform, with three steps near the center to a higher level, was unroofed and may have been a shrine.

The dates of the Talus Unit do demonstrate that people were living in the large pueblos and the smaller sites at the same time. Suburbia is nothing

Talus Unit No. 1, at the base of the cliff behind Chetro Ketl, resembles several typical unit pueblos side-by-side when viewed from directly above.

The platform in Talus Unit No. 1 with three steps may have been an open shrine.

new. The Talus Unit was at least two stories high. Ladders from the roof may have enabled the people of the canyon to reach a roadway at the top of the cliff that leads to Pueblo Alto.

Pueblo del Arroyo

In the eleventh century the population of Chaco Canyon burgeoned. During the fifty years between 1025 and 1075 the population doubled. Pueblo del Arroyo's tree-ring dates are spread from 1052 to 1103, showing that it was built during the population explosion. It was a Florescent Bonito Phase town with an estimated 284 rooms, fourteen kivas, and room blocks three and four stories high. It was one of the last of the major Chacoan towns constructed. The evidence indicates that the central section was constructed first, sometime around 1075, some forty years after Pueblo Bonito and Chetro Ketl began. It was oriented to face east rather than south and was set away from the cliffs.

The most significant aspect of Pueblo del Arroyo

is a McElmo Phase tri-wall structure on the west side. This ruin consists of three concentric circular masonry walls with cross walls creating a series of long arcing rooms between the walls and an open area, which possibly once held a kiva, in the center. Attached to the outer wall are several masonry rooms and kivas. Originally the tri-wall complex contained seventy or eighty rooms. It is probable that the complex was covered by timber and dirt roofs with roof hatchways for entrances. The tree-ring dates indicate construction about 1109, which would make it slightly younger than the main pueblo. There is a tri-wall structure at Aztec Ruin north of the San Juan River, one on the Chacra Mesa south of Chaco Canyon, and a number of others in the Mesa Verde–Montezuma Valley area. The tri-wall was probably constructed or inspired by Mesa Verde peoples who moved into the area and were living side by side with the Chacoans.

Tri-wall structures probably were ceremonial in character and performed the same kind of com-

Pueblo del Arroyo was a Florescent Bonito Phase site. The circular McElmo Phase tri-wall structure constructed later than the pueblo was probably roofed and served a ceremonial function similar to the great kivas. The smaller of the two side-by-side kivas near the center of the room block was Mesa Verdean with a flat roof. The larger was typical Chacoan with a dome-shaped cribbed roof. (Photograph taken with the assistance of John Q. Royce.)

munity service as the great kivas. No great kiva has been found at Pueblo del Arroyo, although some indications point to one in the courtyard. The people of the Pueblo del Arroyo may have utilized the great kivas of Pueblo Bonito until the tri-wall was constructed to fill their ceremonial needs, or, more likely, they were a part of the Pueblo Bonito community.

Pueblo del Arroyo does have an indisputable Mesoamerican connection. In the long room just to the east of the kiva facing the courtyard, the skeletons of three macaws were found. These parrots are not native to the Southwest, nor were they bred here during prehistoric times because only the remains of adult birds have been found. The birds were especially prized for their colorful feathers used by the Anasazi as a part of their religious regalia. The scarlet macaw is a large parrot that must have been brought live from southern Mexico—a long, long way to carry a live bird, especially if made in a single journey. These birds are long lived; perhaps they moved

north from settlement to settlement. The authors flew over the terrain from Casas Grandes in Chihuahua, Mexico, to Chaco Canyon. An Indian could have followed this route without crossing any mountains and without ever being far from water.

Near this long room are two kivas of different types: the smaller of the two was roofed with long timbers that extended from wall to wall and finished with small sticks and mud making a flat roof with a hatchway over the fire pit. The other and larger kiva is a typical Chacoan kiva with a bench supporting horizontal log pilasters from which circular tiers of logs were laid to create a dome-shaped cribbed roof. The space between the dome and the surrounding walls was filled with soil and rubble to create a flat roof with a hatchway entrance to the kiva below. The subfloor ventilating system eliminated the necessity for the deflector found in many kivas to protect the fire from draft.

These two kivas represent the continued remodeling done by the Chacoans. Several two-story rooms were removed to make space for these kivas. And the rooms torn out had been built above still earlier kivas that had been filled with trash to provide a foundation for the room blocks. This constant rebuilding and remodeling indicates the Chacoans may not have had a master plan from the outset of each pueblo but rather a general overall concept of the architectural form of the complex.

The masonry of Pueblo del Arroyo equals the finest in Chaco. The veneer is generally very closely fitted, light-colored sandstone tablets. It is possible that the dark brown sandstone of the north cliff used to build Pueblo Bonito and Chetro Ketl had been exhausted by the time Pueblo del Arroyo was constructed, and that the stone used here came from the main cliff. The tablet-like stones used in the walls required a minimum of mortar and have enabled these walls to stand for a thousand years.

Casa Rinconada Group

The Anasazi great kivas built during the eleventh and twelfth centuries were the counterparts of the cathedrals of western Europe that were constructed about the same time. These structures represented for both cultures an outpouring of religious fervor and an enormous amount of labor, probably voluntary even if organized to some extent. In all, the great kivas signify a considerable economic expenditure in manpower and materials.

Casa Rinconada is surrounded by several small pueblos (residential units), five of which appear below counterclockwise as follows: Bc59, Bc51, Tseh So (Bc50), Bc58, Bc57. The "Bc" designations were given to these sites when they were excavated by the University of New Mexico in the 1930s. Casa Rinconada and its surrounding small pueblos were contemporaneous with the larger pueblos on the north side of the canyon. These residences are part of the Hosta Butte Phase of Chaco Canyon. Archaeologists originally thought they were an earlier and more primitive phase of development, but excavations have revealed that they were occupied about the same time as the great pueblos of Chaco Canyon.

The small pueblos on the south side of the canyon consist of ten to fifty rooms each. They are generally only one or two stories high and with

Casa Rinconada great kiva and surrounding small pueblos on the south side of the Chaco Wash were contemporaneous with the great pueblos on the north side. Sites to the left of Casa Rinconada, Bc59, Bc51, and Tseh So have been excavated. Just below the great kiva are two unexcavated mounds. There are many unexcavated small pueblos in Chaco Canyon. (Photograph taken with the assistance of L. A. Villarreal.)

212

relatively poor masonry. The total number of rooms may have exceeded 300 in the immediate vicinity of Casa Rinconada, and all were a part of the Casa Rinconada complex. This total exceeds the number of rooms in any of the large pueblos except Pueblo Bonito and Chetro Ketl. Except for the interior architecture, the excavations indicated the life-style of the Hosta Butte people was very much like that of the Bonito Phase people living across the wash.

Casa Rinconada, though larger, was a more-or-less typical Anasazi great kiva, having a circular, partially subterranean chamber with a flat roof constructed several feet above ground level and supported by four interior pillars. Casa Rinconada was about sixty-three feet in diameter with a one-room public entrance at ground level to the south and multiroom antechamber and other attached rooms on the north. One of the north rooms contained an altar. Inside the main chamber, a bench encircled the outer edge, which would seat 100 people (more could have been included within the kiva). There were also four roof-support sockets, a fire box, east and west vaults, cists, a fire screen, niches, windows, and a subfloor passage and circular trench.

The Chacoans built and used Casa Rinconada during the last half of the eleventh century. It was reconstructed; the second floor was rebuilt about four inches higher than the first. At that time the fire box was altered, the bench and floor vaults were changed, and the subfloor passage was filled and abandoned. The subfloor passage was an unusual feature that connected the north room of the north antechamber with the interior of the kiva. The passage was about three feet deep, three feet wide, and roofed over. The apparent purpose was to allow a costumed or masked figure to appear suddenly in the center of the kiva.

The small ruin located next to the parking area for the Casa Rinconada trail is Tseh So (Bc50). This village consisted of twenty-six ground-floor rooms and four kivas. There may have been some second-story rooms. Tseh So and its companion site to the south, Bc51, were inhabited simultaneously and belonged to the Pueblo III Hosta Butte Phase. Bc51 included forty-five rooms and six kivas.

Kin Kletso

Kin Kletso is a cliff-side pueblo located about one-fourth mile northwest of Pueblo Bonito. It is a pueblo built by the McElmo Phase people who came into Chaco Canyon from the Northern San Juan Region—Mesa Verde and Montezuma Valley.

During Chaco Canyon's golden age, its three phases, Bonito, Hosta Butte, and McElmo, coexisted side by side. Early Classic Bonito began about 1020, Hosta Butte about 1040, and McElmo about 1050, and all ended about the same time in the early 1100s. These people were all Anasazi Indians; their differences lay in where they lived and how, in their architecture and town planning. The Hosta Butte people lived on the south side of the wash in scattered villages; the Bonito people lived in the large, well-ordered pueblos; and the McElmo people—the last to arrive—built more compact pueblos of large shaped sandstone blocks set in courses two stones thick.

The McElmo people brought their own style of kivas and built them into the room blocks. They didn't build great kivas, but probably constructed the Pueblo del Arroyo tri-wall unit to serve the same purpose. In some cases they adopted the Chaco-style kivas as they did in the two central kivas at Kin Kletso.

Kin Kletso is a one-occupation site with no evidence of earlier habitation. The Northern San Juan people came to Chaco, selected a site, and constructed a pueblo. At the west end on top of a huge boulder they built a tower-kiva fifteen feet tall and surrounded by walls and rubble fill. Inside was a simple hearth, and a T-shaped doorway on the east side.

The two visible centrally located kivas are both constructed on one story of fill and fit the Chaco style, with eight horizontal log pilasters, subfloor ventilator shafts, and a central fire pit. These had cribbed dome-shaped roofs. There were two smaller keyhole-shaped Mesa Verde–style kivas on the east side of the complex. The masonry and the smaller room sizes of Kin Kletso indicate the Mesa Verde style.

Kin Kletso was constructed in three phases. The first was the west half of the pueblo, the second the east half except for the two small kivas which were constructed during the last phase. The construction probably lasted for about fifty years from 1076 to 1124.

Text continued on page 216

213

Casa Rinconada (built and used during the last half of the 1000s) was a more-or-less typical Anasazi great kiva: circular, partially subterranean, and roofed in the fashion of the restored great kiva at Aztec Ruin. The subfloor passage allowed a figure to appear suddenly in the middle of the kiva during ceremonies. (Photograph taken with the assistance of John Q. Royce.)

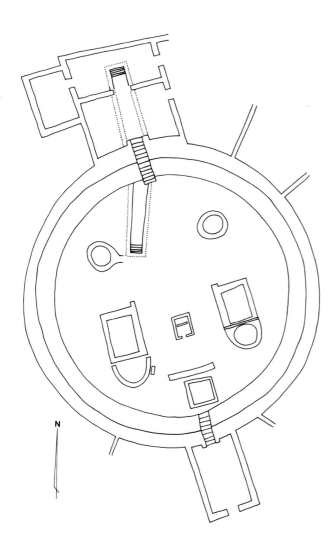

Plan of Casa Rinconada great kiva showing the subfloor passage, fire box, fire screen, parallel vaults or foot drums, seating pits for the roof-support columns, and the north antechamber rooms (after Vivian and Reiter 1960).

Two of the smaller sites that belong to the Casa Rinconada Group on the south side of Chaco Canyon across from Pueblo Bonito. These small pueblos stood one and two stories high and were somewhat scattered apart rather than all incorporated into one large building like their neighbors across the canyon. These Hosta Butte Phase buildings were constructed with poorer masonry than that used by their neighbors, yet they apparently built and held their ceremonies at Casa Rinconada, the finest great kiva in the entire Chaco Basin.

Kin Kletso (occupied between 1050 and 1100), a McElmo Phase site located just northwest of Pueblo Bonito, and probably built by the same people who constructed the tri-wall structure at Pueblo del Arroyo. The two central kivas were Chacoan in style, the smaller kivas on the east end were Mesa Verde style.

Interestingly, two very late dates, 1171 and 1178, were obtained from charcoal in the fill of one of Kin Kletso's rooms. These dates would extend the classic period at Chaco for fifty years, as the beginning of the abandonment of Chaco Canyon has been calculated to be about 1125, when construction ceased. However, these samples could have nothing to do with Kin Kletso's occupation since they were found in deposits made after the room was abandoned.

Peñasco Blanco

Construction at Peñasco Blanco may have begun earlier than at any of the other large Chaco Canyon pueblos. The tree-ring dates indicate an early burst of construction around 900 that continued through the Pueblo III, Bonito Phase, until at least 1088.

It is located on West Mesa on the south side of Chaco Canyon with a view of Chaco Wash, Escavada Wash, and Chaco River. The ruin is oval-shaped, contained some 160 ground-floor rooms, and was, in some portions of the pueblo, four stories high. Peñasco Blanco went through the several stages of masonry development from the more primitive slab walls, through the banded masonry to the rub-

ble-cored veneer evidenced by Pueblo Bonito and Chetro Ketl. The large depression to the northwest is an unexcavated great kiva. Two other kivas are visible outside the pueblo and several within.

Along the Peñasco Blanco Trail about three-quarters of a mile from Casa Chiquita, the Anasazi rock artists pecked out a cluster of petroglyphs depicting a bighorn sheep, a man, and a geometric design containing two spirals. These petroglyphs are located high on the northwest canyon wall. Beyond these at canyon-floor level are other examples of rock art that include several humanoid figures, spirals, footprints, and some recent graffiti.

Text continued on page 218

216

Rock art on the trail to Peñasco Blanco.

Peñasco Blanco, a large oval-shaped ruin located on the mesa top. Next to it was a great kiva. There were three kivas in the courtyard and five within the room block.

On the trail to Peñasco Blanco beneath a shallow overhang across the wash to the southwest, the Anasazi painted a star, crescent moon, human hand, and below, to the left, the sun. The complex represents the eastern sky just before sunrise and may portray Venus as a morning star or, possibly, the supernova of A.D. 1054.

Across the Chaco Wash on the canyon wall a pictograph complex shows a crescent moon, bright star, and human hand, painted beneath the overhang. Somewhat below and to the left are three red circles on a yellow background that probably represent the sun. This cluster may portray a supernova that was visible in Chaco and worldwide in A.D. 1054. It could equally well represent Venus in the morning sky. Michael Zeilik, an astronomer, points out that the portrayal of the sun, Venus (or the supernova), and the crescent moon as they appear to the viewer looking westward are astronomically impossible; however, with one's back to the wall, looking upward, as if seeing the moon and Venus rising in the eastern sky, the display is astronomically correct, either for the rising of Venus or the supernova. The hand points toward the moon and star as they would appear in the eastern sky just before sunrise, and the sun lies just below the horizon.

Una Vida plan.

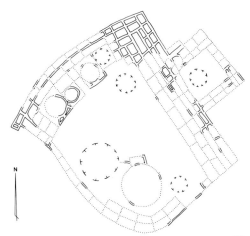

Una Vida. This unexcavated Bonito Phase ruin had about a hundred first-floor rooms and six kivas.

Una Vida and Kin Nahasbas

Una Vida is a Pueblo III, Bonito Phase, medium-sized pueblo with about a hundred first-floor rooms, six kivas, and possibly a great kiva. It was occupied at the same time as Pueblo Bonito and Chetro Ketl. Una Vida, however, has not yet been excavated. The ruin was stabilized in 1960 by the National Park Service, and at that time and later, tree-ring and wood specimens were taken. Basically the ruin appears now as it did when first seen by archaeologists.

Above is an aerial view from the southwest clearly showing the L-shaped outline of the pueblo and the kiva depressions in the northwest room block. The photograph shows the ruin from about the same angle as the plan (top of page). The aerial view reveals the mounds covering collapsed rooms on the northwest and northeast sides of the pueblo and the

219

arcing row of rooms that connected the northwest and northeast wings enclosing a plaza area. It is from this kind of evidence that archaeologists can map the approximate layout, ground plan, or arrangement of an unexcavated pueblo site.

Una Vida is located immediately adjacent to the park headquarters with surfaced trails leading from the parking lot. On the face of the cliff behind the ruin is some interesting Anasazi rock art depicting humanoids, spirals, hand prints, and a number of four-legged animals—probably bighorn sheep.

A great kiva, Kin Nahasbas, was constructed a few hundred feet west of Una Vida on a sandstone point bounding a small canyon about sixty feet up the southern slope. As in the case of Casa Rinconada, Kin Nahasbas was not directly connected to any other building; it was not in the courtyard of the pueblo as is the case of the great kivas of Pueblo Bonito and Chetro Ketl. It was probably constructed between 1030 and 1070. Its style is much the same as Casa Rinconada except that it had no underground entrance and no southern antechamber.

Another interesting aspect of Kin Nahasbas is its possible part in the Chaco signaling system. Many of the Chaco structures have been linked to the Chacoan system of transmitting signals by line-of-sight contact from one pueblo to another. The system extended from the canyon to outlying villages and towns. In many cases the only spot in the pueblo from which another pueblo could be seen was at the top of the tower-kiva. Una Vida, however, was built on the canyon floor and was not visible to other pueblos or signal stations, but the great kiva Kin Nahasbas situated on the top of the adjoining hill allowed contact with another signal station and with the tower-kiva in Una Vida's east wing. The desire for signal contact may account for the enormous extra effort involved in the excavation into bedrock to construct the kiva at the top of a steep hill.

Pueblo Alto

The Pueblo Alto trail begins behind Kin Kletso, winds over the talus slope to a crack in the cliff, and continues upward to the top of the mesa. From here the trail turns eastward skirting the top of the cliff for about a half mile giving the hiker an excellent view of Kin Kletso, Pueblo del Arroyo, Pueblo Bonito, Chetro Ketl, and much of the canyon from above.

There are several visible ancient steps, particularly the Jackson Stairs (page 200) in the canyon behind Chetro Ketl, used by the Anasazi to descend from the mesa top into the canyon below. Steps are rather unusual in Anasaziland. In most situations where the cliffs were to be traversed—as in Mesa Verde and Canyon de Chelly—the Anasazi used only hand and toeholds. The trail passes the Jackson Stairs and bends westward across some ancient farming terraces to the Alto ruins complex made up of four ruins on the mesa top to the north of Chaco Canyon: Pueblo Alto, East Ruin, New Alto, and Rabbit Ruin. Pueblo Alto is at the center and is the principal ruin with some 110 one-story living and storage rooms and eleven kivas. It lies about two-thirds of a mile north of Pueblo Bonito and was connected to Bonito by an ancient road.

New Alto is 400 feet to the west of Pueblo Alto. It is a square, multistory McElmo Phase ruin with twenty-eight rooms and one kiva built into the room block. Rabbit Ruin is a rubble-covered mound lying about 800 feet north of Pueblo Alto. The East Ruin is a twelve-room, one-kiva ruin that bounded an open plaza between it and Pueblo Alto.

These sites flourished during classic times just preceding the abandonment of Chaco. New Alto is among the latest constructions at Chaco and is attributed to the immigrants from the Northern San Juan–Mesa Verde area that built Kin Kletso. This complex is unique both in its placement and architecture, and it is possible that the Anasazi utilized it as a commercial center, as a market, and as a center for the storage and transfer of goods.

Pueblo Alto is a U-shaped pueblo with a curved row of rooms across the southern part of the plaza and with unusually high walls and large rooms. The walls were of such height that until the site was

New Alto, just west of Pueblo Alto, is a McElmo Phase ruin with twenty-eight rooms and a single kiva in the room block.

East Ruin (foreground), Pueblo Alto (center), and New Alto on the mesa north of Chaco Canyon looking west to the junction of Escavada and Chaco washes (above).

Pueblo Alto (110 one-story rooms and 11 kivas) was partially excavated in 1976 by W. James Judge who suggests the pueblo may have been designed and built as a hostelry for the accommodation of pilgrims and merchants (below).

carefully examined between 1976 and 1978 by the National Park Service Chaco Center, archaeologists had assumed it was multistoried as were all other classic Chacoan towns. Ten rooms and several kivas were carefully examined. Few artifacts attributable to normal habitation were found in the rooms, suggesting that they were not inhabited as living quarters—at least not as living quarters on a permanent basis. W. James Judge, who directed the excavation, has suggested that Pueblo Alto may have been designed and built as a sort of hostelry to accommodate pilgrims or merchants.

This complex, located on the dry, treeless mesa, constituted the terminus of several ancient Anasazi roads. These roads, including the Great North Road that has been traced as far north as the Kutz Canyon near Bloomfield, entered the plaza between Pueblo Alto and the East Ruin through an opening in the east-west wall connecting the two sites. In recent years aerial photography has revealed more than four hundred miles of ancient Chacoan roads. Robert B. Powers of the Southwest Cultural Resources Center suggests that most of the roads were constructed between 1075 and 1140. The roads, for the most part, are only shallow depressions ranging from very narrow up to forty feet wide, marked only by vegetation of a slightly different color. They are difficult to make out on the ground but are more apparent from the air. Powers raises the question as to why they were so wide and what were they used for, particularly since the Anasazi had no beasts of burden or wheeled vehicles. The roads connected Chaco Canyon with outlying communities, which would indicate they were used for communication between sites, but they also lead to quarries, water sources, and small settlements. He concludes that whether the roads were for trade, processions, resources, defense, or ease of travel is as yet unknown.

What did the Chaco Phenomenon represent? Perhaps the Chaco Canyon pueblos served as a ceremonial center. Or perhaps the area was a market and commercial center. From its position at the south end of the north road system, Pueblo Alto could have been a warehouse and marketplace for the Chaco outliers. Although the argument for Chaco as a pilgrimage and trade center is persuasive, neither religious pilgrimages nor organized trade were practiced by the other Anasazi, many of whom live in far more favorable environments than the Chaco Basin. If organized trade and pilgrimages were part of the Chaco Phenomenon, it was an aberration from the social organizational framework of all other Anasazi.

Outliers

Chaco Canyon lies near the center of the Chaco Basin—a relatively flat semiarid region—bounded on the north by the San Juan Valley, on the west by the eastern slopes of the Chuska Mountains, on the south by the divide between the headwaters of the Chaco River tributaries and the Puerco River of the West, on the southeast by the Continental Divide, and on the northeast by the divide between the Chaco River and Canyon Largo. This region roughly matches that of northwest New Mexico bounded by Bloomfield, Shiprock, Gallup, and Grants. It was in this region that the Chaco culture flourished.

A decade or so ago archaeologists compared such things as the construction and finish of the masonry walls, the size of the rooms, the design of kivas, and the existence of great kivas with the buildings at Chaco Canyon and concluded that some seventy Chaco Canyon outliers ranged from Lowry in the Montezuma Valley of Colorado to Guadalupe near Albuquerque. To Chacoanists the term *Chacoan outlier* still refers to sites that exhibit Chacoan architectural features.

The term *outlier* suggests a close connection with Chaco Canyon. What kind of connection, whether economic, religious, or political, is unknown. The enigma is, in part, whether these outlying sites were actually outliers or colonies, whether they contained enclaves or small migrant settlements of Chaco Canyon people, or whether they were merely influenced by them.

The Chaco road system provides the most persuasive evidence to suggest which sites constitute outliers. At least thirty sites located within the Chaco Basin are or may be connected to Chaco Canyon by ancient roads and are generally recognized as outliers. They range from sites as large as Pueblo Pintado and Kin Bineola to rather small settlements such as Newcomb and Kin Ya'a.

Chaco specialists have suggested that there are additional outliers outside the Chaco Basin. Salmon Ruin at the north terminus of the Great North Road is an outlier and so may be the Chimney Rock Ruin to the northeast and Casamero to the south. Other sites such as Aztec may have housed only an enclave of Chacoans. It is now known that the presence of great kivas or cored-masonry walls does not necessarily provide evidence of a Chacoan influence, since these architectural elements are found at numerous Anasazi sites not in any way connected with Chaco.

Text continued on page 229

Pueblo Alto from the northeast showing portions of the seven ancient Anasazi roads leading into the complex. The Great North Road has been traced from here as far north as the Kutz Canyon near Bloomfield.

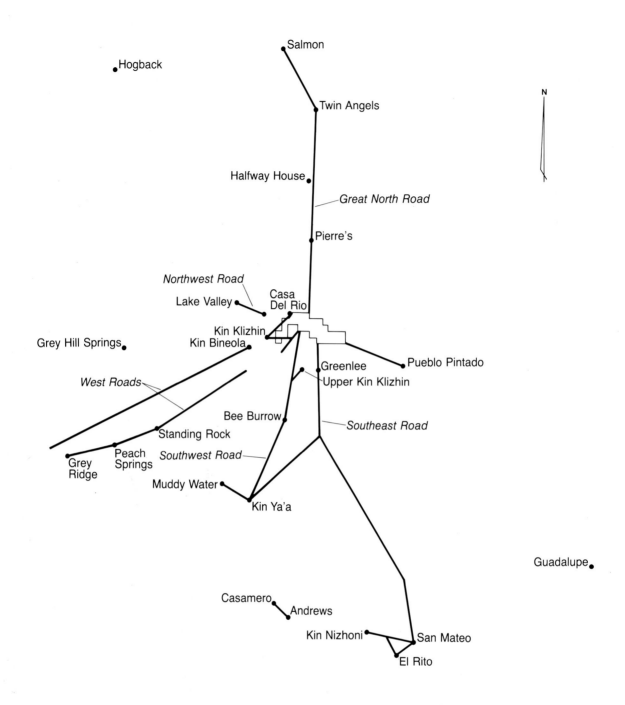

The Chaco system of roadways linked Anasazi communities throughout the Chaco Basin with Chaco Canyon proper. The map shows the known segments of roadways (more than 400 miles) recognized through a combination of aerial photography and ground checking. Obviously, many more miles of roadways existed in the past but have been destroyed by modern farming or are yet to be discovered.

Pueblo Pintado plan.

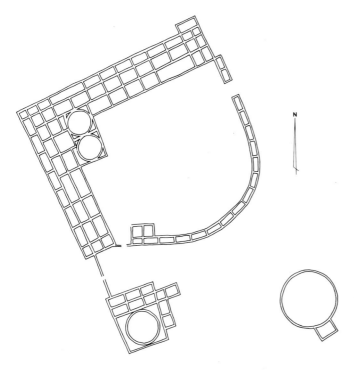

First Lt. James H. Simpson saw Pueblo Pintado in 1849 and described the masonry: "Indeed, so beautifully diminutive and true are the details of the structures as to cause it, at a little distance, to have all the appearance of a magnificent piece of mosaic work" (Lister 1981:10). The ruin lies seventeen miles east of the visitor center at Chaco Canyon on Highway 197 west of Cuba. The photograph reveals the extent of the ruin—it had some sixty ground-floor rooms, four kin kivas in the pueblo, and fourteen to sixteen kivas in the plaza with a great kiva to the southeast. Some buildings stood three stories high.

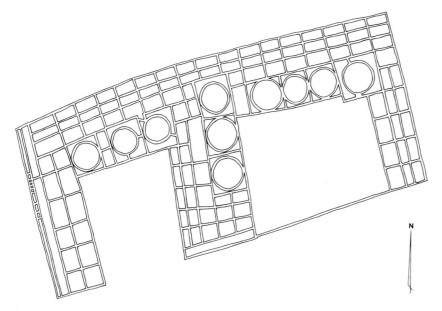

Kin Bineola plan.

Kin Bineola is a great E-shaped structure some 350 feet long and 150 feet wide containing 105 ground-floor rooms, 58 second-floor rooms, and 34 third-floor rooms with 10 kivas and one great kiva. The tree-ring dates show construction from A.D. 940 (Early Bonito Phase) to 1120 (Late Classic Bonito Phase). Kin Bineola is one of the principal Chacoan outliers located directly west of Chaco Canyon.

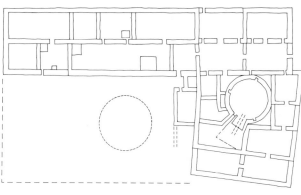

Casamero Ruin, a probable Chacoan outlier situated about fifty miles south of Chaco Canyon and some four miles north of Prewitt, New Mexico, was a small pueblo (about thirty rooms) with one kiva, but the presence of a very large great kiva (seventy feet in diameter) located just south of the ruins indicates Casamero was central to a community of some fourteen known nearby habitations. Its occupation span: 1050–1220.

Casamero plan.

Guadalupe Ruin, built high on a ridge overlooking Salado and Tapia canyons northeast of Mount Taylor. Surrounded by flat lands where ancient cultivated fields are still visible was an Anasazi Chacoan outlier with some twenty-five rooms and three kivas. Cynthia Irwin-Williams considers Guadalupe Ruin to be a part of the Chacoan regional pueblo system that failed and was abandoned along with most of the rest of Chaco by 1140.

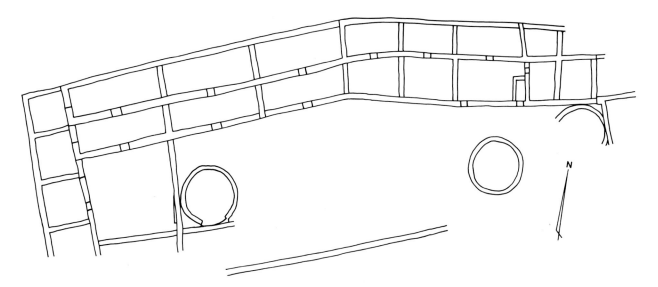

Guadalupe Ruin plan.

Kin Ya'a is one of the Chaco Canyon outliers located about twenty-four miles south of the Chaco Canyon visitor center on part of the Chaco ancient road network. The tree-ring dates available show 1106, indicating the ruin was inhabited in the Late Classic Bonito Phase. Here the Anasazi built a four-story tower-kiva for use as a part of the Chaco signal network in addition to three kin kivas, nine second-story rooms, and twenty-six one-story rooms.

Tsin Kletzin (photographed from the east) lies on the South Mesa about a mile and a half by foot trail beginning at Casa Rinconada. The available tree-ring dates are all late—A.D. 1111–13; this small, compact building is generally assigned to the McElmo Phase. There are at least forty-five ground-floor rooms and four kivas, and it was possibly three stories high. It may have been a part of the Chacoan signal system because of its high location on the mesa.

Why were there outliers? A number of Chacoanists have suggested that the network of outliers was designed to bring goods into Chaco Canyon from more favorable environments around the perimeter of Chaco Basin, things such as timbers for construction, food, and pottery that were exchanged for tur-

quoise jewelry and mosaic items. In addition, they see Chaco Canyon as a redistribution center for food: when one area was short, the others could support it. Others feel that Chaco Canyon was a sort of religious mecca. Still others argue that Chaco Canyon and all its habitation and community buildings was the creation of the outliers and was utilized by them as a center for religious ceremonies and for handling their trade and political alliances.

Pueblo Bonito and Chetro Ketl, each with five hundred rooms and enclosed plazas, were the largest Chacoan pueblos and were built at a convergence point of incoming roads. This suggests to Robert P. Powers that they were powerful centers of the Chacoan system, that their occupants controlled a network of outlying sites, and that they were not just ordinary towns but were quarters for a chiefly or priestly elite. Other large Chacoan towns may have served a similar function.

None of these hypotheses have been clearly demonstrated. So little is really known. About all we know is that there were sites in the Chaco Basin that were connected to Chaco Canyon by a network of roads. The Chaco outliers remain one of the tantalizing mysteries of ancient Anasazi culture.

Cibola (Modern Zuni Region) Connection

Francisco Vasquez de Coronado arrived in the Zuni vicinity in July 1540, looking for the "Seven Cities of Cibola" (there were six Pueblo IV villages in existence at the time). Coronado never found the fabled cities of gold, but the name, nevertheless, attached to the region.

The Cibola region extended westward from modern Zuni, in western New Mexico, as far as Springerville, Arizona, and Quemado, New Mexico, and east to the Continental Divide that angles southwestward thirty or forty miles east of Zuni at the Zuni Mountains. The northern border of the region is more difficult to define since here it merged, in prehistoric Pueblo II and III times, with Chaco. This is also sometimes called the upper Little Colorado River drainage, because it does encompass the headwaters of the Little Colorado River, the Zuni River, and the Puerco River.

Development has been continuous in the Cibola region from Basket Maker times to the present. A sizeable Basket Maker III site has been found at Cerro Colorado north of Quemado, New Mexico, and contemporaneous pottery sherds occur at Allentown and White Mound in Arizona. Pueblo I villages have been excavated at White Mound and Kiatuthlanna,

229

Grey Hill Springs, another Chacoan outlier to the west of Chaco Canyon, is a Pueblo II (Early Bonito Phase) and Early Pueblo III (Early Classic Bonito Phase) site. The most unique feature of the site is a circular wall on the top of a twenty-foot-high natural pillar. It was probably an unroofed structure known as a "stone circle," the function of which is unknown.

Grey Hill Springs stone circle.

Arizona. Development continued in the region during Pueblo II and III, particularly in the northern sector. Some archaeologists have suggested that the beginnings of the Chaco culture occurred in late Pueblo II and early Pueblo III times in the northern Cibola region at sites such as the Village of the Great Kivas, northeast of Zuni, or its forerunners. They further suggest that the organization central to the Chaco culture shifted northward into Chaco Canyon during the late eleventh century to coincide with the Chaco building spurt.

Another view suggests that a close connection existed between Chaco Canyon and Cibola and that the towns and villages of the Cibola region were full participants with Chaco Canyon during the Florescent Pueblo Bonito Phase at Chaco and therefore were Chaco outliers. Inclusion of the Cibola sites would increase the number of Chaco Canyon outliers and make more viable the concept of supportive outliers, since the Cibola region is a far more productive region than the Chaco Basin.

The Chaco Canyon–Cibola connection hypothesis adds to the dimensions of the Chacoan culture. If we accept in full the outlier concept, Chaco Canyon in its halcyon days controlled, influenced, or traded with Anasazi towns and villages located in a great arc from what is now St. Johns, Arizona, to Cortez, Colorado. It appears unlikely, however, that the smaller numbers of Chacoans actually controlled larger populations living in the more favorable environments of both the Cibola and Northern San Juan regions. The kind and extent of the relationship between Chaco Canyon and Anasazi sites outside the Chaco Basin is not yet fully understood.

Little Colorado River–Zuni Region

The Little Colorado River–Zuni region is a crescent-shaped territory extending from the Continental Divide east of Zuni, New Mexico, along the Zuni and Little Colorado River valleys to Cameron, Arizona.

Zuni

The home of the ancestral Zunis at the east end of the crescent is referred to as Cibola, from the "Seven Golden Cities of Cibola" reported by Alvar Nuñez Cabeza de Vaca. After being shipwrecked on the coast of the Gulf of Mexico in 1528, he had heard about them in his wanderings through Texas and New Mexico before his rescue. Following a reported sighting of these cities of gold in 1539 by Fray Marcus de Niza, Vázquez de Coronado mounted an expedition in 1540 to search for them, but all he found were six Zuni pueblos. These pueblos were clustered around Halona, which later became the modern Zuni Pueblo.

The east end of the Little Colorado River–Zuni region is watered by the Zuni and the Puerco rivers and has broad grass and brush-covered valleys and pinyon and juniper woodlands. It has been continuously occupied by the Anasazi and their descendants from Basket Maker to modern times.

Village of the Great Kivas

The Village of the Great Kivas located northeast of Zuni represents one of numerous twelfth-century villages located in small valleys off tributaries to the Zuni River. Archaeologist Frank H. H. Roberts excavated this site in the late 1920s and named it for its two great kivas. In addition there were eighty-six ground-floor rooms and seven small kin kivas. Most of the village's deceased inhabitants had been buried with their heads pointing either southeastward or northeastward toward points on the horizon where the sun would have risen at the winter and summer solstices. This may reflect affiliation with the Winter or Summer People as in the present-day pueblos.

Atsinna (El Morro)

By the 1200s these villages in the Cibola district increased in size, and some were built on the mesa tops. Atsinna, built on top of El Morro, was a multistored pueblo with about 1,000 rooms built around a plaza. The living area was surrounded by a heavy rectangular wall against which all the interior suites abutted. The south side may have had a gate or opening, but this has never been verified. Atsinna has a round kiva and a rectangular kiva showing perhaps influence from the neighboring Mogollon Indians. There is also a smaller ruin on the northern part of the rock, across the box canyon. When Atsinna and some of the other large pueblos in the area were abandoned, their inhabitants probably went to live in what later became historic Zuni's six towns.

El Morro lay along the trail from Zuni to Acoma and the Rio Grande valley. At El Morro's base was El Estanque del Penol—the Pool by the Great Rock—mentioned in the journal of Diego Perez de Lujan in 1583. This was one of the very few sources of water on the entire route. The Indians had apparently used this trail for centuries, leaving a variety of rock art figures along the base of the rock later covered with inscriptions by many Spanish and Anglo passersby. Juan de Oñate carved in Spanish the following inscription: "Passed by here the Adelantado Don Juan de Oñate, from the discovery of the Sea of the South, the 16th of April of 1605." After the reconquest by the Spaniards following the Pueblo Rebellion of 1680, Don Diego de Vargas inscribed the following in Spanish on Inscription Rock: "Here was the General Don Diego de Vargas who conquered for our Holy Faith, and for the Royal Crown, all of New Mexico at his own expense, year of 1692."

Other Precolumbian Anasazi sites in defensive settings were built to the south of Zuni in Pueblo IV times, but only Atsinna has been stabilized. By the late 1300s Atsinna and other eastern sites were abandoned, and the people moved into the Zuni (Halona) district. Here, during Pueblo IV, five other pueblos were constructed and were being occupied when the Spaniards arrived.

Puerco Indian Ruin

In the Petrified Forest National Park are the ruins of a Pueblo III Anasazi site called Puerco Indian Ruin. Prior to 1200 the Indians in this part of the Little Colorado River valley lived in small summer settlements, but during the 1200s they moved onto the banks of the Puerco River and constructed a rectangular 124-room pueblo around a plaza. They used sandstone masonry for a series of one-story rooms built three deep with the living quarters in the front and storage rooms in the rear. The roofs were designed as work areas, and the rooms were entered through a hatchway in the roof. These rooms were built without doors.

The Anasazi of the Little Colorado River valley occupied the southwestern border of Anasaziland where they came in contact with their Mogollon and Sinagua neighbors to the south and southwest. The square kivas of the Puerco Ruin evidence such Mogollon contact. The village was built on a small mesa with an escarpment on the south and east sides. Pecked into the "desert varnish" of many boulders tumbled from the cliff edges are numerous rock art figures, including mountain sheep and other animals, humanoid stick-men possibly representing kachinas, faces, scrolls, kachina masks, a heron holding a frog in its bill, human feet, and many abstract designs. This ruin is a feast for rock art lovers because most of the figures appear white against a dark background, making them easy to recognize.

Village of the Great Kivas on the Zuni Reservation. The site is named for two great kivas that lie outside the pueblo. Chacoanists consider the Village of the Great Kivas to have been one of the Chacoan outliers because it flourished during the 1000s and 1100s.

Atsinna Pueblo ruin atop El Morro (above). Note the outline of the rectangular pueblo built around a plaza containing a large kiva. A small portion of the northeast corner of the room blocks has been excavated. Atsinna was occupied by the Anasazi during the 1200–1300s.

El Morro: (*morro* = cliff) is a huge escarpment of rock (below) jutting into the valley lying along the ancient trail from Acoma to Zuni. On the high mesa—the cleared area at the upper left—are the ruins of Atsinna, a 1,000-room pueblo. At the base of the cliff is a permanent pool of water making El Morro a resting place for travelers, both prehistoric and historic, many of whom left graffiti on the rock now a part of El Morro National Monument.

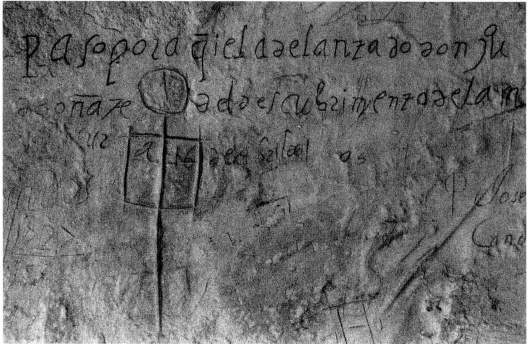

A small excavated portion of Atsinna (above) showing the large kiva in the plaza. Atsinna was defense oriented, built on a high mesa, and the ruins reveal no ground-level openings. The pueblo was abandoned by the late 1300s.

The oldest Spanish inscription (below) on Inscription Rock, El Morro National Monument is "Passed by here the Adelantado Don Juan de Oñate, from the discovery of the Sea of the South, the 16th of April of 1605."

Long before Spanish and Anglo travelers inscribed their messages on Inscription Rock, the prehistoric Anasazi pecked and incised figures of animals such as these four mountain sheep, hands, and geometrics into the rock surface. They, too, had used the great pool at the base of the rock and built pueblos on its top and in the valley nearby.

The modern Zuni Pueblo, the Halona of early Spanish accounts, was one of six Pueblos IV Zuni villages located along a twenty-five-mile stretch of the Zuni River that were occupied when the Spaniards arrived.

Excavated portions of Puerco Indian Ruins (above), part of a single-story rectangular pueblo built around a plaza with each set of living quarters consisting of three rooms attached front to back with roof-top entrances—there were no ground-floor doors. Puerco Ruin was occupied from 1100 to 1200 and again from 1300 to 1400.

Partially excavated room blocks (below) at the southwest corner of the Puerco Indian Ruins of the Petrified Forest National Park.

A portion of the beautiful and easily viewed Anasazi rock art of Puerco Indian Ruins (above).

A rock art panel (below) at Puerco Indian Ruins in Petrified Forest National Park. The figures of animals, kachina spirits, and other symbols have been pecked through the dark desert varnish on the surface of large sandstone blocks fallen from the low cliff edge.

Rock art at Newspaper Rock, Petrified Forest National Park, Arizona. Like many other such panels, this cluster of figures probably represents a shrine where the story of a past migration is probably expressed by the continuous line wandering among numerous symbols of clans and spiritual figures.

About a mile to the south of the Puerco Ruin is Newspaper Rock. This huge sandstone block is covered with petroglyphs: hand and foot prints, animals, figures, possible clan symbols, and abstract designs. The Puerco was a permanent stream with a marshy floodplain adaptable for farming and with ample brush and trees to provide a habitat for wild fowl and game, seemingly an ideal drought proof place to live; yet this pueblo was abandoned about 1350.

The Indians of the Puerco Ruin participated in the Great Migrations of the fourteenth century in which the Northern San Juan people moved to the Rio Grande valley, the Kayenta people moved southward to the Hopi Mesas, and the Zuni Indians retreated to a core of pueblos near Zuni.

Ancestral Hopi Region

The desolate, dry, forbidding Little Colorado River valley from St. Johns, Arizona, westward beyond the Petrified Forest National Park, to Holbrook and Winslow, including the southern end of the Black Mesa, is the home of the ancestral Hopis. Sites from Basket Maker III through Pueblo IV have been found scattered throughout Hopi country, and people have most certainly lived in the Little Colorado River valley for at least 10,000 years.

Hopi Mesa Sites

There are four Hopi Mesas at the south end of Black Mesa: Antelope Mesa, First Mesa, Second Mesa, and Third Mesa in order from east to west from Keams Canyon, Arizona. The Black Mesa itself extends from the Hopi Mesas north about sixty miles to Kayenta. The mesa is a great block of tilted sandstone and shale sloping to the south so that its aquifers feed the many springs at the southern edge, which is why the Hopi live there. During the 1200s (at the end of Pueblo III) a major population movement took place to the southern end of Black Mesa and into the Little Colorado River valley. Large Pueblo IV sites such as Awatovi and Oraibi were constructed on the Hopi Mesas. Others were built along the river to the south. The most likely ancestors of the

Hopi were the people from the Kayenta region, from the Grand Canyon, and from the Virgin River territory. Others came from the Little Colorado River valley from villages such as Homolovi.

During the period from 1300 to 1500 the ancestral Hopi retreated to the core area around the Antelope, First, Second, and Third mesas. The forerunners of the present-day villages were built on the slopes or in the valley bottoms. A few like Oraibi and Awatovi were built on the mesa tops. Following the Pueblo Rebellion of 1680, when they feared Spanish reprisals, pueblos like Walpi and Shongopovi were moved to the narrow mesa fingers.

Awatovi stands on Antelope Mesa south of Keams Canyon and can be visited (four-wheel drive is preferable). Pedro de Tovar was dispatched by Coronado in 1540 with seventeen horsemen from Cibola (Zuni) to seek Tusayán (Hopi). Awatovi was the first Hopi pueblo he encountered.

The kiva murals from this Pueblo IV site are outstanding and can be seen at the Museum of Northern Arizona at Flagstaff and at Harvard University's Peabody Museum.

Awatovi was the ony Hopi pueblo that accepted the Spaniards after the reconquest following the revolt, and, as a consequence, it was destroyed by enraged Hopi, probably from First Mesa, during the winter of 1700–1701. It was never reoccupied.

The modern pueblos of Walpi on First Mesa and Oraibi (the oldest continuously occupied town in the United States) on Third Mesa are particularly significant because they represent a continuous occupation from prehistoric Anasazi times. These Hopi, too, were successful in resisting Spanish Catholicism.

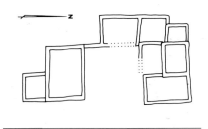

Agate House is a partially restored Pueblo III hamlet at the south end of the Petrified Forest National Park. The bright colors in the agatized wood used by the Anasazi to build this small pueblo come from iron, manganese, and carbon. The rooms were built in what is now referred to as the Rainbow Forest. Above, plan of Agate House.

239

Ancient Awatovi (above), an ancestral Hopi town on Antelope Mesa, was occupied as early as the late 1200s and is probably the first town in Hopi country to be visited by the Spaniards in 1540 and the first Hopi town to be converted to Christianity in 1629. It alone welcomed the friars back after the Pueblo Revolt of 1680 and, as a consequence, was destroyed in 1700 by the other Hopi; the men were killed and the women and children taken captive.

A portion of Awatovi (below) was excavated during the 1930s by J. O. Brew from Harvard University. The exposed rooms and walls provide a setting for the view the ancient Awatovians saw to the south from their homes.

The Homolovi ruins (above) are made up of four large Pueblo IV (1300–1540) sites situated along the Little Colorado River near Winslow, Arizona. Homolovi is recognized by the Hopi Indians as the home of some of their pre-Spanish ancestors. Unfortunately, artifact seekers have seriously vandalized these important sites thereby destroying valuable pages of human history. Virtually all of the visible depressions in the rubble mounds resulted from the pot hunters.

Dating from at least the early 1300s, Oraibi (below) on Hopi Third Mesa is the oldest continuously occupied town in the United States. Parts of the town have begun to fall into ruin as people have steadily moved out over the past eighty years. However, old Oraibi still serves as the place where a great many important ceremonies take place, for which most Third Mesa Hopi return every year.

Modern Walpi, on the Hopi First Mesa, has been continuously occupied since the Pueblo Rebellion of 1680. Prior to then Walpi stood on a lower terrace of First Mesa, closer to the valley bottom farmlands. The prehistoric Anasazi of the Kayenta, Canyon de Chelly, and many Little Colorado River sites moved into the Hopi Mesas after 1300.

Wupatki

Beyond the southwestern border of Anasaziland are sites sharing Anasazi influence, several located in the Wupatki National Monument north of the San Francisco Peaks about twenty miles from Flagstaff. This country was sparsely inhabited prior to eruption of the Sunset Crater (variously dated 1065, 1066, or 1067), which spread a blanket of cinders and ash over the Wupatki Basin. This covering caused the soil to retain ground moisture, enhancing dryland farming. The Sinagua Indians quickly expanded into this ash-covered zone where they were soon joined by Anasazi immigrants from the Kayenta region and by Mogollon and Hohokam from the south.

These easily accessible ruins lie near the loop road that winds through ponderosa pines, past Sunset Crater, north and east, down from 7,000 feet elevation through the lava beds, to 5,000 feet onto a spectacular table-land covered with multicolored sage growing out of a bed of black cinders and volcanic ash. Along the road are beautiful vistas of the Painted Desert and the Little Colorado River valley.

More than 2,000 individual sites have been found in the basin. There are the Wupatki, Wukoki, Citadel, and Lomaki pueblos and many small one-, two-, and three-room masonry units, probably used as field houses for the outlying farms. The masonry walls (sandstone blocks, three stones wide, set in mud mortar), a number of kivas, and much Kayenta pottery are hallmarks of the Anasazi.

The Wupatki Pueblo, with more than 100 rooms partially excavated, is reachable by trail a short distance from the monument headquarters (visitor center). Below the room blocks, built castle fashion on a huge rock promontory at the head of the canyon,

Wupatki (above) lies eighteen miles north of Sunset Crater, a volcano that erupted around 1064 spewing black ash over the whole landscape. The large oval structure in the foreground is a restored masonry ball court reflecting strong Hohokam influence from the south.

is a large, circular, open dance plaza that may have served the same function as the Anasazi great kivas—a community gathering place. The pueblo is Sinagua, but Hohokam influence exists here in the form of an ovoid masonry ball court. The Precolumbian game was played with a rubber ball by the Maya, Zapotec, Aztec, and other Mesoamerican Indians from very early times but on courts of different design than this one. No one yet knows how the game was played here. Wupatki Anasazi influence appears in the form of an unexcavated kiva across the canyon to the north.

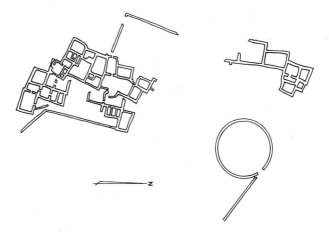

Plan of Wupatki.

Wupatki, a Sinagua village occupied from about 1120 to 1210, contains considerable evidence of Anasazi influence. In the foreground is a large dance plaza called the "amphitheater." The partially restored ruin is located near the Wupatki National Monument headquarters.

Lomaki (below), a short distance north of the Citadel and part of the same settlement, was built on the edge of an earth crack during the 1190s. It contains nine rooms, some of which were two stories tall. The only permanent source of water was the Little Colorado River some ten miles to the east.

The Citadel (above) crowns the circular butte above Nalakihu. It was a multistoried pueblo containing about fifty rooms. The defensive nature of the Citadel is evidenced by the single entrance on the south (back) side. Along the sides of the butte ancient farming terraces are still visible.

Northwest of Wupatki is the Citadel Ruin and a small pueblo named Nalakihu (below). Both were part of an Anasazi-influenced Sinagua village occupied from the late 1100s to the middle 1200s. To the south of the Citadel is the Citadel Sink, a natural water entrapment, and in the background, the San Francisco Peaks.

Wukoki was built atop a huge boulder about three miles east of Wupatki. The outlines of an ancient field can be seen across the wash in the background.

Citadel Ruin (west of the visitor center) resembles a medieval fortress. A circular wall enclosing some thirty ground-floor rooms circumscribes and caps a volcanic butte. The only entrance was a narrow opening in the wall on the south. The Citadel overlooks a large and deep depression in the ground called a sink, beyond which, on the horizon, are the San Francisco Peaks. Below the Citadel are the ruins of Nalakihu—a ten-room, single-story pueblo. On the slope of the butte between the two pueblos were several individual small rooms placed on stone-walled agricultural terraces. Their function is unknown, although they look like field houses.

From the Citadel eight other small pueblos are visible. These and other nearby habitations made up a village occupied during the twelfth and thirteenth centuries. To the north is a short spur off the loop road leading to the parking area near Box Canyon. Here along the hiking trail are three small pueblos. Lomaki, one of them, is a beautiful little building

hanging over the upper end of the canyon. Wukoki, to the east of the visitor center, is another small fortress-type pueblo located across a shallow canyon from an ancient field. A large amount of Kayenta-Anasazi pottery has been found here.

Down the valley to the east, winding through the Painted Desert, the Little Colorado River flows toward the Grand Canyon. It was the ultimate source of water for the people of Wupatki if the impounded runoff water in the canyons dried up.

About the middle of the 1200s these Sinagua-Anasazi people left the Wupatki region and moved south below the Mogollon Rim to the Verde River valley where they constructed pueblos such as Tuzigoot and Montezuma Castle.

Northern Rio
Grande Valley

The Rio Grande originates high in the San Juan Mountains west of Creede, Colorado, just across the Continental Divide from the headwaters of the San Juan River. It winds southeastward out of the Rocky Mountains to Alamosa, Colorado, and then flows southward by Taos, Espanola, Bernalillo, and Albuquerque. This region, north of Albuquerque, constitutes the northern Rio Grande valley.

In this region are Taos, San Ildefonso, Cochiti, Jemez, Santa Clara, Zia, and a number of other modern pueblos, and several excavated and partially restored Pueblo IV ruins: Puyé, Bandelier (Frijoles Canyon Ruins), Tsankawi, Pecos, and Kuaua. Pueblo IV has been referred to as the Rio Grande Classic, for it was here (and in the Acoma-Zuni-Hopi ancestral sites to the west) between 1300 and the arrival of the Spaniards that the Anasazi culture was preserved and carried into historic times.

The northern Rio Grande valley was occupied to some extent during Pueblo II and III, but toward the end of Pueblo III Anasazi populations began to move into the area from Chaco and the Northern San Juan. None of the sites actually reflects an assemblage of Chaco or Northern San Juan features. However, the migrants from Chaco and the Northern San Juan brought with them all the ingredients of the Pueblo III culture: masonry pueblos, cliff-dwelling settlements, kin kivas, great kivas, and an egalitarian social organization with a duality of ceremonial and leadership obligations.

Pueblo IV was not a time of regression of the Anasazi culture, but rather of gradual evolution and change brought about by different surroundings. Pueblo IV Anasazi culture developed and flowered in the Rio Grande valley and in the Zuni-Hopi country. The Hopi produced beautiful black-on-yellow and a polychrome yellow and red ceramics by firing with coal. Coal firing was then unique in the

New World when it was discovered by the Hopi during the early 1300s—about the same time coal was first used as a fuel in England. In the Rio Grande valley and earlier at Zuni the technique of painting pottery vessels with glaze paints heralded yet another new idea. There were other changes in the Anasazi way of life during Pueblo IV. Populations were consolidated into large pueblos, such as Puyé, Pecos, Kuaua, and Atsinna, with multistoried rooms built around large plazas. Some, like Pecos and Atsinna, were built in defensive settings to resist attack. The plazas were used for public ceremonies replacing the great kivas of Pueblo III. Kin kivas, too, were no longer in vogue; instead kiva societies whose membership cut across lineage lines built and used kivas, thus sharply reducing the number of small kivas included in the pueblos.

Unfortunately none of the prehistoric Pajarito Plateau towns (Tyuonyi and the Frijoles Canyon sites at Bandelier, Tsankawi near Los Alamos, and Puyé) is well dated. Each may have earlier construction beneath the Pueblo IV ruins that would indicate building periods extending from the 1300s into the mid-1400s. These sites, however, are representative of Pueblo IV construction in the northern Rio Grande valley.

Puyé

The Puyé Ruins, on the Santa Clara Indian Reservation located west of Espanola, New Mexico, are a combination of cliff dwellings and a mesa-top pueblo. The cliff dwellings are arranged on two levels extending for more than a mile down the Santa Clara Canyon. The dwellings in the cliffs here were different from those of Mesa Verde or Kayenta, where the dwellings were built of masonry in cliff overhangs. At Puyé and in the Frijoles Canyon at Ban-

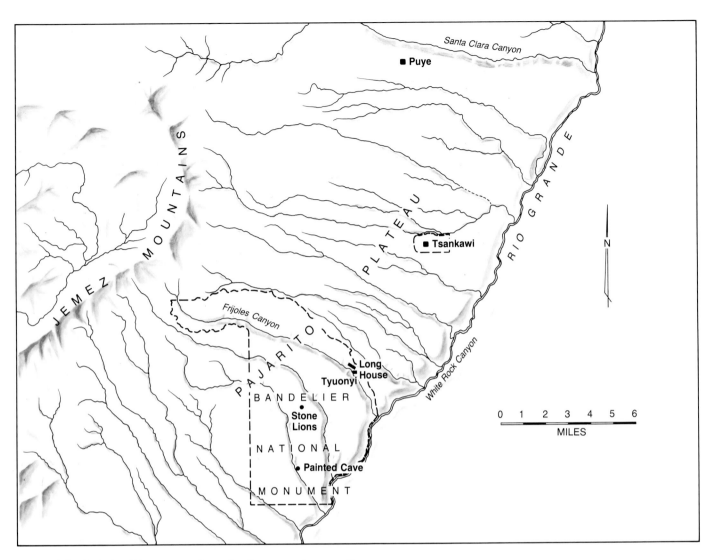

The Pajarito Plateau consists of a flat-topped mass of
whitish volcanic tuff (solidified ash) extending between
the Jemez Mountains, an ancient volcano, and the
deeply incised Rio Grande canyons. The plateau is cut
up by many deep canyons, providing a suitable
environment for Pueblo IV Anasazi to build their
pueblos and raise their crops. Puyé and Bandelier
National Monument are on the Pajarito Plateau.

248

delier, cavate rooms were carved out of the soft volcanic tuff and fronted by multistoried masonry-walled rooms. The masonry consisted of loaf-size, irregular-shaped blocks made out of porous volcanic rock.

Atop the cliff are the ruins of a large rectangular mesa-top pueblo built around an open plaza with multistoried masonry-walled rooms, and a circular kiva outside the pueblo on the east side. The pueblo contains some one thousand rooms and housed perhaps 350 families.

The archaeological data are sparse. Although Puyé was one of the first Rio Grande sites to be excavated, no detailed report of the excavation was ever published. It is impossible to say with certainty whether or not the cliff dwellings were contemporaneous with the pueblo. The cliff dwellings and the pueblo were probably constructed no earlier than the late 1300s and were abandoned before the Spaniards arrived in the mid-1500s. This apparent contemporaneous occupation of a cliff dwelling and pueblo also occurred at Frijoles Canyon, Tsankawi, and other Pajarito Plateau locations.

The evidence is circumstantial, yet it points to the conclusion that these towns combined the cliff dwelling and pueblo aspects of Anasazi culture. In addition, the pueblo–cliff dwelling dichotomy of these settlements may be evidence of the duality of social organization (Summer and Winter People) found in modern pueblos and probably during Pueblo III at Chaco Canyon and in the Northern San Juan.

Tsankawi

Tsankawi is an unexcavated Tewa ruin built upon the Pajarito Plateau, a long mesa of volcanic ash that stretches along the west side of the Rio Grande from just south of Bandelier National Monument to north of the Puyé Ruins. It encompasses Bandelier National Monument. The pueblo sits on a finger of the Tsankawi Mesa. The plan of the pueblo can still be made out—a series of room blocks around a plaza, two kivas located within the plaza, and several other kivas outside the pueblo. Like Puyé and Frijoles Canyon this Pueblo IV town combined cliff dwellings and a mesa-top pueblo. The cliffs to the south are pocked with cavate dwellings and are inscribed with rock art.

Tsankawi is a Tewa word that translates to "gap of the sharp, round cactus." The San Ildefonso Indians claim it to be one of their ancestral villages. We have no accurate dating here, but people may have lived on the mesa as early as 1150, and the

Tsankawi, a Pueblo IV town on the Pajarito Plateau east of Los Alamos (Rory Gauthier).

pueblo and adjoining cliff dwellings were occupied into very early historic times.

Immigrants from the Four Corners began to settle on the Pajarito Plateau in the early 1300s, when they built scattered settlements on the mesa tops. Later, as their numbers increased, larger settlements were built until finally they occupied towns such as Frijoles Canyon, Tsankawi, and Puyé.

Bandelier–Frijoles Canyon

The most heavily visited Anasazi ruins in Bandelier National Monument west of Santa Fe, New Mexico, lie in Frijoles Canyon near the park headquarters. The ruins fall into two major categories—those situated on the valley floor, such as Tyuonyi, and those built along the base of the cliff on the north side of the canyon. Both the valley floor pueblo and the cliff dwellings are Pueblo IV, built after the Great Migration of 1300, probably by migrants from the Northern San Juan. The canyon was abandoned prior to the arrival of the Spaniards in the early 1500s.

Text continued on page 254

The Puyé Pueblo was about half excavated many years ago. The green sage-covered area to the right of the plaza contains unexcavated room blocks. Note the great kiva at the lower end of the pueblo. (Photograph taken with the assistance of John Q. Royce.)

Puyé Ruins are a combination of cliff dwellings and mesa top pueblo. This Pueblo IV (1300 to historic times) site was probably built by Anasazi who migrated from the Northern San Juan to the northern Rio Grande valley. These Indians lived both on the top of the mesa in multistory room blocks surrounding a plaza and along and in the cliff face, with a total of 1,000 rooms housing 2,000 people. These ruins are located in the Santa Clara Indian Reservation near Española, New Mexico. (Photograph taken with the assistance of John Q. Royce.)

Restored second-story room (above) in the Puyé Pueblo.

Restored two-story cliff dwelling (below), Puyé. The horizontal rows of holes in the cliff on either side mark where other buildings stood.

Frijoles Canyon, Bandelier National Monument Visitor
Center, and Frijoles Canyon ruins, with the Jemez
Mountains in the background.

252

Model showing what Tyuonyi might have looked like during the fourteenth and fifteenth centuries when the Anasazi lived there. A single narrow passage allowed entrance to the inner plaza from the outside. Three subterranean kivas lay beneath the north side of the plaza.

Tyuonyi Pueblo with 300 ground-floor rooms in tiers from three to eight deep and two and three stories high, arranged around a plaza, housed some 500 people. Three kivas were built on the north side of the plaza. The pueblo and the cliff dwellings were probably occupied simultaneously, and all belong to Pueblo IV (1300–1540). (Photograph taken with the assistance of John Q. Royce.)

Frijoles Canyon, Bandelier National Monument. In the foreground is a large kiva, the first ruin on the trail to the Frjoles Canyon ruins. Next on the trail is the Tyuonyi Pueblo. Further on are dwellings along the cliff base; three (of more than thirteen) house units have been excavated and partially restored. The largest cliff site is Long House. These habitations make up a Pueblo IV town built after 1300 by Anasazi and their descendants who migrated from the Northern San Juan and Chaco Canyon regions to the northern Rio Grande valley. (Photograph taken with the assistance of John Q. Royce.)

Tyuonyi is the largest of several ruins on the valley floor. More than 300 ground-floor rooms are arranged around a central plaza in tiers ranging from three to eight deep. Each row of rooms, like the spokes of a wheel, seems to represent the suite of rooms occupied by a household. Additional second- and third-story rooms would have brought the total room count to between 450 and 500, providing housing for up to 500 people. The arrangement of these rooms follows the standard Anasazi pattern, although the corners of the building are rounded by creating pie-shaped room blocks. The builders used rough blocks of volcanic lava and tuff laid in abundant mud mortar to construct these buildings. Three circular underground kivas lay beneath the north end of the plaza. Only one has been excavated; the other two are marked by visible depressions.

People could enter the plaza only through a narrow passageway between tiers of rooms on the east side. Provisions existed to constrict this passage if necessary. Since all the suites of rooms opened onto the plaza, the inhabitants of Tyuonyi were protected against unwanted visitors.

The name *Tyuonyi* means "olla" in the Keresan

A restored house block of the Sun House cliff dwelling, a part of the Talus House ruin, located opposite Tyuonyi. These reconstructed rooms illustrate the appearance of all the Pajarito Plateau cliff sites when the Anasazi lived in them.

Pueblo language. The residents of Cochiti Pueblo, who speak Keresan, apply the name *Tyuonyi* to their ancestral town, now the ruins in the Frijoles Canyon, including the pueblo and over two miles of ruins along the north cliffs.

The cliffs in Frijoles Canyon are formed of massive deposits of volcanic tuff, the same material the Anasazi used to the build masonry walls at Tyuonyi and along the cliffs. The Pueblo IV peoples built houses against this north cliff and even burrowed into the soft tuff face to form additional rooms. Consequently, visitors can see the bases of masonry-walled rooms constructed in front of the cliff, and rectangular doorways leading into rooms carved wholly out of the tuff.

Paved trails lead visitors past three of some thirteen housing units lining more than two miles of the north cliff. Directly behind Tyuonyi are ruins labeled Sun House and Snake Village by Edgar L. Hewett, who excavated the Frijoles Canyon sites around 1910. Sun House was named after the sun symbol pecked onto the rock face near the top of the cliff above it. The ruin consists of twenty-eight known rooms plus maybe half again as many that have completely collapsed. A low terrace in front of the rooms probably served as a dance plaza.

Snake Village was named after the figure of a feathered serpent painted on the plastered wall of a kiva hollowed out of the cliff. It was considerably larger than Sun House, with many rooms carved out of the volcanic tuff. One series of seven such rooms was all interconnected inside the rock itself. Some cavate rooms have been finished by constructing a masonry wall across the opening, leaving a small rectangular doorway with a smokehole above it. A small block of rooms has been restored by the National Park Service.

The largest contiguous talus ruin has been named Long House. In reality its 356 rooms belong to five distinct room clusters. One cluster has a kiva, and the other four each had a second-story dance plaza on the roofs of dwellings plus distinctive rock art motifs. The rooms were built from one to four deep in front of the cliff and terraced up to three levels. One set of rooms was even stacked four high. Even though most of the buildings have collapsed, visitors can still see the masonry wall bases and the many marks on the cliff face left from the houses. Most of the rock art figures pecked into the cliff face require the right lighting conditions to be seen. They in-

Text continued on page 258

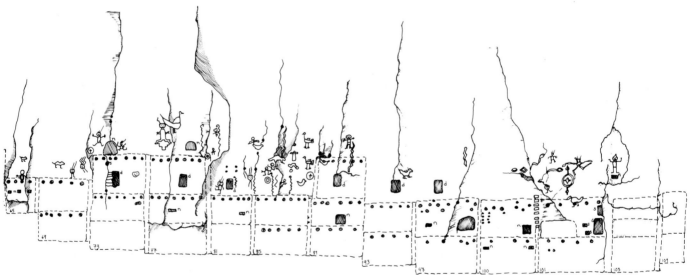

Long House Ruin in Frijoles Canyon (above) has 356 rooms that make up five room clusters. This pueblo had rooms built from one to four deep in front of the cliff and three to four stories high.

A sketch of the cliff wall and a portion of Long House (below) in Frijoles Canyon, Bandelier National Monument, showing the outlines of now collapsed rooms with attendant roof beam sockets, niches, rock art, and doorways and smoke holes into rooms carved wholly within the cliff. (Drawing by Lisa Ferguson.)

256

The flat roofs over many second-story rooms (above) provide a platform suitable for conducting ceremonies in front of a major panel of rock art. Perhaps such decorated "plazas" in the Pueblo IV communities of the Pajarito Plateau had begun to replace the older kin kivas. (Drawing by Lisa Ferguson.)

Some of the Long House rooms (below) were dug partially out of the soft tuff of the cliff face. These partial cavates show evidence of painted interior walls and ceilings blackened from ancient fires.

This macaw, a bird imported from Mesoamerica by the Anasazi, appears on the cliff face above a small talus ruin just to the west of Long House. For hundreds of years the Anasazi had contact with other southwestern tribes and the Indians of Mexico.

clude faces (masks), kachina (humanoid) figures, animals, birds, serpents, shields, and some geometric forms.

A so-called Ceremonial Cave is found near the west end of the talus ruins. This most impressive natural cave is situated 150 feet above El Rito de los Frijoles and is reached by a complicated trail including ninety feet of ladders. Inside the cave is a very well-preserved kiva, whose roof has been restored, and evidence for more than twenty-two masonry-walled rooms. The name *Ceremonial Cave* is a misnomer since the many rooms suggest that Pueblo IV people lived in the cave and simply used the kiva for their kin-group rituals.

The Bandelier National Monument visitor center is situated on El Rito de los Frijoles at the bottom of Frijoles Canyon, some ten miles south of Los Alamos. A self-guided trail takes the visitor west from the center along the canyon past the big kiva, Tyuonyi Pueblo, and several excavated cliff dwell-

Ceremonial Cave (actually a habitation site) in Frijoles Canyon, 150 feet above the canyon floor reached by 90 feet of ladders, contains a small restored kin kiva and the remains of numerous dwelling rooms.

ings including Talus House (Sun House and Snake Village), Long House, and the Ceremonial Cave.

Bandelier's Living Shrines

Two sites within Bandelier National Monument take on a very special interest for students of archaeology. Not only are these two sites excellent examples of prehistoric Anasazi shrines, but they both continue in use today as active shrines. Both are maintained by the Indian inhabitants of Cochiti Pueblo, which helps to confirm the inferred cultural continuity from the pre-Spanish Anasazi culture to the culture of the historic Pueblo Indians of New Mexico and Arizona.

One of these shrines, the Stone Lions, lies on the mesa top three miles southwest of Tyuonyi. The figures of two crouching mountain lions (pumas) have been carved into the top of volcanic tuff boulders protruding slightly out of the ground. This gives the appearance of the lion figures crouching on the ground surface. Each animal is about six feet long, including two feet of tail. The lions face southeast in the southwest portion of a stone enclosure formed with large volcanic tuff blocks, many of them standing up to five feet tall. The enclosure forms a rounded pentagon about twenty feet across. A similar stone-lined passageway leads directly southward for sixteen feet from the southeast corner of the enclosure, providing proper ritual access.

Old photographs show traces of vandalism, but the shrine has survived and continues in use. Our photographs taken in 1983 show an oval ring of antlers encircling the crouching lions. Most are deer antlers, but several elk antlers also were included. Within the circle of antlers and between the two lions lies a concentration of pottery fragments, obsidian and chert flakes, lumps of volcanic basalt, several crow feathers, and a fragment of cotton cloth. A bovine leg bone and a limpet shell with a feather occupy a central position between the lions, while a dance headdress made from the skull and antlers of a pronghorn antelope stands between the ends of the tails. Twenty-six tiny pouches of cloth in four colors—red, black, white, and yellow—are tied on a string around the trunk of a pinyon tree growing out of the stone enclosure's southwest corner. This tree's overhanging branches support two feather prayer plumes above the lions.

Proximity of the Stone Lion shrine to the pre-Spanish Pueblo IV village of Yapashe argues for the first use of the shrine while the village was inhabited.

Stone Lion Shrine in Bandelier National Monument: two crouching mountain lions carved in prehistoric times from a volcanic tuff boulder, and encircled by whitened deer and elk antlers within a low stone enclosure, make up a living shrine still in use by the Indians of Cochiti Pueblo.

The lions actually face toward the ruin. Most of the pottery fragments represent Pueblo IV styles, although they could have been picked up much later. The name *Yapashi* refers specifically to the shrine enclosure.

In Pueblo Indian religion, the mountain lion spirit provides important assistance to hunters and represents the direction north. The Stone Lion shrine lies less than one-half mile northwest of the village of Yapashe where the historic Cochiti say their ancestors lived. During historic times, people from many pueblos in the Rio Grande valley and from as far away as Zuni have visited this shrine.

The second shrine consists of many figures painted on the back wall of a symmetrical rock shelter or cave located in the north cliff of Capulin Canyon about three miles south of Yapashe and the Stone Lions shrine. Painted Cave is roughly thirty feet above the base of the volcanic tuff cliff that must have been climbed by supplicants using a series of hand and toeholds. The route enters the cave at its west end through a small room cut partly into the cliff and decorated with layered rows of red dots, diamonds, triangles, and zigzags with a star near the center. Within the cave itself, most of which can be seen from the valley floor below, are numerous painted figures rendered in red, white, and black. The paintings include many recognizable kachina

An enclosure of large tuff boulders surrounds the Stone Lion Shrine leaving a lined passageway leading south out of the extreme left of the picture. Modern-day offerings have also been placed around the trunk and in the branches of the tree growing out of the enclosure.

figures and kachina masks, human-like figures behind large shields, cloud and lightning symbols, various animals such as wolves and a snail, some Christian symbolism, several monster-like figures, men on horseback, and many others whose meaning is less apparent. Many of the figures such as a church, bell, humans on horseback, and an elk drawn in perspective are clearly of post-Spanish origin, but several others could easily predate the Spaniards' arrival. They at least reflect pre-Hispanic motifs and ideas. In the floor of the cave were pecked depressions from three to nine inches in diameter plus engraved outlines of both moccasins and shoes and the tracks of turkeys. A room cut into the base of the cliff below the Painted Cave contains a number of grinding slabs and hand stones.

Text continued on page 263

Painted Cave in Capulin Canyon of Bandelier National Monument contains many figures painted in a variety of colors by Pueblo Indians from late prehistoric times down to the present day. Like many prehistoric rock art panels, this cliff recess houses an important shrine.

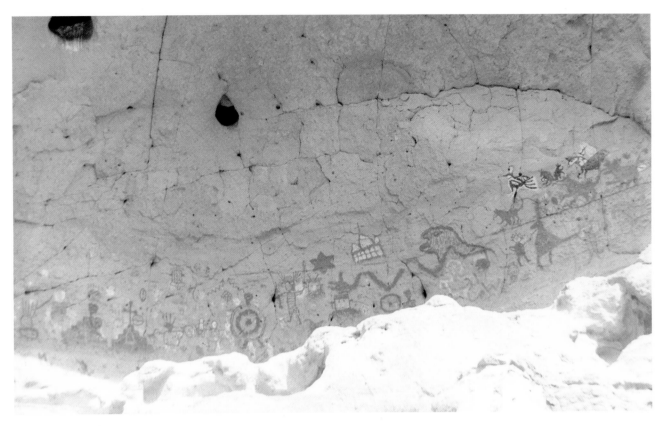

Painted Cave figures include kachina figures and masks, humanoid figures, Christian symbols, and monster figures. These figures are part of a living Indian shrine that has been embellished and added to from Pueblo IV Anasazi to recent times.

This small recess in Painted Cave displays rows of geometric figures that may have been painted by prehistoric Anasazi.

Painted Cave detail of a monster, animals, kachina masks, and humanoid figures.

Since both these shrines are still used by modern Pueblo peoples, they should be treated as sacred places. Visitors should not enter the sacred portions nor remove any objects from the shrines. The National Park Service preserves the context for these shrines, both of which serve as more than religious places. They provide direct links to a long history reaching far beyond the beginning of written records in the Anasazi Southwest.

Pecos

The Pecos Ruin stands on the Pecos National Monument located about twenty-five miles southeast of Santa Fe, New Mexico. Indians lived in the Pecos River valley in scattered settlements as early as 1100. By 1300 room blocks of one or two stories had been built at Pecos, and by 1450 Pecos Pueblo had reached maximum size. It was a large, quadrangular, multi-storied village. In 1591, Castano de Sosa described the pueblo:

> The houses in this pueblo are in the manner of houseblocks. They have doors to the outside all around, and the houses are back to back. The houses are four and five stories. In the galleries there are no doors to the streets. They go up little ladders that can be pulled up by hand through the hatchways. Every house has three or four apartments so that from top to bottom each house has fifteen or sixteen rooms. The rooms are worthy of note, being well whitewashed. . . .

The pueblo probably housed some 2,500 Indians.

Little excavation has been done on the original or North Pueblo, but four kivas have been partially restored. This unit lies at the north end of a low ridge. Between the North Pueblo and the excavated and restored mission church and convento, the South Pueblo forms a linear block of rooms that have been partially excavated. The South Pueblo may have been constructed after the arrival of the Spaniards. Between the two pueblos is a restored kiva. A low wall, hardly high enough to be a major defensive structure, encircles the ridge. The people dumped their trash down the ridge between the pueblos and the

The ruins of the stabilized Pecos South Pueblo are located on the south end of the ridge next to the ruins of the church and convento. A wall encircled the ancient town. Unexcavated mounds cover the ridge to the north at the end of which is the unexcavated ruin of the North Pueblo (Cicuyé). Visitor trails lead from the Pecos National Monument headquarters through the ruins of the church, convento, and pueblo. Pecos was a Pueblo IV–V Towa town begun around 1300 and completed by 1450. It was abandoned because of severe population loses from diseases such as smallpox brought by the Spaniards and the raids of Plains Comanche Indians. (Photograph taken with the assistance of John Q. Royce.)

wall. As the space filled, it became necessary from time to time to extend the wall outward.

Pecos Pueblo was located in a strategic spot between the Pueblo villages of the northern Rio Grande, and the hunting tribes of the Great Plains. The Pecos people traded grain to the Plains Indians for meat and hides. This was a mixed blessing, however, because continuous raids by the Apache, and especially the Comanche, and smallpox finally forced the few remaining Pecos Indians to abandon the pueblo and move westward.

The Franciscan order of monks established the first of four mission churches at Pecos. It was known to be standing by 1625, but we do not know when it was built. The Nuestra Señora de los Angeles de Porciuncula, Pecos was started shortly after the convento was completed and furnished in 1663. The mission was burned at the time of the Pueblo Revolt of 1680, shortly after which the Indians built a large kiva in what had been the convento courtyard.

Alfred V. Kidder excavated the South Pueblo, the mission churches, and the convento between 1915 and 1929. As Richard B. Woodbury observes, "The Pecos excavations started a new era in American archaeology by showing the importance of stratigraphic information for reconstructing cultural history and by emphasizing the recovery of data over the collection of objects for museums" (Woodbury

Ruins of Pecos Mission and Convento. The Franciscan Order of monks established the first of four mission churches, Nuestra Senora de los Angeles de Porciuncula, Pecos, sometime before 1625. The convento was built and furnished sometime around 1663. The first church was burned during the Pueblo Revolt of 1680 and replaced by a new one when the Spaniards returned. (Photograph taken with the assistance of John Q. Royce.)

Pecos convento plaza showing the restored kiva in the foreground. At the time of the Pueblo Revolt of 1680, the Pueblos burned the church and built a kiva in the plaza.

1981:15). Here in 1927, at the invitation of Kidder, a conference of archaeologists agreed upon the designations for the Anasazi stages: Basket Maker I, II, and III followed by Pueblo I through V, covering Pueblo Indian history to 1870.

Pecos is a beautiful and easily visited site just off I-25 east of Santa Fe. The kiva in the convento courtyard, has been restored, and one can climb down into it. A trail leads from the visitor center through the church and convento ruins past the South Pueblo. The boundary wall of the pueblos has been partially restored on the east side. Between the South Pueblo and the North Pueblo is another restored kiva. The trail leads around the unexcavated mounds of the North Pueblo and back to the visitor center.

Like the pueblos and mission churches of Salinas, Pecos was part of the eastern periphery of Anasaziland.

Kuaua

Kuaua could well be named the "Ruins of the Kiva Murals" because of the spectacular mural reproductions on the walls of Kiva III in the south courtyard. During the 1934 to 1939 investigation and restoration of this Pueblo IV site, archaeologists discovered eighty-seven layers of plaster in the kiva with multicolored murals on some of the layers. Kiva III had been plastered, painted, and replastered over a period of more than two hundred years. The dazzling murals at Kuaua and those we have mentioned from the kivas at Awatovi (on the Hopi Mesas) and the Hopi-like paintings of Pottery Mound on the Puerco River may, Richard B. Woodbury suggests, be only the lucky survivors of a great flowering of art in Pueblo IV times. The similarity of style and subject matter of the paintings at these three sites may indicate a southwestern religious pattern built on a widespread symbolism of birds, serpents, animals, and deities.

The first portion of Kuaua was established around 1300 when the small pueblo on the south side (called the Lummis section) was built. These forty rooms included two kivas in the room blocks. The round kivas in the courtyard to the north and the pottery indicate that the original construction may have been by the Anasazi migrants from the Northern San Juan; the rectangular kivas in the courtyards and in the room blocks together with glaze-painted pottery suggest that they were soon joined by Mogollon or other Anasazi peoples from the Little Colorado River valley.

Kuaua, Tiwa for "evergreen", is now a part of the Coronado State Monument at Bernalillo, New Mexico. It was one of the Tiguex (Tiwa) towns, so called by the Spaniards, in the region near Albuquerque. The town was built from south to north, creating a rectangular pueblo surrounding three plazas with a total of five courtyard kivas and more than 1,200 rooms. The room blocks were constructed of adobe bricks laid in courses producing housing units several stories high. The oldest section of the pueblo includes the plaza to the south with two round kivas and the square Kiva III containing the painted murals. This section burned around 1350 and was rebuilt, and then it may have been abandoned from about 1400 to 1475. Evidence suggests that the burning resulted from a raid or warfare.

The north and east buildings and plazas were completed in the late 1400s.

Kuaua was still occupied at the time Coronado and his army arrived in New Mexico in 1540, but it had been abandoned by the time of the second Spanish expedition in 1581.

The excavation and restoration of Kuaua was done under the direction of Gordon Vivian and supported by the School of American Research, the Museum of New Mexico, and the University of New Mexico. The most significant part of the project, however, was the transfer of all of the plaster layers from Kiva III to the laboratory at the University of New Mexico, where each layer was peeled off and preserved. At that time the murals from Layer N-41 (the forty-sixth layer) were reproduced on portions of the west, south, and east walls, and the murals from Layer G-26 (the sixty-first layer) were reproduced on portions of the east, north, and west walls. The original murals are now displayed in the Coronado State Monument Museum.

A Zuni interpretation of the iconography of the Kuaua kiva murals suggests the identity and interpretation of some of it, but as with all ancient Anasazi rock art, no one knows what it means. Layer N-41 mural begins on the west wall just to the right of the ingress ladder and represents (Zuni interpretation) a winter ceremony including, counterclockwise: a duck or *Eya*, *Paiyatuma* with a rabbit stick under his wing, a goose or *Owa*, *Ka'nashkule* (priest-clown) with a rain altar above his head, Gray *Newekwe* with jimson weed, *Ko'kothlanna*, the great god, surrounded by falling rain, yellow deer or *Maawi*, and a stalk of black corn.

Layer G-26 depicts the universe with major gods symbolizing planting, weather control, and hunting. Counterclockwise from the east wall are: a deer (without head), rain jar and bat, *Shulawitsi*, the Fire God, rattlesnake and eagle, Yellow Corn Maiden, Blue Corn Maiden, eagle spewing seeds, and Lightning Man (pages 267–269).

Salinas

Las Salinas was a seventeenth-century Spanish Mission–Indian pueblo combination that failed before the Pueblo Revolt of 1680. The Franciscan friars, subsidized by the viceroy of New Spain, were dispatched from Mexico to Christianize the Indians of New Mexico. After the Indians had been subjugated by force, the friars had them build missions within, or next to, existing pueblos around what is now

Kuaua Ruin in the Coronado State Monument near Bernalillo, New Mexico. The block of rooms to the right of the visitor's center was the first constructed—probably by the Anasazi migrants from the Northern San Juan—early in Pueblo IV, around 1300. Next constructed were the buildings around the west plaza (to the right in the photograph) with the three kivas in the plaza: two round kivas and the restored covered rectangular kiva that contains the most spectacular known kiva murals. Room blocks were subsequently built around plazas making a total of 1,200 rooms and five courtyard kivas in the town. The pueblo was occupied when the Spaniards arrived in 1540 but had been abandoned when they returned in 1581. (Photograph taken with the assistance of John Q. Royce.)

Mountainair, New Mexico. The missions were completed by 1630. The missions and the pueblos were abandoned before 1680. Although the pueblos had been occupied for hundreds of years, the joint occupation lasted less than fifty years. The Spaniards and the Pueblo Indians departed, never to return.

The salt flats east of Mountainair, near Willard, are the remnants of a huge lake that filled the Estancia Basin 20,000 years ago. The salt left after the lake dried up was a trade commodity both for the prehistoric people and the Spaniards who gave the region the name Las Salinas. The Salinas Pueblo ruins include three Indian pueblos with Spanish mission sites: Gran Quivira, Abó, and Quarai. They make up the Salinas National Monument.

There is evidence of prehistoric occupation of the Estancia Valley going back as much as 10,000 to 12,000 years and of an occupation by sedentary people from Basket Maker times. Mogollon-style pottery, jacal walls, and pithouses lead us to believe that the region was occupied by Mogollon peoples from about 500 through 1000. Anasazi and additional Mogollon folk arrived sometime in the late 1200s or early 1300s and built Gran Quivira, Quarai, Abó, and other pueblos. They came from the northern Rio Grande and perhaps from the Cibola district.

The kiva walls at Kuaua are painted with beautiful restorations of many figures painted by the Kuauans over many decades. In the southwest corner is pictured a human figure that may be a priest-clown next to a goose and duck. This was part of the forty-sixth repainting. The originals are displayed in the museum building.

Yellow deer, black corn, and a headless deer. Over the centuries, the Kuaua Indians repainted the walls of this kiva some eighty-seven times, each time painting over their previous work, sometimes with murals and sometimes without.

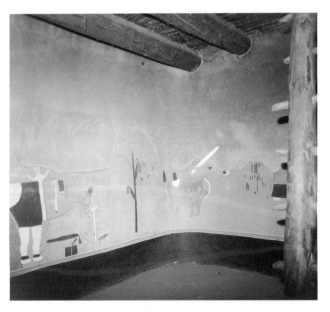

During Pueblo IV there was a burgeoning of Anasazi kiva painting in the Rio Grande valley and the Little Colorado River valley. The murals at the Coronado State Park (Kuaua), both the originals in the museum and the restorations in the kiva, are accessible to visitors.

Bertha P. Dutton describes these figures in her book *Sun Father's Way* as an eagle spewing seeds and Lightning Man.

This may be a depiction of the gods of planting, weather, and hunting (sixty-first repainting) showing a rain jar and bat, Fire God, rattlesnake and eagle, and Corn Maiden.

The Indians of Quarai spoke the southern Tiwa language, while those of Abó and Gran Quivira spoke the Tompiro language, both belonging to the Tanoan language family. These settlements seem to have been typical Pueblo IV towns with masonry walls, contiguous residential rooms (built around plazas) in which kin kivas were situated. Gran Quivira was the largest of these, as large as Pecos, housing perhaps 3,000 people in Pueblo IV times.

The Salinas Pueblos occupied the southeastern frontier of the Pueblo IV Anasazi distribution. These people traded salt, corn, and cotton cloth to the nomadic Indians to the east (called the Jumanos by the Spaniards) for buffalo meat and hides. Because of the presence of these nomadic trading Indians at Gran Quivira, it was referred to by the Spaniards as the *"Pueblo de las Humanas."*

The Salinas Pueblos were initially bypassed by Coronado and his army, but the Spanish incursion had a secondary effect. It may have precipitated the movement of Hopi and Zuni peoples from the west into the Salinas district in the middle 1540s. They brought the practice of cremation and influenced the development of Tabirá pottery.

The Spanish friars arrived in the 1620s and began building mission churches. Dry weather, white man's diseases, demands of the missionaries, a feudal system based on encomiendas requiring the Indians to pay an annual tribute of cotton cloth or corn, and raids by the Apaches resulted in the gradual aban-

donment of the Salinas pueblos in the 1670s. Many died of starvation. Those who survived joined pueblos along the Rio Grande or migrated to the El Paso region. These pueblos were never reoccupied after the Pueblo Revolt of 1680.

Gran Quivira

Located twenty-six miles south of Mountainair, New Mexico, Gran Quivira occupies a dry limestone hill, at an elevation of 6,600 feet, between Chupadero Mesa to the west and the Gallinas Mountains to the east. By some trick of fate, this impoverished village where some 450 people died of starvation in 1668, got the name of "Quivira"—the legendary city of gold in Kansas that was the object of Coronado's expedition in the 1540s.

The site contains seventeen house mounds, nine kivas, the historic ruins of the chapel of San Isidro (built between 1629 and 1631), and the San Buenaventura Mission (page 271). The masonry of the pueblo room blocks was poor; the walls were haphazardly constructed and the mortar was weak. Because of this poor construction, the maximum height could not have been more than two stories.

Excavated House A, just east of San Buenaventura Mission, was built over the remains of older construction. Gordon Vivian suggests the other mounds may also represent at least two periods of construction, some of which may have occurred in historic times. More likely the earlier construction took place in Pueblo IV during the 1300s, and the later was Pueblo V. The plan was generally rectangular construction facing a plaza. Most of the ground-floor suites or apartments consisted of three rooms. This pattern of construction is similar to that of Pecos, Bandelier, and Puyé. We have previously discussed the concept of suites for family units in connection with Mug House and other towns at Mesa Verde, Chaco Canyon, Pecos, and other pueblos during Pueblo III an IV.

The room blocks at Gran Quivira were scattered around the hillside with plaza areas containing detached circular kivas between the small pueblos. These kivas were probably not kin-group kivas like those built during Pueblo III at Mesa Verde, but more likely they were similar to the society kivas found in the modern Pueblos. Five interior rooms in Mound 7 show some ceremonial characteristics. The doors were plugged, and the walls contained several coats of plaster. The courtyard kivas appear to have been destroyed some years before the abandonment. This suggests the Indians adapted the in-

269

Gran Quivira (also called "Pueblo de Las Humanas") in Salinas National Monument from the east. The Pueblo was begun in early Pueblo IV times, around 1300, along with neighboring Abó, Quarai, and several other towns. These settlements occupied a province called Las Salinas by the Spaniards after a nearby salt basin. Spanish friars moved into the towns during the 1620s and directed Indian laborers to build mission churches. San Isidro chapel, to the left, was built between 1629 and 1631. The kivas in the foreground were probably not kin-group kivas but rather were more akin to the modern Pueblo kiva society structures. Kiva F, the large one with benches around the inside may have been a great kiva. (Photograph taken with the assistance of John Q. Royce.)

terior rooms to serve as kivas after the missionaries forced them to fill their old kivas. In this way the Indians, unknown to the friars, could secretly perform their old rituals.

Kiva D in the plaza south of Mound 7 has been excavated. It was a circular kiva seventeen feet in diameter, dug to a depth of eight or nine feet. Its roof was supported by four upright poles. The fire pit was in the center and the above-floor ventilator was installed on the east side. This east-west axis is typical of the kivas at Gran Quivira and resembles the typical Mogollon orientation rather than the Anasazi southern one. The use of this style kiva through Pueblo IV may indicate a continuity of, or influence by, Mogollon peoples, or a population mix similar to that of Chaco Canyon and Aztec in earlier times.

Kiva F located in the East Plaza approaches a great kiva in size—more than thirty-five feet in diameter—with a low, wide bench around the walls. Beneath the rectangular room blocks of Mound 7, at the center of the excavated ruins, is a circular pueblo of over two hundred rooms with a kiva (Kiva C) in the center. Although smaller, this pueblo was constructed in much the same manner as the circular pueblos, Tyuonyi, at Bandelier and Peñasco Blanco at Chaco Canyon. This older construction, dating from the 1300s, had substantially better masonry than the later structure on top.

San Buenaventura Mission (church and convento) in the foreground built on the west side of Gran Quivira Pueblo. The Pueblo town contained seventeen house mounds, only two of which have been excavated, and at least nine kivas. It was constructed during both Pueblo IV (before the arrival of the Spaniards) and Pueblo V. Most of the apartments consisted of three rooms facing a plaza. The mission and pueblo were abandoned prior to the Pueblo Revolt of 1680. (Photograph taken with the assistance of John Q. Royce.)

Abó

Abó, a Tompiro Pueblo IV–V ruin, is situated about nine miles west of Mountainair, New Mexico, and is part of the Salinas National Mounment.

It was only after a six-day battle in 1601 that the Spaniards, under the command of Vincente de Zaldivar, were able to overcome the resistance of the Indians from Abó, Quarai, and perhaps other pueblos. Less than thirty years later San Gregorío de Abó Mission was built by the Franciscan missionaries— or more precisely, by the Pueblo Indians directed by the friars—next to the northeast side of the pueblo. The Indians of Abó got along well with the Franciscans as evidenced by the many Tompiros who retreated with the Spaniards to settlements near El Paso when the Salinas pueblos began to decline in the 1670s. By the time of the Pueblo Revolt of

1680, Abó and all the Salinas pueblos had been abandoned.

The mission church and attached convento buildings were excavated in the 1930s by J. H. Toulouse, but he left the pueblo ruins virtually untouched. Toulouse did find a kiva in the courtyard of the mission built about the same time as the church.

The excavated mission complex is fenced and open to the public. To the west and southwest of the Abó Misson and straddling the arroyo lie the rubble remains of a sizeable pueblo. In the late 1800s Adolph Bandelier was told by local residents that portions of three-story buildings once stood in parts of the historic pueblo. Two- and three-story buildings surrounding a long rectangular plaza along the east side of the arroyo mark the houses of the Abó

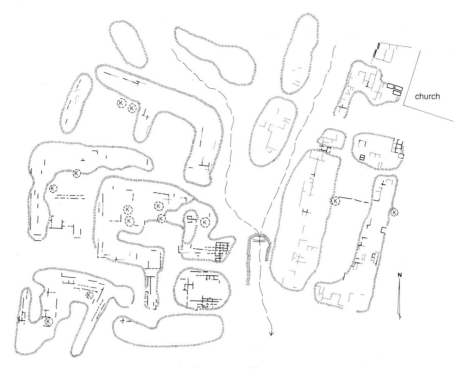

church

Ground plan (above) of the rubble house mounds at Abó Pueblo in the Salinas region at which the Spaniards established a mission church. The mounds lying east of the arroyo and nearest the church represent the historic Tompiro Pueblo laid out in a large rectangle around a central plaza. West of the arroyo are the many house mounds of the earlier pre-Spanish pueblo.

Only the mission church and convento at Abó have been excavated (below), at the Salinas National Monument pueblo of Abó. The Pueblo V unexcavated ruin lies in the background extending to the arroyo, while earlier Pueblo IV mounds lie to the right of the arroyo and range beyond the picture.

Indians during Spanish colonial times. Two rooms, excavated in 1981–82, may be seen on the south side of the northern mound in this complex. Several kivas were located within the plaza and along the east side of the pueblo. Sometime during the 1800s, Spanish colonists constructed several houses—one on the west side of the plaza and another on the southeast mound—with stones gathered from ruins of the Indian pueblo.

Across the arroyo to the west are numerous low rubble mounds representing the prehistoric Abó Pueblo, first established around 1300. Most of these buildings stood only one-story high. They were arranged around small plazas and courtyards where kivas were located, presenting plans resembling the letters L and E. None have been excavated. Artifical catchments along the arroyo and unreliable springs in the canyon to the south provided water to the occupants of both pueblos.

Abó's location served as a hub for trails connecting with the other Salinas pueblos, with the Rio Grande valley to the west, and with the Great Plains to the east. Consequently, Abó became a trading center for products from all three regions, exchanging locally produced pottery, salt, and pinyon nuts for such items as obsidian and chalcedony (to make tools); buffalo meat and hides; and turquoise, shell, macaw feathers, and copper bells for personal adornment and ritual needs. The Spaniards exploited this trade network to amass these same items for shipment south into Spanish Mexico. They may have built the complex of rooms around the walled yard attached to the west side of the church in which to store and load the goods on ox-cart trains.

Diseases introduced by the Spanish, raiding Apaches from the plains, and droughts decimated the Indian population of the Salinas pueblos. By the 1670s, the last remaining inhabitants abandoned their homes and moved southward to the vicinity of El Paso, Texas.

Quarai

Located a few miles north of Mountainair, Quarai Pueblo and Mission occupies one of the most picturesque settings in the Southwest. The Indian pueblo began during very late Pueblo III and was continuously occupied throughout Pueblo IV and V, until general abandonment of the Salinas region in the 1670s. At its peak, masonry room blocks enclosed at least six plazas with kivas. The rooms standing up to three stories high were constructed of the bright red Abó sandstone. A few of the later rooms, located just north of the small church, have been excavated.

Adolf Bandelier estimated that some 600 people occupied Quarai Pueblo. They probably farmed in the broad valley to the west and on terraced hillsides to the north and south. Permanent springs in the wash provided water and may have irrigated terraces on the floodplain downstream to the east. Residents of Quarai imported obsidian and chalcedony from the Rio Grande valley to manufacture a wide variety of tools. Styles of arrowpoints and hide scrapers indicate strong influence from the plains.

Fray Estebán de Perea began construction of *La Purísimna Concepción* church in 1628. Together with the convento or friar house, storerooms, workshops, and other buildings, the church constituted the mission of Quarai. The ruins of the mission have been excavated and may be visited as a part of Salinas National Monument.

Quarai was abandoned in 1674 by its Tiwa-speaking inhabitants, who first went to Tajique Pueblo twelve miles to the north and shortly after to Isleta Pueblo south of Albuquerque. The Franciscan mission functioned for only about forty-five years.

Living Descendants of the Anasazi

The Pueblo Indians of the existing twenty-nine pueblos of the Rio Grande valley, the Zuni-Acoma region of New Mexico, and the Hopi Mesas of Arizona are the living descendants of the Anasazi Indians who occupied much of the Colorado Plateau of southwestern Colorado, southern Utah, northern Arizona, and northwestern New Mexico from the first millennium B.C. to the Great Migration of 1300. The modern Pueblo Indians may include a partial admixture of some ancient Mogollon as well as the Anasazi, but today's Pueblo culture seems to derive almost wholly from the Anasazi.

The Great Migration marked the end of the Pueblo III Anasazi, as they abandoned the Northern San Juan, Chaco Basin, and Kayenta to resettle in the Rio Grande valley and the Zuni and Hopi regions to begin the Pueblo IV stage that extended to historic times. According to the Spanish records, at the time the Juan de Oñate colonization was beginning in 1598, there were 134 pueblos with population estimates ranging from 16,000 to 248,000. These figures—the number of pueblos and particularly the number of Indians—are suspect. We know that during historic times, sixty-one pueblos were aban-

Quarai Mission and Pueblo, part of the Salinas National Monument, located north of Mountainair, New Mexico. La Purísima Concepción church was begun in 1628. To the west of the mission was a large pueblo of a thousand rooms built around five plazas, a portion of which is visible to the upper left of the church ruins. None of the room blocks have been excavated.

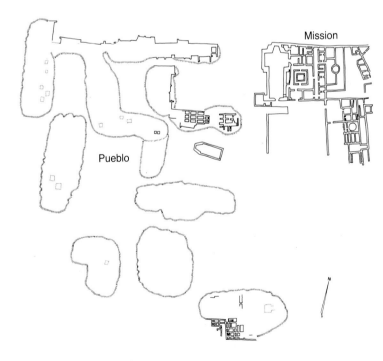

Mission

Pueblo

Ground plan of the collapsed rubble house mounds of Quarai Pueblo in the Salinas district of New Mexico. This southern Tiwa pueblo had been flourishing through trade with the Indians of the Great Plains when the Spaniards established a mission here. House blocks were arranged around numerous plazas in which some kivas were located.

doned, including Gran Quivira, Abó, Quarai, Pecos, Puyé, Awatovi, Hawikuh, and Kuaua.

The efforts of the Spanish friars to foster Catholicism and eliminate all Pueblo religion and customs that were not consonant with Christianity, together with the Indian resentment of the incursion of the Spaniards into the pueblos—especially the whippings, torture, and public executions—precipitated the Pueblo Revolt of 1680 that drove the Spaniards out of New Mexico—for a few years. Diego de Vargas finally completed an often bloody reconquest by 1692.

Plains Indian raids on both the Pueblos and the Spanish settlements increased. The Spaniards had introduced horses into North America; some escaped captivity and were acquired by Indians of both the Southwest and the Plains. The Plains Comanche and Apache used horses in their raids, enabling them to devastate the easternmost pueblos, such as Pecos and Gran Quivira. After the successful Mexican revolt against Spain, New Mexico became a part of the Republic of Mexico in 1821. For twenty-five years the pueblos were substantially ignored by the Mexicans and unprotected against Plains Indian raids. After the Mexican War, New Mexico and Arizona were ceded to the United States in 1846, which ended the warfare and raids and the power of the Catholic church over the pueblos.

The Anasazi are one of the very few cultures of the world that show a continuity and homogeneity of culture from 700 B.C. (Basket Maker II) to modern times and a remarkably consistent culture from Pueblo III (1100 to 1300) to the present day. The Pueblo culture has, of course, been influenced during historic times by the Spaniards, Mexicans, and Anglo-Americans, yet despite these influences the religious ceremonies, marriage customs, duality of government, and language have remained remarkably constant since Coronado's incursion in 1540. Even diet and housing did not begin to change radically until well into the twentieth century.

Despite the continuity in Pueblo culture, regional variations reach back into prehistoric times. There are four language families. The Tanoan family in the Rio Grande valley includes four living languages—Northern Tiwa, Southern Tiwa, Tewa, and Towa—and two dead languages—Tano and Tompiro. Tanoan is related linguistically to the language of the Kiowa, a Plains Indian tribe. Keresan is the language of the middle Rio Grande valley. The Zuni speak Zunian. The Hopi villagers speak Shoshonean, a Uto-Aztecan language related to the Numic languages of the Great Basin, and ultimately to the

Nahuatl tongue of the Aztecs in Mexico. All these languages are used in the pueblos today.

Pueblo Languages

Language Family	Language	Pueblo
Tanoan		
	Northern Tiwa	Taos
		Picuris
	Southern Tiwa	Isleta
		Sandia
		[Kuaua]
		[Quarai]
	Tewa	San Juan
		Santa Clara
		San Ildefonso
		Nambé
		Pojoaque
		Tesuque
		[Puyé]
		[Tsankawi]
	Towa	Jemez
		[Pecos]
	[Tano]	Hopi-Tewa (Hano)
		[Galisteo Basin pueblos]
	[Tompiro]	[Abó]
		[Gran Quivira]
Keresan		
	Keresan	Cochiti
		Santo Domingo
		San Felipe
		Santa Ana
		Zia
		Laguna
		Acoma
		[Tyuonyi]
		[Yapashe]
Zunian		
	Zunian	Zuni
		[Halona]
		[Hawikuh]
		[Atsinna]
Shoshonean		
	Hopi	Walpi
		Sichomovi
		Mishongnovi
		Shipaulovi
		Shungopovi
		Oraibi
		Hotevilla
		Bacabi
		Moencopi
		[Awatovi]
		[Sikyatki]
		[Kawaika]
		[Kokopnyama]
		[Homolovi]

[ ] Indicates an abandoned pueblo or a dead language.

The present-day Pueblo of Acoma, properly called "Sky City" because of its location atop a steep-sided mesa, lies about twenty-five miles southeast of Grants, New Mexico. Its Keres-speaking inhabitants, along with the other modern Pueblos, are the living descendants of a more than 2,500-year Anasazi cultural history. Acoma preserves the traditional feeling of its heritage, including the heavy-walled mission church marking the arrival of Spanish missionaries and colonists. (Photograph taken with the assistance of John Q. Royce.)

Anyone who has seen the Anasazi ruins of Mesa Verde, Chaco Canyon, or Kayenta can see the close resemblance to the modern pueblos—Taos, Acoma, Zuni, or the pueblos of the Hopi Mesas. Pueblos built with room blocks of masonry, one, two, or three stories high, facing a plaza with subterranean kivas, with room access by ladders, were common at the beginning of the twentieth century. The small doorways and roof entry to living rooms have given way to full-sized doors, and some pueblos have admitted electricity and running water. Nevertheless, the original pueblo housing methods remain little changed during historic times.

More significant is the survival of the egalitarian society, in which adherence to custom is enforced by the approval or disapproval of the members of the Pueblo community and any active reach for political power is effectively proscribed. Although marriage customs vary among the pueblos, they are enforced, and the kinship groups or clans govern the marriage relationships so as to protect the integrity of the Pueblo community. Ceremonial activities are still conducted by the kin group or kiva societies with responsibility shifting between the Summer People and the Winter People.

Perhaps the most remarkable quality of the Anasazi's 2,700-year cultural history (700 B.C. to the present day) lies in their tremendous achievements in architecture, crafts, water and soil management, and communications networks without surrendering their egalitarian values. So many other human societies readily accepted direction for public works and government from a privileged elite class for the supposed security of a larger urban civilization. Yet, the Anasazi and their modern-day Pueblo Indian descendants have shown dramatically how a social system based on equality and cooperation can survive changes in technology and social complexity. Pueblo culture has even survived quite successfully the powerful impact of Spanish conquerors and Christian missionaries, both of whom attempted to replace traditional Pueblo beliefs and practices with their own. The vitality in living Pueblo culture allows us to breathe life into the ancient pithouse, kiva, great kiva, pueblo, and cliff-dwelling ruins of the American Southwest.

Glossary

A short definition of terms employed
in this volume specifically relating
to Anasazi culture.

Adobe: Mud, sometimes mixed with fibers, dried in the sun, used as bricks or mortar.

Anasazi: Ancient Pueblo Indians of the southwest United States. It is a Navajo Indian word meaning "ancient enemies" or "ancient ones."

Anasaziland: The area of the Southwest occupied by the Ancient Anasazi on the Colorado Plateau from the Rocky Mountains west to the Grand Canyon and south to the Little Colorado River valley.

Antechamber: A small, partially underground room built on the south side of pithouses that provided access and ventilation to the pithouse dwellings.

Archaeological Site: Any remnant of human construction, occupation, or use such as a small storage cist, village, pueblo, reservoir, irrigation system, or rock art.

Archaic: A broad stage of human cultural development in North America characterized by nomadic hunters and gatherers. The Desert Culture peoples of the Great Basin and the American Southwest preceding the Anasazi belonged to the Archaic stage.

Atlatl: A hand-held stick as an arm extension used for throwing a spear or dart. The word comes from the Aztec language Nahuatl.

Banquette: A bench-like shelf around the internal periphery of a kiva or pithouse.

Basket Maker stages: Basket Maker I: A postulated stage (pre-500 B.C.) during which the ancestral Anasazi were nomadic hunters and gatherers.

Basket Maker II (Basket Maker): Preceramic Anasazi stage extending from 700 B.C. to A.D. 450.

Basket Maker III (Modified Basket Maker): A.D. 400–450 to 700–750, the period in which pithouse villages, pottery, and the bow and arrow developed and corn, beans, squash, and domesticated turkeys were grown.

Bering land bridge: Dry land connection between Alaska and Siberia exposed by a lower sea level during the last Ice Age allowing passage of people and animals from Asia to North America.

Cavate: Small cave dug out of the cliff side used for habitation, storage, or ceremonial purposes.

Ceremonial structure: A construction archaeologists regard as having been utilized for religious or community purposes rather than for habitation.

Chaco Basin: The geographic region centered on the Chaco Canyon in northwestern New Mexico, bounded on the north by the San Juan River, the west by the Chuska Mountains between Gallup and Shiprock, on south by the ridge north of and paralleling Interstate 40, and on the east by the Continental Divide and New Mexico Highway 44.

Chaco Phenomenon: A flash of Anasazi cultural development by the Chaco Canyon peoples between A.D. 1070 and 1130 resulting in spectacular pueblo and road buildng at Chaco Canyon and around the Chaco Basin.

Chinking: The process of inserting small stones (spalls) into the soft adobe mortar of masonry walls during construction to bond the mortar and strengthen the walls.

Cibola region: The geographic region surrounding modern Zuni, New Mexico, extending west to the Petrified Forest, south to Springerville, Arizona, east to the Continental Divide, and north to the ridge lying north of modern Interstate 40.

Cist: A roofed pit for storing food or a storage recess in the wall of a building.

Clan: A formalized lineage group, usually with a name or symbol such as the bear, wolf, or squash.

Cliff dwelling: A pueblo constructed against a cliff wall, generally under an overhang, by the Anasazi in Pueblo III and IV. Cliff dwelling ruins are found at Mesa Verde, Kayenta, Canyon de Chelly, Bandelier, and Puyé.

Concentric wall structures: A bi-wall or tri-wall ceremonial structure, built by the Anasazi, arranged in a circle or a D-shaped plan. Examples are Hubbard Site at Aztec, the round structure in Pueblo del Arroyo at Chaco Canyon, Sun Temple at Mesa Verde, and Horseshoe House at Hovenweep.

Convento: Residence of the priest and friars located next to the mission church.

Copper bells: These small cast copper bells were trade items from Mexico—the only known Anasazi metal objects.

Coursed masonry: A technique for building walls of successive horizontal layers of building stones.

Cribbed roof: A form of roof construction used on many kivas where logs are extended horizontally from pilaster to pilaster forming a hexagon or octagon (or more) upon which additional tiers of logs are fitted in decreasing concentric rings to form a beehive-type roof.

Culture: The sum of nonbiological customs, mores, and methods of providing food, clothing, and shelter involved in the life-style of any group of people. These essentials are modified and passed along from generation to generation.

Dance platform: A level area used for ceremonies: on the ground supported by terrace walls or on areas of pueblo roofs (generally Pueblo IV) partially surrounded by residential rooms.

Deflector: A low barrier, generally a vertically placed stone slab, between the doorway or ventilator entrance and the fire pit in kivas and pithouses.

Desert Culture People: Nomadic peoples who lived in the Great Basin and the Southwest from the end of the last Ice Age to Basket Maker II (700 B.C.).

Dressed stone masonry: A masonry style where building stone surfaces have been pecked, chipped, or ground to produce a relatively smooth finish.

Dry-wall masonry: Stone walls laid up without mortar.

Duality of social organization: Modern Pueblo Indian social organization dividing periods of responsibility for rituals and matters of government and society between the Winter and Summer People. Evidence of such duality existed as early as Pueblo III times.

Great Basin: A geographic area covering some 185,000 square miles centered in Nevada and including portions of California, Oregon, and Utah without drainage to the sea resulting in the creation of salty lakes such as the Great Salt Lake.

Grinding bins: A small stone-lined bin in which a metate is fixed at the proper angle for grinding grain. The Anasazi often placed several grinding bins side by side, allowing several women to work simultaneously grinding maize.

Foot drums: Recesses in the floor covered with wooden planking producing a drum-like sound when danced upon.

Fret (fretwork): Ornamental design in painting or in relief on stone consisting of continuous running lines in short straight segments. It may also be painted on pottery, the only occurrence in Anasazi culture.

Hamlet: A settlement housing between 15 and 100 people.

Hematite: Red-colored iron ore.

Hohokam culture: Prehistoric neighbors of the Anasazi living in Southern Arizona from 300 B.C. to A.D. 1450. They were the builders of Casa Grande near Phoenix.

Horseshoe house: A concentric bi-wall structure typical of Hovenweep constructed in the form of a D or horseshoe.

Hunting and gathering: The subsistence pattern of obtaining food by hunting game for meat and gathering wild seeds, fruit, and nuts.

Jacal (wattle-and-daub) construction: Wall construction utilizing a framework of posts interlaced with horizontally woven branches plastered over with mud.

Kachinas: Supernatural beings, associated with the Pueblo Indian's origin myth, that taught and guided their ancestors. By using the Kachina masks and following proper rituals, Pueblo Indians could evoke the powers of these supernatural beings.

Keres: A Pueblo Indian language spoken by the modern pueblos of Cochiti, Zia, Acoma, and others, and possibly by the Anasazi of Frijoles Canyon (Bandelier).

 Keyhole-shaped kivas: A circular kiva with a recess on one side producing a keyhole shape (when viewed from above).

Kivas (a Hopi word): Kin-group kiva: Generally a subterranean circular room less than twenty feet in diameter and about seven to eight feet high with a ceiling hatchway for access. Especially during Pueblo III and before, the kiva was associated with living quarters and utilized by related family groups for meetings, rituals, weaving, making of tools and clothing, storytelling, and instruction of children. A hallmark of Anasazi culture.

Great Kiva: Large (forty-five feet in diameter) generally circular, partially subterranean and roofed structure built by the Anasazi of the Northern San Juan and Chaco Canyon for rituals and community use.

Tower-Kiva: A kiva found at Chaco Basin sites built on top of a rubble-filled platform, usually within a room block, and probably constructed for community use.

 Kokopelli: The ubiquitous hunch-backed flute player depicted in rock art and sometimes on pottery throughout Anasaziland.

Koshare: A costumed dancer who satirizes proper behavior by clowning.

Lintel: A load-bearing member of wood or stone spanning the opening in a doorway or window.

Loom anchors: Loops of flexible branches securely buried in the kiva floor to which was fastened a horizontal pole serving as the lower portion of the loom frame.

Macaw, scarlet: A large red and green parrot found in tropical Mesoamerica. This bird was a popular trade item with the ancient Anasazi.

Mano and metate: The mano was the hand grinding stone drawn back and forth across the metate or fixed stone receptacle with a concave upper surface. Corn was placed on the metate and ground with the mano.

Mealing room: A room in the pueblo containing several grinding bins with metates used as a communal corn grinding room.

Mogollon Indians: Anasazi neighbors to the south occupying central Arizona and southern New Mexico as far north as the Mogollon Rim and the south edge Zuni-Cibola regions.

Montezuma Valley: A valley extending from the Mesa Verde in Colorado to the Abajo Mountains near Monticello, Utah, occupied by some 30,000 Anasazi during Pueblo III.

Neolithic: The New Stone Age (the age prior to metallurgy) characterized by polished stone tools, agriculture, domestic animals, and settled communities but without use of writing or metal tools.

Niche: A small opening or excavation in the wall of a habitation room, pithouse, or kiva for the storage of small items.

Northern San Juan Region: The geographic region occupied by the Anasazi prior to 1300 in southern Colorado, Utah, and extreme northwestern New Mexico located north of the San Juan River.

Outliers (Chaco Canyon): The name given to settlements in or near the Chaco Basin considered by some archaeologists to be satellites of Chaco Canyon.

Pajarito Plateau: The plateau between the Jemez Mountains and the Rio Grande from Española to the Bandelier National Monument in New Mexico including Los Alamos. The Pueblo IV sites of Puyé, Tsankawi, and Tyuonyi are located here.

Paleo-Indians: Nomadic Indians of North America, hunters of big game, who are believed to have followed now extinct large animals (mastodons and mammoths) across the Bering land bridge. They occupied portions of the Southwest between 10,000 and 8,000 B.C.

Pecked masonry: Masonry stones shaped or dressed by striking or pitting with a hammerstone.

Petroglyph: Rock art figures pecked or incised into the face of cliffs or rocks.

Pictograph: Rock art of painted figures.

Pilaster: Rectangular upright column of masonry, usually set against a wall, and upon which the roof rested.

Pithouse: Semisubterranean, usually circular or squarish living quarters of the earlier Anasazi. Pithouses were the forerunners of kin-group kivas.

Point (projectile point): A chipped stone tip for a spear, dart, or arrow. A spear head or arrowhead.

Portico: A covered colonnade across the front of a building.

Pueblo: The name given by the Spaniards to Pueblo IV–V Indian towns of the American Southwest, towns composed of multistoried, flat-roofed, adjacent buildings constructed of masonry or adobe. The Pueblo Indians were the residents of Anasazi towns, villages, and cliff dwellings from A.D. 700 to modern times and are now residents of or associated with the Hopi and Zuni pueblos and other pueblos of the Southwest such as Taos, Zia, and Acoma.

Pueblo stages: Pueblo I (A.D. 700–750 to 900): The stage marked by aboveground rectangular living rooms and the first use of the pithouse as a kiva.
Pueblo II (A.D. 900 to 1070–1100): Development of the unit pueblo, kiva, and masonry construction.
Pueblo III (A.D. 1070–1100 to 1300): Stage of the great centers of population: Mesa Verde, Chaco Canyon, Kayenta, and Cibola. During this stage (sometimes referred to as "classic"), the Anasazi built large multiroom and multistory pueblos and cliff dwellings. At the end of Pueblo III (by 1300) the Mesa Verde, Chaco Canyon, and Kayenta centers were abandoned. The Great Migration moved these people to the Rio Grande and Little Colorado River valleys.
Pueblo IV (A.D. 1300–1540): During this stage the Anasazi were located in the Rio Grande valley, the Zuni (Cibola) region, and the Little Colorado–Hopi Mesas region. This last prehistoric stage ended with the arrival of the Spaniards.

Ramada: A roofed structure with no walls, supported by four corner poles, often constructed in front of Anasazi living and storage rooms.

Recess (kiva architecture): The space above the banquette between pilasters or the indentation on the southside of a keyhole kiva.

Region: A large definable unit of geographic space that encompasses a similar cultural pattern among its inhabitants.

Restoration: The process of reassembling the fallen parts of ancient structures into their original condition.

Rubble-cored walls: Rubble of small stones, dirt, and clay used as a fill between facings of stone masonry.

Rock art: A term used in reference to all types of figures that were pecked, incised, carved into or painted on cliffs or stone faces.

Salado culture: Prehistoric neighbors of the Anasazi who lived in central Arizona between about A.D. 1150 and 1350.

Shoshonean: A family of languages spoken by small bands of nomadic Indians of the Great Basin and adjacent areas living by gathering seeds, fruit, and nuts and hunting small game. Ancestors of the Shoshoneans date back to about 8,500 to 2,000 B.C., and some may have been ancestors of the Anasazi. The Hopi also speak a Shoshonean language.

Shrine: A place or construction especially hallowed or sacred. The Anasazi revered cliffs or caves decorated with rock art, kiva and tower combinations, and receptacles containing sacred objects.

Sill: Horizontal rock or timber used as the base of a doorway or other opening.

Sinagua culture: Prehistoric neighbors of the Anasazi. About A.D. 600 the Sinagua moved into the area around modern Flagstaff near the San Francisco Peaks. They fled during the eruption of Sunset Crater but moved back into the region in the late 1000s and were influenced by the Anasazi from the adjacent Kayenta region. In the 1200s they moved south to the Verde Valley below the Mogollon Rim.

Sipapu: A small lined hole placed in the floor of a kiva or pithouse to symbolize the place of the original emergence by the Anasazi ancestors from the underworld. The word comes from the Hopi word *sipap.*

Spalling (masonry): The reduction of irregular stones by chipping to the desired size and shape.

Stabilization: The process of partially rebuilding existing portions of ancient structures for purposes of preservation.

Stage: A degree or level of cultural development within the course of human cultural history.

Standardized pueblo unit: See Unit pueblo.

Style: The characteristic of an object, structure, or thing that brings it within a recognized fashion or mode. The Anasazi evidenced established and recognizable styles of masonry, architecture, pottery, baskets, tools, and clothing.

Suite: Living and storage rooms occupied by a single household that are clustered around an outdoor work space.

Talus slope: Rock debris at the base of a cliff.

Tanoans: A family of languages spoken by many of the modern Pueblo Indians in the Rio Grande valley from Taos to Isleta. The inhabitants of Pecos, Tsankawi, Kuaua, and the Salinas pueblos spoke Tanoan languages.

Toehold trail: The Anasazi pecked a series of small depressions in the cliff walls just large enough to hold the toes and the ball of the foot and to provide hand grips, enabling them to ascend and descend steep rock faces.

Tower (Anasazi): Round, oval, or rectangular masonry structure, often several stories in height, probably used for ceremonial or religious purposes.

Town (Anasazi): A settlement housing between 1,200 and 3,000 people and containing a communal ceremonial center.

Trash dump: An area in front and generally to the south of living quarters and courtyard where the Anasazi deposited garbage and unusable items such as broken pottery, stone tools, and worn-out clothing.

Tree-ring dates: Dendrochronology, a method of determining the age of timber through the pattern combinations of annual growth rings of trees. The chronology now stretches back more than 2,000 years in the American Southwest.

Tusayán: The name the Zuni gave the Spaniards referring to the region northwest of Zuni occupied by the Hopi.

Unit pueblo: A standardized pueblo building unit: with storage and living rooms, courtyard and kiva, and rubbish dump constructed on a north-south axis.

Ute Mountain Tribal Park: Part of the Ute Mountain Ute Indian Reservation located on the southern border of the Mesa Verde National Park containing numerous Anasazi cliff dwellings.

Ventilator: A tunnel leading from the ground surface into pithouses and kivas to provide a flow of outside air.

Village (Anasazi): A settlement housing between 200 and 500 people.

Wing wall: A low partition wall built across the interior south end of pithouses and kivas.

Winter and Summer People: The social organization of the modern Pueblos providing for a dual division of responsibility for rituals and other social and governmental activities between the Winter People and Summer People group. The Hopi and Zuni recognize this duality only for ceremonial purposes.

Selected Bibliography

Adams,Richard E. W.
1977 *Prehistoric America* (Boston: Little, Brown and Co.).

Anyon, Roger, and T. J. Ferguson
1983 *Settlement Patterns and Changing Adaptations in the Zuni Area After* A.D. *1000.* Paper presented for the Anasazi Symposium, San Juan Archaeological Research Center and Library, Bloomfield, New Mexico.

Amsden, Charles Avery
1949 *Prehistoric Southwesterners from Basketmaker to Pueblo* (Los Angeles: Southwest Museum).

Barnes, F. A.
1982 *Canyon Country Prehistoric Rock Art* (Salt Lake City: Wasatch Publishers, Inc.).

Breternitz, David A., Arthur H. Rohn, and Elizabeth A. Morris
1974 "Prehistoric Ceramics of the Mesa Verde Region", ed. by Watson Smith, *Museum of Northern Arizona Ceramic Series* no. 5 (Flagstaff: Northern Arizona Society of Science and Art, Inc.).

Brew, J. O.
1946 *Archaeology of Alkali Ridge, Southeastern Utah, with a Review of the Prehistory of the Mesa Verde Division of the San Juan and Some Observations on Archaeological Systematics,* Papers of the Peabody Museum of American Archaeology and Ethnology no. 21, Harvard University. (Cambridge, Mass.).
1979 "Hopi Prehistory and History to 1850," in *Handbook of North American Indians, Southwest,* ed. by William C. Sturtevant, vol. ed. by Alfonso Ortiz, vol. 9, (Washington, D.C.: Smithsonian Institution).

Brody, J. J.
1984 "Chacoan Art and the Chaco Phenomenon" in *New Light on Chaco Canyon,* ed. by David Grant Noble (Santa Fe: School of American Research).

Canby, Thomas Y.
1982 "The Anasazi, Riddles in the Ruins," *National Geographic* 162(5):554–92.

Cattanach, George S., Jr.
1980 *Long House, Mesa Verde National Park, Colorado,* U.S. National Park Service Archeological Research Series 7-H (Washington, D.C.).

Corbett, John M.
1962 *Aztec Ruins National Monument,* National Park Service Historical Handbook Series no. 36 (Washington, D.C.).

Cordell, Linda S.
1979 "Prehistory: Eastern Anasazi," in *Handbook of North American Indians, Southwest,* ed. by William C. Sturtevant, vol. ed. by Alfonso Ortiz, vol. 9, (Washington, D.C.: Smithsonian Institution).
1984 *Prehistory of the Southwest* (Orlando: Academic Press).

Dean, Jeffry S.
1969 *Chronological Analysis of Tsegi Phase Sites in Northeastern Arizona,* Papers of the Laboratory of Tree-Ring Research, no. 3. (Tucson, Ariz.).

Dozier, Edward P.
1970 *The Pueblo Indians of North America* (New York: Holt, Rinehart and Winston).

Dutton, Bertha P.
1963 *Sun Father's Way* (Albuquerque: University of New Mexico Press).
1983 *American Indians of the Southwest* (Albuquerque: University of New Mexico Press).

Eddy, Frank W.
1977 *Archaeological Investigations at Chimney Rock Mesa: 1970–1972,* Memoirs of the Colorado Archaeological Society, no. 1 (Boulder).
1981 "Upland Anasazi Settlement Adaptations at Chimney Rock Mesa," in *Proceedings of the Anasazi Symposium 1981,* ed. by Jack E. Smith (Mesa Verde: Mesa Verde Museum Association).

Earley, Frank Lee
1976 *Chaco Canyon,* Museum of Anthropology, Arapahoe Community College, Museum Study Series no. 2 (Littleton).

Euler, Robert C., George J. Gumerman, Thor N. V. Karlstrom, Jeffery S. Dean, and Richard H. Hevly
1979 "Colorado Plateaus: Cultural Dynamics and Paleoenvironment," *Science* 205:1089–1101.

Euler, Robert C., and George J. Gumerman (eds.)
1978 *Investigations of the Southwest Anthropological Research Group,* Proceedings of the 1976 Conference, Museum of Northern Arizona (Flagstaff).

Gillespie, William B.
1984 "Environment of the Chaco Anasazis" in *New Light on Chaco Canyon* ed. by David Grant Noble (Santa Fe: School of American Research).

Grant, Campbell
1978 *Canyon de Chelly, Its People and Rock Art* (Tucson: University of Arizona Press).

Hargrave, Lyndon L.
1970 *Mexican Macaws Comparative Osteology and Survey of Remains from the Southwest,* Anthropological Papers of The University of Arizona no. 20 (Tucson: The University of Arizona Press).

Haury, Emil W.
1974 "The Problem of Contacts between the Southwestern United States and Mexico," in *The Mesoamerican Southwest* ed. by Basil C. Hedrick, J. Charles Kelley, and Carroll L. Riley (Carbondale and Edwardsville: Southern Illinois University Press).

Hayes, Alden C.
1974 *The Four Churches of Pecos* (Albuquerque: University of New Mexico Press).

Hayes, Alden C., D. Brugge, and W. J. Judge
1981 *Archeological Surveys of Chaco Canyon, New Mexico,* in National Park Service Publications in Archeology 18A (Washington, D.C.).

Hewett, Edgar L.
1938 *Pajarito Plateau and Its Ancient People* (Albuquerque: University of New Mexico Press).

Hibben, Frank C.
1975 *Kiva Art of the Anasazi at Pottery Mound* (Las Vegas: KC Publications).

Irwin-Williams, Cynthia (ed.)
1972 *The Structure of Chacoan Society in the Northern Southwest: Investigations at the Salmon Site 1972,* Eastern New Mexico University Contributions in Anthropology, vol. 4. no. 3 (Portales).
1973 *The Oshara Tradition: Origins of Anasazi Culture,* Eastern New Mexico University Contributions in Anthropology, vol. 5, no. 1 (Portales).

Jennings, Jesse D.
1956 "The American Southwest: A Problem in Cultural Isolation," in *Seminars in Archaeology, 1955* ed. by Robert Wauchope, Memoirs of the Society for American Archaeology 11 (Salt Lake City).
1966 *Glen Canyon: A Summary,* Univeristy of Utah Anthropological Paper 81 (Salt Lake City).
1978 *Ancient Native Americans* (San Francisco: W. H. Freeman).

Jernigan, E. Wesley
1978 *Jewelry of the Prehistoric Southwest* (Albuquerque: University of New Mexico Press).

Judd, Neil M.
1954 *The Material Culture of Pueblo Bonito,* Smithsonian Miscellaneous Collections 124 (Washington, D.C.).
1964 *The Architecture of Pueblo Bonito,* Smithsonian Miscellaneous Collections 147 (1) (Washington, D.C.).

Judge, W. James
1984 "New Light on Chaco Canyon," in *New Light on Chaco Canyon,* ed. by David Grant Noble (Santa Fe: School of American Research).

Judge, W. James, W. B. Gillespie, Stephen H. Lekson, and H. W. Toll
1981 *Tenth Century Developments in Chaco Canyon,* Archaeological Society of New Mexico Anthropological Papers 6 (Santa Fe).

Kidder, Alfred V.
1924   *An Introduction to the Study of Southwestern Archaeology, with a Preliminary Account of the Excavations at Pecos,* Papers of the Southwestern Expedition 1 (9) (New Haven, Conn.). Published for the Phillips Academy by Yale University Press. Reprint in 1962.
1958   *Pecos, New Mexico: Archaeological Notes,* Papers of the Robert S. Peabody Foundation for Archaeology 5 (Andover, Mass.).

Kubler, George
1972   *The Religious Architecture of New Mexico* (Albuquerque: University of New Mexico Press).

Lindsay, Alexander J., and Jeffery S. Dean
1981   *The Kayenta Anasazi at* A.D. *1250: Prelude to a Migration,* Proceedings of the Anasazi Symposium 1981, ed. by Jack E. Smith (Mesa Verde: Mesa Verde Museum Association).

Lister, Robert H., and Florence C. Lister
1978   *Anasazi Pottery* (Albuquerque: University of New Mexico Press).
1981   *Chaco Canyon Archaeology and Archaeologists* (Albuquerque: University of New Mexico Press).
1983   *Those Who Came Before* (Tucson: University of Arizona Press).

Lyons, Thomas R., and Robert K. Hitchcock
1977   "Remote Sensing Interpretation of Anasazi Land Route System," in *Aerial Remote Sensing Techniques in Archeology,* Thomas R. Lyons and Robert K. Hitchcock, eds. Reports of the Chaco Center 2 (Albuquerque: U.S. National Park Service and the University of New Mexico).

Marshall, Michael P., John R. Stein, Richard W. Loose, Judith E. Novotny
1979   *Anasazi Communities of the San Juan Basin* (Santa Fe: Public Service Co. of New Mexico, and Historic Preservation Bureau, Department of Finance and Administration of New Mexico).

Martin, Paul S., and Fred T. Plog
1973   *The Archaeology of Arizona: A Study of the Southwest Region* (Garden City, N. Y.: Doubleday).

Martin, Paul S., Lawrence Roys, and Gerhardt von Bonin
1936   *Lowry Ruin in Southwestern Colorado,* Field Museum of Natural History Publication 356, Anthropological Series 23 (1) (Chicago).

McGregor, John C.
1965   *Southwestern Archaeology* (Urbana: University of Illinois Press).
1982   *Southwestern Archaeology* 2d ed. (Urbana: University of Illinois Press).

Morris, Earl H.
1921   *The House of the Great Kiva at the Aztec Ruin,* Anthropological Papers of the American Museum of Natural History 26(2) (New York).
1925   "Exploring the Canyon of Death: Remains of a People Who Dwelt in Our Southwest at Least 4,000 Years Ago Are Revealed," *National Geographic* 48(3):263–300.
1938   "Mummy Cave, *Natural History* 4(2):127–38.

Nickens, Paul R.
1981   *Pueblo III Communities in Transition: Environment and Adaptation in Johnson Canyon,* Memoirs of the Colorado Archaeological Society, no. 2 (Boulder).

Noble, David Grant
1981   *Ancient Ruins of the Southwest* (Flagstaff: Northland Press).

Nordenskiöld, Gustaf
1893   *The Cliff Dwellers of the Mesa Verde, Southwestern Colorado: Their Pottery and Implements,* trans. by D. Lloyd Morgan (Stockholm and Chicago: P. A. Norsted and Söner), reprint 1980 (Glorieta, N.M.: Rio Grande Press).

Olsen, Nancy H.
1981   *Mesa Verde Anasazi Rock Art: A Visual Communication System?,* Proceedings of the Anasazi Symposium 1981, ed. by Jack E. Smith (Mesa Verde: Mesa Verde Museum Association).

Osborne, Douglas
1964   "Solving the Riddles of Wetherill Mesa," *National Geographic* 125(2):155–211.

Parsons, Elsie (Clews)
1939   *Pueblo Indian Religion,* 2 vols. (Chicago: University of Chicago Press).

Peckham, Stewart
1977   *Prehistoric Weapons in the Southwest,* Museum of New Mexico Press Popular Series Pamphlet no. 3. (Santa Fe: Museum of New Mexico Press).

Pike, Donald G.
1974   *Anasazi, Ancient People of the Rock* (New York: Crown Publishers).

Plog, Fred
1979 "Prehistory: Western Anasazi," in *Handbook of North American Indians, Southwest,* ed. by William C. Sturtevant, vol. 9 ed. by Alfonso Ortiz, (Washington, D.C.: Smithsonian Institution).

Powers, Robert P., William B. Gillespie, Stephen H. Lekson
1983 *The Outlier Survey,* Division of Cultural Research, U.S. National Park Service, Reports of the Chaco Center, no. 3 (Albuquerque).

Powers, Robert P.
1984 "Outliers and Roads in the Chaco System" in *New Light on Chaco Canyon,* ed. by David Grant Noble (Santa Fe: School of American Research).

Reed, Erik K.
1964 "The Greater Southwest," in *Prehistoric Man in the New World,* ed. by Jesse D. Jennings and Edward Norbeck. (Chicago: University of Chicago Press).

Rohn, Arthur H.
1971 *Mug House, Mesa Verde National Park, Colorado,* U.S. National Park Service Archeological Research Series 7-D (Washington, D.C.).
1977 *Cultural Change and Continuity on Chapin Mesa* (Lawrence: Regents Press of Kansas).
1981 *Budding Urban Settlements in the Northern San Juan,* Proceedings of the Anasazi Symposium 1981, ed. by Jack E. Smith (Mesa Verde: Mesa Verde Museum Association).

Schaafsma, Polly
1980 *Indian Rock Art of the Southwest* (Albuquerque: University of New Mexico Press).

Schwartz, Douglas W.
in press *Dynamics of Southwestern Prehistory* (Santa Fe: School of American Research).

Schroeder, Albert H.
1979 "Pueblos Abandoned in Historic Times," in *Handbook of North American Indians, Southwest,* ed. by William C. Sturtevant, vol. 9 ed. by Alfonso Ortiz (Washington, D.C.: Smithsonian Institution).

Smith, Watson, R. B. Woodbury, and N. F. D. Woodbury (eds.)
1966 *The Excavations of Hawikuh by Frederick Webb Hodge* (New York: Museum of the American Indian).

Steen, Charles R.
1977 *Pajarito Plateau Archaeological Survey and Excavation* (Los Alamos: Los Alamos Scientific Laboratories).

Stuart, David E., and Rory P. Gauthier
1981 *Prehistoric New Mexico, Background for Survey,* ed. Thomas W. Merlan (Santa Fe: Historic Preservation Bureau).

Tanner, Clara Lee
1976 *Prehistoric Southwestern Craft Arts* (Tucson: University of Arizona Press).

Viele, Catherine W.
1980 *Voices in the Canyon* (Globe: Southwest Parks and Monuments Association).

Vivian, Gordon
1979 *Excavations in a Seventeenth-Century Pueblo, Gran Quivira,* Archeological Research Series, no. 8 (Washington, D.C.: National Park Service).

Vivian, R. Gordon, and Paul Reiter
1960 *The Great Kivas of Chaco Canyon and Their Relationships,* Monographs of the School of American Research 22 (Santa Fe).

Waters, Frank
1963 *Book of the Hopi,* reprint 1982 (New York: Penguin Books).

Watson, Don
1961 *Indians of the Mesa Verde* (Mesa Verde: Mesa Verde Museum Association).

Wendorf, Fred, and Erik K. Reed
1955 "An Alternative Reconstruction of Northern Rio Grande Prehistory," *El Palacio* 62 (5–6): 131–73.

Wenger, Gilbert R.
1980 *The Story of Mesa Verde National Park* (Mesa Verde: Mesa Verde Museum Association).

Willey, Gordon R.
1966 *An Introduction to American Archaeology, Vol., 1: North and Middle America* (Englewood Cliffs, N.J.: Prentice-Hall).

Williamson, Ray A., Howard H. Fisher, and Donnel O'Flynn
1977 "Anasazi Solar Observations," in *Native American Astronomy,* ed. by Anthony F. Aveni (Austin: University of Texas Press).

Woodbury, Richard B.
1979 "Zuni Prehistory and History to 1850," in *Handbook of North American Indians, Southwest,* ed. by William C. Sturtevant, vol. 9 ed. by Alfonso Ortiz (Washington, D.C.: Smithsonian Institution).
1979 "Prehistory Introduction" in *Handbook of North American Indians, Southwest,* ed. by William C. Sturtevant, vol. 9 ed. by Alfonso Ortiz (Washington, D.C.: Smithsonian Institution).
1981 "Chaos to Order: A. V. Kidder at Pecos," in *Pecos Ruins,* ed. by David Grant Noble (Santa Fe: School of American Research).

Woodbury, Richard B., and Ezra B. W. Zubrow
1979 "Agricultural Beginnings, 2000 B.C.–A.D. 500," in *Handbook of North American Indians, Southwest,* ed. by William C. Sturtevant, vol. 9 ed. by Alfonso Ortiz (Washington, D.C.: Smithsonian Institution).

Wormington, H. M.
1969 *Prehistoric Indians of the Southwest,* Denver Museum of Natural History, Popular Series no. 7, 2d. ed. (Denver).

Acknowledgments

This book would not have been possible without the full cooperation and assistance of the United States National Park Service and particularly Robert C. Heyder, superintendent, and Allen S. Bohnert of the Mesa Verde National Park; William R. Germeraad, superintendent of Canyon de Chelly National Monument; John Hunter, superintendent, Kevin McKibben, Chris Judson, and Sari Stein of Bandelier National Monument; Walter P. Harriman, former superintendent, and Tom Vaughan, superintendent of Chaco Culture National Historical Park, and W. James Judge, chief of the Division of Cultural Research; John Loleit of the Navajo National Monument; and Susie Schofield of Salinas National Monument.

Our special thanks also go to Richard B. Woodbury who reviewed the text and offered numerous helpful suggestions; John Q. Royce who doubled as a pilot and aerial photographer; L. A. Villarreal who took a number of the aerial photographs and was the cataloger for the nearly 4,000 photographs and negatives that formed the core of the project. Artists Lisa Ferguson and Joan Foth contributed paintings and drawings to show things the camera eye could not.

Index

293